D1452844

Refiguring Chaucer in the Renaissance

Edited by Theresa M. Krier

Gainesville Tallahassee Tampa Boca Raton
Pensacola Orlando Miami Jacksonville

UNIVERSITY PRESS OF FLORIDA

REFIGURING CHAUCER

in the Renaissance

03 02 01 00 99 98 6 5 4 3 2 1

LIBRARY OF CONGRESS CATALOGING-IN-PUBLICATION DATA
Refiguring Chaucer in the Renaissance / edited by Theresa M. Krier.
p. cm.
Includes bibliographical references (p.) and index.
ISBN 0-8130-1552-9
1. Chaucer, Geoffrey, d. 1400—Influence. 2. English literature—Early modern, 1500–1700—History and criticism. 3. Spenser, Edmund, 1552?–1599—Knowledge—Literature. 4. Chaucer, Geoffrey, d. 1400—Appreciation—England. 5. Medievalism—England—History—16th century. 6. Medievalism—England—History—17th century. 7. Influence (Literary, artistic, etc.) 8. Middle Ages in literature. 9. Renaissance—England. 10. Canon (Literature) I. Krier, Theresa M., 1953–.
PR1914.R44 1998
821'.1—dc21 97-8740

Page from 1602 printing of Thomas Speght's edition of Chaucer, showing maniples found in *Troilus and Criseyde*. Reprinted by permission of the University of Virginia Library.

The University Press of Florida is the scholarly publishing agency for the State University System of Florida, comprised of Florida A&M University, Florida Atlantic University, Florida International University, Florida State University, University of Central Florida, University of Florida, University of North Florida, University of South Florida, and University of West Florida.

University Press of Florida
15 Northwest 15th Street
Gainesville, FL 32611
http: //nersp.nerdc.ufl.edu/~upf

Contents

Preface

The subject of this volume has dictated our using many different early editions (and editors and printers) of our writers: among modern editions, we rely on *The Riverside Chaucer.* For Spenser, we use either the *Variorum* edition, A. C. Hamilton's edition of *The Faerie Queene* (Longman), or Smith and de Selincourt's Oxford *Poetical Works,* depending upon the requirements of the particular chapter.

We're indebted to the many studies of Chaucer's roles in literary history and British culture, a phenomenon that's interested readers and writers since 1400. This endowment notwithstanding, there are still many paths to pursue within this field, on the way to the reciprocal engagement of traditional literary history with contemporary theoretical work. We hope that the chapters in this volume contribute to this project and spur others. I'm grateful to everyone who's supported this project: Notre Dame colleagues Dolores Warwick Frese, Graham Hammill, Katherine O'Brien O'Keeffe, Kathy Psomiades, Jennifer Warlick, Ewa Ziarek, Andrew Elfenbein; Ellen Martin, who helps me think through the possible relationships of early literatures and psychoanalysis; various audiences who heard earlier versions of some of these essays at conferences, especially at the Medieval Congresses in Kalamazoo, Michigan, the MMLA in Minneapolis, and the conference of the Arizona Center for Medieval and Renaissance Studies; the anonymous readers for the press; Beth Ammerman, who provided much of the labor in compiling the bibliography; typists and computer aces Sherrie Reichold, Cheryl Reed, and Margaret Jasiewicz; the press's able editors—Walda Metcalf, who began the project with us when it was hatched all too many years ago, and Meredith Morris-Babb, Judy Goffman, and freelance copyeditor Sally Antrobus. This book is made possible in part by support from the Institute for Scholarship in the Liberal Arts, College of Arts and Letters, University of Notre Dame. Most immediately, I owe a happy debt to the contributors for their patience and their constant provocations to thinking, especially to Judith Anderson, who shared her editorial experience, and to all the members of my multispecies family for providing stability as well as constant drama—especially my two good gray horses Pepper and (the late) Cruiser.

Grateful acknowledgments are made to the following publishers for permission to quote from copyrighted works.

Addison Wesley Longman: Edmund Spenser, *The Faerie Queene*, ed. A. C. Hamilton (reprint 1977, by permission of Addison Wesley Longman Ltd.).

British Library Board: Devonshire Manuscript, British Museum Additional MS 17492, folio 29.

Cambridge University Press: *The Dramatic Works in the Beaumont and Fletcher Canon*, ed. Fredson Bowers (1966–); Carolyn Spurgeon, *Five Hundred Years of Chaucer Criticism and Allusion, 1357–1900* (1925).

Houghton Mifflin Company (by permission of Houghton Mifflin Company): *The Riverside Chaucer*, general ed. Larry D. Benson, 3d ed. (copyright 1987 by Houghton Mifflin Company); G. Blakemore Evans, ed., *The Riverside Shakespeare* (copyright 1974 by Houghton Mifflin Company).

The Johns Hopkins University Press: *The Works of Edmund Spenser: A Variorum Edition*, ed. Edmund Greenlaw, F. M. Padelford, C. G. Osgood, et al. (reprint, 1966, copyright The Johns Hopkins University Press).

Liverpool University Press: Sir Thomas Wyatt, *Collected Poems*, ed. Kenneth Muir and Patricia Thomson (1969).

Oxford University Press (by permission of Oxford University Press): Ludovico Ariosto, *Orlando Furioso*, trans. Sir John Harington, ed. Robert McNulty (1972); Henry Howard, Lord Surrey, *Poems*, ed. Emrys Jones (1964); Walter W. Skeat, ed., *Chaucerian and Other Pieces* (1894–97); William Shakespeare, *The Complete Works*, ed. Stanley Wells and Gary Taylor (1986); G. Gregory Smith, ed., *Elizabethan Critical Essays* (1904); Edmund Spenser, *Poetical Works*, ed. J. C. Smith and E. de Selincourt (1912, rpt. 1970).

University Microfilms: *The Works of Geoffrey Chaucer*, ed. Thomas Speght (London: John Harefinch, 1687) (*English Books 1641–1700*, C3736 Wing Reel No. 59).

University of Virginia Special Collections Department, Alderman Library: *The Workes of Our Ancient and learned English Poet, Geffrey Chaucer*, ed. Thomas Speght (London, 1602).

CHAPTER I

Receiving Chaucer in Renaissance England

THERESA M. KRIER

The parts that Geoffrey Chaucer plays in British letters from the time of his death through the Restoration have stimulated literary scholars since the late nineteenth century. Into the first decades of the twentieth century Chaucer functioned not only as presiding genius of English poetry but also as a threshold between the man of letters, who practices connoisseurship, and the professional scholar. Studies of Chaucer's place in British letters during the three centuries after his death have continued through multitudinous kinds of scholarly method and ideology, and into the last quarter of this century, when they have been refreshed first by the kind of work on *imitatio* and literary precursors associated with Yale, second by feminist criticism and gender studies more broadly, and third by revisionist interest in the literary culture of the fifteenth century.[1] From virtually the year of his death, it has been a part of the story of British letters that Chaucer's works exemplify, variously, a paradoxically canny innocence and a courtly idealism; styles both plain and aureate, low and high; interpretive possibilities both open and hidden; many means of characterization; strategies for negotiating complex social positions; forms, tropes, *topoi,* and devices that made possible many new things in lyric and narrative; and fictional worlds the vitality and high color of which became a resource for a remarkable array of writers; indeed, that his works have formed what could be taken by writers and readers of the next three centuries as an authentic literature, within which they could speak themselves. Gratitude to Chaucer for this unintended gift does not simply occur within English literary history; from the time of Chaucer's death through the seventeenth century, the documents of gratitude to him and the invention that his work elicits constitute one of the chief accounts of such a history, a major narrative thread of the formation of English letters.

This gratitude with which Chaucer and the works attributed to him are so often met in the Renaissance is a remarkable feature of English literary history, worth dwelling on here. In England in the sixteenth and early seventeenth centuries, the time span of this book, the gratitude is ardent and abundant; it is acknowledged even by those of neoclassical bent; it is characteristic of readers, writers, editors, and publishers alike; it extends to many kinds of Chaucerian writing—fabliau and romance, courtly and bourgeois, lyric, narrative, prose; it is gratitude for Chaucer as universal or general figure of the poet as well as for his specific works. Gratitude for the resource that Chaucer proved to be for English Renaissance letters and national identity gives rise to tropes that became long-lived topoi: Chaucer as master and teacher, Chaucer's refinement and garnishing of the vernacular, Chaucer's bounty and abundance, Chaucer the delver into rich mines of wisdom, Chaucer the wellspring of poetry, Chaucer the treasure-house; Chaucer at once mellifluous and satiric, thus the very form of the poet who mingles counsel with delight; Chaucer as the most hospitable host and also the glad receiver of English poets' later hospitality; Chaucer as revered, white-haired father of England's youngest poetry ("Art, like yong grasse in the spring of *Chaucers* florishing," Thomas Nashe calls it).[2] Writers representing diverse, not to say conflicting interests in matters political, religious, poetic, economic, scientific, or historical enlist Chaucer into service or align themselves with him. And all of this hardly begins to address the manifold ways in which his lyrics, tales, genres, authorial self-representations, and other features of his craft were to prove a resource for poets and dramatists of scope.

How can we, late twentieth-century readers and scholars, approach this phenomenon of gratitude to Chaucer without naïveté but without cynicism? Is it even possible to speak of gratitude in sixteenth- and early seventeenth-century English culture (to come to the frames of this book) in terms besides those of a Maussian analysis?[3]

For Mauss, the gift is something intentionally given, and it structures constraints: intentional generosity creates a burden to the recipient, an obligation to acknowledge and reciprocate. Furthermore, any one gift is by definition limited because specific. Chaucer's work is taken or constructed as a gift by readers and writers in the sixteenth and seventeenth centuries, as we have come to see during the writing of this book. But these readers and writers, otherwise so woven into the tensions of a gift economy, often enjoy in this gift a liberation from any intentionality of a giver. In this respect, Chaucer's work is received less as an intentional gift in a structure of exchange than as a world is received, there to be used, inexhaustible. As William Flesch argues, "[t]he world's generosity consists in its being able to absorb all skepticism about its objects and still promise the plenitude of its generality. This is not the Cartesian or Heideggerian generosity that *gives* being; it is rather a generosity that *assures* being."[4] And again, "It is one of the important consolations of viewing the world not as a collection of objects but as a *kind* of place, as a locus of generality, that such generality promises to be inexhaustible" (85). Chaucer frequently functions for the Renaissance as a world or a place in this sense; I think this is one reason that sixteenth-century printers and editors continually enlarged the list of works attributed to Chaucer, because of a wish to increase what they felt as the resource of his generality, which came to be felt as inexhaustible. (For another, more explicitly political explanation of the swelling of Chaucer's complete works in the sixteenth century, see John Watkins's chapter in this volume.)

Furthermore, although readers and writers focused on Chaucer in the Renaissance sometimes manifest ambivalence and anxiety about how to manage a relation to him, it would be difficult to argue for much hostility toward him; in fact a pervasive affection for him and a sense that he makes possible one's own inventiveness and elevations of craft are the things that need more explanation, especially in light of fifteenth-century writers' much more frequent self-deprecation before Chaucer. For example, Chaucer may become less formidable or excessive a precursor as temporal distance from him grows: it is likely that the increasing pressure of the Reformation in England, and a gradual alienation from forms of spoken Middle English, contributed to the new sense of distance from, and unservile gratitude toward, Chaucer among men of letters in the sixteenth century. Seth Lerer's study of the transitional work of Caxton, Hawes, and Skelton, at the turn of the fifteenth century, is relevant here: Lerer situates their work in emergent differences in purpose and function between manuscript and print, and in the relatively settled political situation after the Wars of the Roses.[5] Moreover, aggression is not identical to hostility. Aggression indeed enters responses to Chaucer in the sixteenth and seventeenth centuries, but it is most often aggression understood as an energy, even a fierceness, of willingness to use Chaucer in a strong sense: to engage with specific works, to grapple with him, to acknowledge that he elicits one's own invention and discovery of poetic authority. (The chief exception may be the late-Elizabethan aristocrat Sidney, whose breeding and expectations led to responses to Chaucer much different from those of most of the writers and editors discussed in this volume, born into the middle classes.) Sometimes the concomitant affect is gladness, sometimes darker or less secure postures. (See especially the chapters of Craig Berry, Carol Martin, and Glenn Steinberg in this volume.) I turn altogether, therefore, from the complex philosophical and ethnographic discourses in which Mauss figures prominently to a psychoanalytic account of gratitude that more effectively articulates the peculiar kind of gift that Chaucer was to become for the English Renaissance.

Gratitude entered psychoanalytic discourse controversially but fleetingly, twinned with envy, when Melanie Klein placed these two conditions at the heart of her developmental theory. In the 1957 book *Envy and Gratitude,* she argues that envy and gratitude are innate, arising from the death instinct and the life instinct, respectively, and that they develop as responses to the maternal breast, with its power to provide or withhold food and comfort. As the infant comes to perceive this provider as separate from himself—that is, insofar as nurture and love are deposited elsewhere than in himself—envy is stirred, with its particular wish to spoil the desired external object, to destroy its creativity. But gratitude is also awakened: as the infant internalizes the "good breast" as a steadfast good object, and identifies with it so as to feel that he possesses goodness of his own, he founds a capacity for a later, generous mode of relating and a capacity to experience gratitude. Klein says a "good [internal] object is established, which loves and protects the self and is loved and protected by the self. . . . Through processes of projection and introjection, through inner wealth given out and re-introjected, an enrichment and deepening of the ego comes about. In this way the possession of the helpful inner object is again and again reestablished and gratitude can fully come into play."[6]

This passage is notable for its sustained attention to gratitude; in her book and the papers that led up to its composition, Klein gives a good deal more attention to envy than to gratitude. Because her argument required a condition derived from the life instincts, as envy derived from the death instinct, gratitude fit the structure of her argument. But she and other Kleinians have little to say about gratitude. It remains largely implicit, for instance, that while envy arises in earliest infancy (Klein's "paranoid-schizoid position"), gratitude must be a later achievement of the "depressive position." Nor does she dwell on the mechanisms by which this comes about. A few British psychoanalytic writers will fill out this gap. D. W. Winnicott, for instance, insists on the relevance of the environmental role of the caretaker in the arousal of envy and gratitude. Gratitude becomes possible when, over time, the good-enough mother *receives* the infant's projections of "good breast," "good object." The mother's taking and holding of the infant's projections, and her subsequent reciprocation by sending such projections, transformed, back to the infant, who has also been changed by the encounter, eventually allow the infant to internalize the constancy of the object that he has both projected and discovered.[7]

Gratitude, for Winnicott, would be a character formation allowing the capacity to "use" an object, even to use objects "ruthlessly" (this would include the way that strong poets in Harold Bloom's sense use earlier poets, although for Winnicott this need not be an oedipal agon). To use an object, in Winnicott's special sense, requires having accepted "the object's independent existence, its property of having been there all the time." The developmental challenge is to place the object "outside the area of the subject's omnipotent control."[8] The infant comes to this realization of the object's independence of his control through destruction of the (fantasied, omnipotent) object—for instance in frustration that the object hasn't perfectly met his desire for food, or comfort, or stimulation—followed by the liberating discovery that the (external, living) object has survived this destruction and sustained its responsiveness to him. The external object's survival is effectually what gives the world, or assurance of the world, to the child. And the ruthlessness of the infant in destroying and recovering objects is an aggression that makes possible his attachment to those objects. (A fuller discussion would need to address the ethics of various kinds of "usings.") As Christopher Bollas puts it, the adult "develops a profound gratitude toward life—for what it offers and for how it can be *taken*. Such an individual conveys not rapacity in the choice and use of objects but almost exactly the opposite: a kind of pleasure in being, a knowledge that there is sufficient experience to go around."[9] This is gratitude for the assurance of being that the world grants, of which William Flesch speaks, and that Chaucer as a world grants to so many Renaissance writers.[10] If the world is a resource to be used, gratitude can be not only a resulting condition but also a structural means of creating an abundant inner world, and apprehensions of a complex, densely populated external world: the person and the world summon or elicit each other. The originary object may or may not be mother; the particular constellations of objects "taken" are infinitely various, the uses to which they are put incalculable, and the integral nature of the taken objects crucial in any single instance. The "usings" that constitute literary *imitatio* are one domain evincing many kinds of using and complicated forms of gratitude. In *imitatio*, writers and works manifest what Elaine Scarry calls a "capacity for excessive reciprocation; what the human being has *made* is . . . this excessive power of reciprocation. . . . The total act of creating contains an inherent movement toward self-amplifying generosity." Receiving the nonintentional gift of the world (or of Chaucer's work), which assures of its inexhaustibility, may permit in the recipient a generosity extended toward the future: future projects, relationships, internal object relations.[11] This seems to me especially likely when the object or gift has something of the status of a person—Chaucer, for instance—and something of the status of a thing (or world)—like Chaucer's writings.

Then gratitude of this kind, a gratitude free to be supple and varied in its acknowledgments of obligation and allowing latitude for diverse ways of taking and using objects, arises not so much from having or being specific desirable things as from an inner, achieved sense that the resources to have or be them are available. Klein speaks of the inner wealth of the person, established through the infant's gradually built up experience of the object constancy of the breast; this object constancy, when and if achieved, is later available for extension to other objects. Envy, then, would include a kind of bemused bafflement or regret not just at others' being or having things but at some things' being possible or available to others, being resources *in potentia* to others but not to oneself. In the context of this book, we may speculate that fifteenth-century readers and writers often felt a kind of passive envy in the burden of Chaucer's generosity: not a Kleinian desire to despoil his creativity but the helplessness of not being able to respond in kind to his power. By the 1530s, however, Chaucer is effectually a "world," a reliably abundant source of provision. The processes and contents of gratitude as a possible feeling and gratitude-as-ability-to-use are thus neither simple nor uniform and need to be sorted out afresh, with more than one possible structure as explanatory model, in any one literary or historical instance.

As a key Renaissance instance of gratitude in the sense articulated by Klein and others in her tradition, of its complex workings, and of its functions in literary culture, I turn briefly to Francis Thynne's 1598 *Animadversions uppon the Annotacions and Corrections. . .*, written in response to Thomas Speght's 1598 edition of Chaucer.[12]

Francis Thynne's *Animadversions* is a defense of his father William Thynne's editing of Chaucer over sixty years earlier. William Thynne, Clerk of the Kitchen to Henry VIII, had been empowered by Henry to search all the libraries of England for Chaucer manuscripts, and had published his great edition in 1532. Francis, born in 1546, was in late middle age by the time he responded to Thomas Speght's 1598 edition with a fierce, detailed defense of his father's editorial decisions—a labor simultaneously on behalf of Chaucer, "to the end Chawcers Woorkes by muche conference and manye iudgmentes mighte at leng[t]he obteyne their true perfectione and glorye" (75). Francis Thynne had a passion for historical precision, and modern descriptions of him have gently mocked his antiquarian bent, which can make him seem pedantic, ineffectual, and irascible.[13] But this is to underrate not only Thynne's annotations on texts but also the motives that spurred the composition of the *Animadversions* in the first place, and the fervent sense of devotion to the past that haunts the work.

Thynne knows that he has a strong claim, through the labors of his father, to Chaucer as a paternal figure, and to insist on both the privileges and the obligations of this family tie that spans nearly two hundred years. It is Chaucer "whom I suppose I have as great intereste to adorne withe my smale skyll as anye other hath, in regarde that the laborious care of my father made hym most acceptable to the worlde in correctinge and augmentinge his work" (4). William Thynne had died before Francis was two years old, and the *Animadversions* as a whole, doing some of the work of mourning, functions to establish both William and Chaucer as paternal objects of constancy for Francis, the son in his fifties at the time of writing. The editorial labors of William endow Francis with the diachronically transmitted gifts of paternity, English national history, and poetic tradition. It is worth remembering that such gifts did not lie ready to hand, as if for the taking, except insofar as they were gradually built up and construed in just this way—as nature was construed, inexhaustible and generous—over the sixteenth century. William Thynne painstakingly recovered and reconstructed a Chaucer who could just as easily not have been recovered at all in any form, the vagaries of time and monarchs being what they are; Francis Thynne's psychic work in recovering both Chaucer and a father he could barely have remembered is even more striking. Father and son alike find strength for creative action by constructing the past as a gift; a proto-Maussian recognition of politic gift reception coexists with expressions of gratitude as affect and noble gesture toward the future. Thus Thynne's prefatory letter to Sir Thomas Egerton, with its excruciatingly complicated expressions of gratitude toward a patron: the treatise is like those gifts of the ancient Romans which were both a good policy and a true pledge of friendship, "for the manye good effects whiche issue from so woorthye cause" (1). Francis takes his own particular tasks to be the edification of learning and his country's honor, and the conservation of Chaucer—which would also be the conservation of his father.

Both William Thynne and Chaucer are poignantly remote from Francis, and it is testimony to the vigor of Francis Thynne's imaginative work that both father figures are so vividly animated and conserved in the *Animadversions.*

The text is populated with good and bad father surrogates and authorities, drawn chiefly from William Thynne's time. There is a repeated concern with recovery and preservation of these fathers' proper names. (Women occur infrequently; when they do it is in the interest of clarifying the genealogical time frame, for example, when certain princesses were wed to certain kings; but their names too need to be saved from the predations of time.) King Henry had authorized William's editorial work; Cardinal Wolsey had been his enemy for Thynne's involvement with John Skelton; good old men, "now of good worshippe" (9), who had been William's clerks, tell the adult Francis a vivid (and historically impossible) anecdote about the wickedness of bishops and the vulnerability of the unlettered poor (9); Henry had in some measure protected William from the anger of the bishops at his inclusion of the anti-episcopal "Pilgrim's Tale" in his first printing of Chaucer (10); Speght's edition suffers because he perpetuates the many errors of his unreliable authority Bale; late medieval kings and barons crop up frequently, as Francis clarifies the dynastic histories garbled by Speght; Richard Chaucer was the poet's grandfather, not his father as Speght thinks.[14]

Thynne's intense focus on familial and material history seems to me to stem directly from his working to make constant internal objects of his father and Chaucer, in the wake of King Henry's disruption of what Francis, like many of his contemporaries, would have preferred to view as a continuous time line from the late fourteenth and fifteenth centuries to himself. The *Animadversions* shows the adult scholar-son populating and filling the world with material objects of interest accessible and alive to him by virtue of his relationships to the two older figures. There is everywhere a concern for accurately remembered family trees, family arms, and family geography. The corrections of Speght's glosses of individual words and etymologies encompass natural history, alchemy, goldsmithing, numismatics, mythography, animal husbandry, heraldry, weapons, and armor. Not all of these corrections are useful or true.[15] Nonetheless, the late medieval world is ardently invoked in Thynne's notes. The tones in which Thynne has directed his points of information and his fields of interest to Speght shift unpredictably from irascibility and injured merit to magnanimity, but in general he seems to move himself toward a stance of generosity through the very process of writing his notes, in part because his evocation of Chaucer's time moves him from rebuke to celebration, or from disappointment and perhaps envy at the appearance of Speght's 1598 edition of Chaucer to an enlivened sense of his own possible contributions, what Klein would call his own inner wealth and resourcefulness, which he can present as a return gift to Chaucer. In this he continues the work of his father, whose motive was "the love he oughte to Chawcers learninge" (71). In neither father nor son does there seem to be an onus of obligation to Chaucer (although they both seem competent in the gift economies of their own periods); the affect seems more a happiness or satisfaction, self-amplifying as Scarry says, in this giving that preserves relationships, despite Henry's having created a history of rupture rather than continuity.

For the title of this volume we've chosen to use the term *Renaissance* rather than *early modern.* Literary history needs the distinctions afforded by conserving both these terms; in this book our emphasis is on the ways that sixteenth- and early seventeenth-century writers defined themselves retrospectively in relation to the fourteenth century, not the ways that they can be situated, prospectively, as early modern.[16] The chronological category of "Renaissance," not without its heuristic usefulness, places Chaucer both as an English medieval poet and as the contemporary of early Italian Renaissance writers; one of his gifts is precisely the conveyance and mediation of Petrarch, Boccaccio, and others to sixteenth- and seventeenth-century English culture. Our title thus refers both to refigurations of Chaucer by Tudor, Elizabethan, and Jacobean readers, writers, and editors and to our own scholarly refigurings of Chaucer's peculiar role vis-à-vis "renaissances" widely separated in time and place.

The chapters in this volume make manifest not so much a diversity of Renaissance Chaucers—one of our early formulations—as the extraordinary range of literary, social, and psychic invention that he makes possible, always as nonintentional contributor to a general, continually emergent English identity. Thus, in our first section, "Forming Canons," John Watkins's chapter on the work that Chaucer does for Wyatt and other early Tudor aristocrats contrasts William Thynne's labor, sponsored by Henry VIII, of compiling and printing his greatly influential edition of Chaucer's works, with the poetic labors in manuscript of the aristocrats who suffered the politico-erotic upheavals of Henry's court. Although we owe to Thynne a relative stabilizing of the medieval manuscript transmission of Chaucer's work and the development of Chaucer as a general poet, accessible to any reader, Watkins argues, the royal patronage of the work was one of the many autocratic, centralizing gestures of Henry's regime, and was intended to augment Henry's own glory and strength. And it was ambitious, restless nobles like Wyatt and Thomas Howard who preserved more purely medieval ways of taking an author by freely borrowing or imitating Chaucer's courtly lyrics and laments, identifying themselves with the speakers of these poems, writing themselves into Chaucer's poetry—most notably for us, in the great Devonshire manuscript, in many ways a testament to a lost medieval past identified with Chaucer and his poetic craft.

Carol Martin, noting the nervous or ambivalent treatments of the *House of Fame* within sixteenth-century editions of Chaucer's works, especially that of Thomas Speght, compares claims for poetry possible in the late fourteenth century, in Chaucer's *House of Fame,* and those possible in the late sixteenth century, in Sidney's *Apologie for Poetrie,* after Boccaccio's defense of poetry and complicated humanist positions on mythopoeia generally. Martin identifies Sidney's emphasis on authority as one line of late-Elizabethan responsiveness to the problem of the truth claims of poetry that Chaucer had negotiated in his narrative poem: while Chaucer declines "externally conferred authority," Sidney's treatise "participates in a hermeneutics suited to compete for power in Elizabethan culture." A number of factors from various spheres would have contributed to this transformation of the role of poet between the late fourteenth and the late sixteenth centuries: the Reformation and Sidney's Calvinist leanings, the challenge to poetry of Plato's *Republic,* Sidney's aristocratic birth and humanist education. The aristocratic Sidney, in fact, demonstrates a wary acknowledgment of Chaucer's importance and a wary acknowledgment of his own affinity for Chaucerian irony that make more sense in Maussian terms of gratitude than in Kleinian terms: for Sidney, Chaucer's works are a gift to English letters, but one that requires caution and an emulative counterinsistence on one's own strength or authority.

Clare Kinney turns to another remarkable phenomenon of Thomas Speght's 1602 printing of Chaucer, his identifying bits of text memorable for their epigrammatic expression of common wisdom by means of tiny pointing hands, marginal maniples. The 221 proverbs or proverblike phrasings, mostly those about love, that Speght identifies in *Troilus and Criseyde* form the matter of Kinney's chapter. To our time Speght's project might well seem a diminishment, a flattening of Chaucer's poetically rich narratives and lyrics. But the commonality of Speght's Chaucerian *sententiae* marks yet another way in which Chaucer's work had become a general gift, available to do many kinds of work. Gerald Hammond remarks how thoroughly proverbs or proverbial phrasings and rhythms pervaded the work of poets of all degrees in the sixteenth and seventeenth centuries, and of the way that apparently easily assimilable commonplaces could conceal hidden depths: "because they were so often compressed, even elliptical, they could . . . take on a parabolic obscurity" pointing to gravity and depth.[17] Speght makes Chaucer responsive to the Renaissance hunger for the reliable truisms of proverbs and proverblike summations. Still, Kinney argues, Speght's proverb hunting poses a difficulty; as reader of the *Troilus* he "forces upon [the poem] a univocality which its very narrative practice perpetually puts in question." No one character, and certainly not the narrator, has the truth in this poem; rather all the characters are given to using proverbial forms to express what they take as the truth about love. Speght seems drawn to expressions of the vicissitudes and unreliability of love, although he never acknowledges the implicit contradictions of the different characters' views. What makes this affinity of Speght's telling, as Kinney discovers, is his complete lack of attention to precisely the passages of the poem that mark movements beyond contingency to a Boethian/Christian divine order. Instead, Speght reconstructs the Chaucer who wrote the *Troilus* as a "classical" authority.

Part II, "Claims for Narrative Poetry: Chaucer and Spenser," includes three chapters examining the ways that Edmund Spenser, Chaucer's greatest successor in narrative poetry, thinks out and represents his own poetic personae, tones, and authority through the instrument of Chaucer's work. Whether Chaucer contributes a theme, a temptation to rework an unfinished tale, a set of aesthetic and spiritual decorums, or models for developing the narrator's presence within stories, Chaucer is always, for Spenser, the other through whom he may think himself as poet. The range of Spenser's Chaucerian tones and genres, and the pervasiveness of Chaucer throughout Spenser's writings, are striking.[18] His Chaucerian store includes, of course, the Squire's Tale, the Franklin's Tale, Sir Thopas, and the *Parlement of Foules* but also the General Prologue and the frame story of the *Canterbury Tales,* the Knight's Tale, the Merchant's Tale, the Wife of Bath's Prologue and Tale, the Monk's Tale, the Nun's Priest's Tale, the Pardoner's Tale, the Tale of Melibee, *The Book of the Duchess, The House of Fame, Troilus and Criseyde,* and *Anelida and Arcite;* it seems likely that he also studied "Jack Upland," the Chaucerian complaint poetry often included as Chaucer's in sixteenth-century editions, the *Boece,* and the translated fragment of the *Roman de la Rose.*

After writing many essays that follow highly specific lexical trails from Chaucer to Spenser, Judith Anderson here ranges over the whole of *The Faerie Queene* in a meditation on Spenser's developments of narrative strategies and positions in relation to his tales, in response to Chaucer's

Canterbury Tales, notably the General Prologue, *Sir Thopas,* and the Tale of Melibee. She argues for a reclamation of authorial "agency, accountability, and . . . responsibility to history" while also insisting on the "doubled, deliberately elusive, and fleeting identity" of Spenser's narrative self-representations. Like the authors of other chapters on Spenser in this volume, Anderson articulates Spenser's Chaucerian epistemological movement (within individual works, or from book to book of *The Faerie Queene*) from assurance to doubt or uncertainty about how to take the world as represented within the narrative. For Anderson, the concomitant poetic feature is the *dédoublement* or division into (at least) two narrative personae; following Paul de Man, she emphasizes the capacity for reflective activity within a consciousness that contains two selves. The vividly mimetic narrator of Chaucer and the fleeting, cagey narrator of Spenser are decentered, masked, impersonating and performing characters whom they inhabit but from whom they are nevertheless distinct. Many of these actions of authorial presence in both poets may be viewed as forms of irony, something that always bears repeating in regard to Spenser.[19] Chaucer, who thought harder about storytelling than perhaps any English writer before Spenser, suggests to Spenser poetic and narrative techniques by which he may dwell, a fleeting presence, within the amplitude of his fictive world yet also embrace it.

Craig Berry's chapter, on doubt in *The Faerie Queene* IV, addresses the linked matters of epistemological uncertainty and gender that Spenser brings together in his engagement with Chaucer's Knight's Tale and Squire's Tale. Spenser's development of romance comes to the fore in this constellation of works, particularly in romance's joining of vulnerability of interpretation with the marvelous, the exotic, the unfamiliar. A line of romance that runs from Chaucer to Spenser—and Shakespeare, we might add—may come to be characterized as a "world" of the kind that (nonintentionally) challenges and exposes the reader willing to take this gift. As Gerald Bruns says of Gadamer on the risks of receiving such gifts: "For Gadamer . . . openness is not simply an open-mindedness or tolerance. . . . It is more like the exposure that occurs in hermeneutical experience, where I find that the other that I seek to understand cannot be contained within the conceptual apparatus that I (or my time, place, and institution) have prepared for it. . . . The other opens me, exposes me, to the subject that calls for understanding. . . . We are placed in the open, in the region of the question."[20] Berry emphasizes a Renaissance ambivalence to Chaucer and to the Middle Ages more generally; Berry's Spenser finds Chaucer a "difficult ancestor" but also Spenser's best ally in carrying the standard of "an English poetic heritage" and confronting the threat of readerly mistaking (a risk not unknown to Chaucer). In the end, Berry's Spenser is not so much defensive as he is exhilarated by the exorbitant poetic challenges he sets for himself as one who receives Chaucer, and by the improvisatory measures that his intricate narratives require.

In his chapter on Chaucer's *Book of the Duchess* and Spenser's *Daphnaïda,* Glenn Steinberg presents a considerably darker and more austere Spenser, but for him too Spenser articulates an aesthetic and spiritual vision by means of an intensive encounter with Chaucer as the other, or better as the opposite, through whom he establishes both identification with and differentiation from a poetry and a poetic unavailable to him. Steinberg argues that the Spenser of the *Daphnaïda* is a man *in extremis,* as fervent in his Calvinism as the poem's protagonist Alcyon is fierce in his grief. Chaucer, to this Renaissance poet, represents a courtly, graceful aesthetic with the capacity to console, and a time when there could be certitude about what were felt to be eternal verities. These consolations do not exist for the Calvinist Spenser, for whom the Reformation has undermined those features of medieval elegy. The aesthetic of *Daphnaïda* is consequently not one of grace and polish but one of rawness and violent excess, its spirituality reaching not to the stability of divine order but to a more perilously grounded sense of divine inscrutability.

Part III, "Gender and the Translation of Genre," opens with another chapter on Spenser. We include it in this last section because the three chapters of part III demonstrate the manifold ways that gender functions as part of Chaucer's "gift" to the English Renaissance: as theme, as narrative resource, as marker of difference among genres, as path of intertextuality, as manifestation of diverse social possibilities for women in the relevant periods.

A. Kent Hieatt, writing about the middle books of *The Faerie Queene,* those on chastity and friendship, argues that they exceed the concerns that new-historical work tends to emphasize through its focus on Books I, II, V, and VI: the representations of Queen Elizabeth, the formation of an English national identity, the unstable politics of courtly life, and so on. New Historicism has little interest in *imitatio* and no concepts that could adequately address the processes or aims of imitation. But it's through imitation that Spenser (like most of his contemporaries) thought out matters of gender, history, politics, ethics, and aesthetics. It is also the way that he makes the past into the future. Specifically, Hieatt argues, Spenser thinks out his relationship to Chaucer via a threefold narrative ramification (Florimell and Marinell, Amoret and Scudamour, Britomart and

Artegall) of the Franklin's Tale, with its emphasis on the failure of mastery to extort love. The converse is also true: Chaucer's work is perhaps Spenser's most powerful and supple instrument for working out his elaboration of romance eros, heroism, and friendship. Developing themes and stories from Chaucer, Spenser invents or finds within himself that which is also, paradoxically, bestowed from without; his invention rises as a consequence of his meeting and entering the world that Chaucer has become for him.

My own chapter takes up the intuition that's appeared now and then in criticism that Shakespeare's *Love's Labour's Lost* is indebted to Chaucer's *Parlement of Foules*. This is a suggestion usually based on similarities of plot, notably the inconclusive endings in which, while the male characters of each work press for marital choice (and the closure of romantic comedy), the female characters claim the authority to defer such choice for a year. I turn instead to the implicit plot of genre and literary history within each work and argue for a purposive progression from narrative verse to lyric (the roundel welcoming summer in the *Parlement*) and from dramatico-narrative verse to lyric (the memorable seasonal songs in *Love's Labour's Lost*). The aim in each case is a particular kind of lyric, the catalogue-based praising of creatures, which in both works descends from the medieval encyclopedic and hexameral traditions. Chaucer draws into the vernacular and makes more general, in Flesch's sense, Latin and French texts of the twelfth and thirteenth centuries (for example, the *Roman de la Rose*); Shakespeare conveys Chaucer himself a step further into the vernacular, delivering (even to the nonliterate, in his performed play) Chaucer and his hexameral, encyclopedic celebrations as a gift to the turbulent vernacular changes of the late sixteenth century.

Helen Cooper's chapter concludes this volume with a discussion of Jacobean playwrights' transformations of tales and characters of *The Canterbury Tales* into dramas, which respond to the complex gender relations that Chaucer had articulated in the Knight's Tale, the Franklin's Tale, the Clerk's Tale, and the Wife of Bath's Prologue and Tale. The main device of plot resolution is the transformation of a tense love triangle into a stable, harmonious quadrangle or its reduction to an equally harmonious pair; in *The Two Noble Kinsmen*, by contrast, the same device becomes an element of radical destabilization. Around this Cooper weaves a web of readings of many Jacobean plays—and of *A Midsummer Night's Dream*, which works in the essay to reveal the manifold ways that Fletcher's plays fail the ethical/aesthetic challenges of Chaucer's intricacies and balances. In Cooper's account, Chaucer plays a large part in the development of the Jacobean plays that we variously, sometimes loosely, group together as tragicomedies and/or romances. *The Canterbury Tales* had played off against one another the genre norms associated with various social estates, chiefly the romance idealism of the Knight (and the real-life aristocrats whose interests he served) and the relative verisimilitude of discourse in the speech of pilgrims of the mercantile estates. But *The Two Noble Kinsmen,* Cooper argues, "charts the decline from the age of chivalry to the age of capitalism"; its "detailed dialogue" with the Knight's Tale ends with a cynical rejection of the balance achieved with such conscious difficulty in its original.

As a transition to the chapters of this book, I turn finally to a late nineteenth-century appreciation of Chaucer, John Ruskin's impassioned *Love's Meinie.* Intended originally to contain "the cream of forty volumes of scientific ornithology,"[21] Ruskin's complete published work becomes an impassioned brief for the vernacular, for the "English labourer" as against industrialization and the homogenization of the landscape by corporate magnates. "England was then [in Chaucer's time] a simple country; we boasted, for the best kind of riches, our birds and trees, and our wives and children" (43). Chaucer has been invoked earlier on the pivotal problem of ornithological nomenclature—Ruskin despises the chaos of Latin names, and he turns to old poets for an alternative:

> In the meantime, you yourselves, or, to speak more generally, the young rising scholars of England,—all of you who care for life as well as literature, and for spirit,—even the poor souls of birds,—as well as lettering of their classes in books,—you, with all care, should cherish the old Saxon-English and Norman-French names of birds, and ascertain them with the most affectionate research—never despising even the rudest or most provincial forms. (22)

Ruskin encourages the naturalist to embrace in his interests not only birds but poems and etymologies; to subordinate the dessicating lust for classification to the generative exercise of naming; to pursue erudition not in remote and foreign (Latinate) taxonomies but in imaginally vivid, historically specific birds of vernacular literature. Of his many examples from medieval poetry, he cites the translation by Chaucer of a passage from the *Roman de la Rose,* a translation in which Chaucer's bird catalogue doubles the number of species of birds named by Jean de Meun. Following both the English and the French, Ruskin offers demonstrations of "word-chasing" (43), a parallel to the activities of ornithologists, as a tribute to the riches of the vernacular. He ends his lecture on the robin with a negative catalogue that stands as a kind of reverse synecdoche, an expansion, of all the poetic, social, political, aesthetic meanings that "Chaucer" has come to mean:

> Since the future life of the English labourer or artisan (summing the benefits to him of recent philosophy and economy) is to be passed in a country without angels and without birds, without prayers and without songs, without trees and without flowers, in a state of exemplary sobriety, and . . . in a state of dispensation with the luxury of marriage, I do not believe he will derive either profit or entertainment from lectures on the Fine Arts. (44)

Taken at face value this is no doubt sentimentality, but a sentimentality performing a certain labor in the particular ways that it continues the long project of making Chaucer part of English culture. Throughout *Love's Meinie,* Chaucer is metonymic for many things that Ruskin wishes to preserve from the diverse threats of big money and power: English birds and flowers, songs, angels, prayers, the pleasures of etymological researches, the laboring classes. By the end, the metonymy reverses itself, so that Chaucer has been disseminated, as it were, into the lives of birds, flowers, honest laborers and their wives and children, into the landscape, into the history of the vernacular. For Ruskin, Chaucer has become a romance spirit of place, a genius of England; like other such figures, he may protect the threatened land. Ruskin can afford this appeal to Chaucer in the late nineteenth century in large part because of the vigorous, unsentimental labors he performed in the sixteenth century before the early seventeenth century's turn toward sentimentality—labors that we describe in this volume.

Notes

1. Book-length studies and collections include Miskimin, *Renaissance Chaucer*; Hieatt, *Chaucer, Spenser, Milton*; Thompson, *Shakespeare's Chaucer*; Donaldson, *The Swan at the Well.* Other studies, useful in part for their instantiation of changing modes of scholarship, include Donaldson and Kollmann, *Chaucerian Shakespeare*; Spearing, *Medieval to Renaissance*; Morse and Windeatt, eds., *Chaucer Traditions*; Lerer, *Chaucer and His Readers*; Hetherington, *Chaucer, 1532–1602*; Maynard, *Connection*; Ord, *Chaucer and the Rival Poet*; Tobler, *Geoffrey Chaucer's Influence*; Wright, *Seventeenth-Century Modernisation.* See also shorter studies: Burrow, "*Sir Thopas* in the Sixteenth Century"; Boughner, "Background of Lyly's Tophas"; Brewer, "Images of Chaucer"; Evans, "Ben Jonson's Chaucer"; Fox, "Thomas More's *Dialogue*"; Machan, "Kynaston's

Troilus"; Ryan, "Chaucer's Criseyde in Neo-Latin Dress." Many others are cited elsewhere in this volume; see bibliography.

2. Nashe, *Strange Newes of the intercepting of certaine Letters,* cited in Spurgeon, *Five Hundred Years of Chaucer Criticism*, 136.

3. See Mauss, *The Gift*. Mauss has been used to great effect by new historicists, students of patronage, and feminist work on drama. William Flesch, *Generosity and the Limits of Authority*, cites several literary studies using Mauss on the gift.

4. Flesch, *Generosity and the Limits of Authority*, 11.

5. Lerer, *Chaucer and His Readers*, chaps. 5 and 6.

6. Klein, *Envy and Gratitude*, 19. Klein's work reveals some contradictory thoughts about gratitude. As in the passage cited here, she takes pains to include it within the early paranoid-schizoid position because she wants to preserve the Eros/Thanatos structure. But, more logically in her thought, gratitude evolves as a response to anxiety and fits better into the later depressive position.

7. Winnicott, "Beginnings of a Formulation" (1962), in his *Psycho-Analytic Explorations*, 450.

8. Winnicott, "The Use of an Object," in his *Playing and Reality*, 88, 89.

9. Christopher Bollas, *Cracking Up*, 92. This is a rare thought about gratitude; current writers on Klein are much more likely to elaborate her work on the death drive.

10. One of the most moving usages of Chaucer in this way, that of Mary Shelton, whose social world was that of the aristocrats variously threatened, imprisoned, and executed by Henry VIII in the 1530s, is reconstructed by Paul Remley, "Mary Shelton and Her Tudor Literary Milieu." The kind of assurance of world focused in Shelton's uses of Chaucer is striking in contrast to the Henrician period's refusal of assurance of life to aristocrats and civil servants.

11. Scarry, *The Body in Pain*, 317–18. Thus Gabriel Harvey imagines for the dead Gascoigne a heavenly future of mutual poetic courtesy and feasting: "This pleasure reape: and shake thou hands / With auncient cuntrymen of thine: / Acquayntaunce take of Chaucer first / And then with Gower and Lydgate dine." Cited in Spurgeon, *Five Hundred Years*, 114.

12. Francis Thynne, *Animadversions*, ed. Furnivall, with preface by G. H. Kingsley.

13. Thus Kingsley, in his preface, describes Thynne speculatively as "a kindly, fussy, busy, querulous old man . . . an amiable but irritable old gentleman" (12).

14. A small, poignant twentieth-century mistake perpetuates the very threat of devouring time to proper lineage that worried Thynne: in the introduction to his facsimile of the *Works, 1532,* Derek Brewer says that Francis Thynne was the "grandson [not the son, as other scholars think] of the original editor of 1532" (unnumbered, seventh page of printed matter, section VI).

15. Derek Pearsall comments that "he is wrong nearly as often as he is right, wrong where Speght is right, right where Speght is wrong, and sometimes, to make utter confusion, wrong where Speght is wrong, but in a different way." See "Thomas Speght," 84–85.

16. See Bono, "The Birth of Tragedy," 449; Spearing, *Medieval to Renaissance*, 1–14; Marcus, "Renaissance/Early Modern Studies." Polemics against the term *Renaissance* often privilege, needlessly, the earliest uses of the word by Italian humanists and writers on the visual arts. The northern Renaissance, intersecting as it did with the Reformation, was different enough from Italian humanist assumptions to warrant more expansive meanings of the term; this is even more the case in insular Britain, where the rescue and transmission of certain medieval cultural phenomena, e.g., Chaucer, became an important adjunct to the recovery of the ancients, especially after the violent efforts of Henry VIII to obliterate late medieval institutions. The rescue of an imperiled Chaucer, the recreative claiming of poet and works in various projects of national literary self-definition, and a pervasive nostalgia in the construction of a Chaucerian England all attest to the traumatic historical ruptures bequeathed to British culture by Henry's actions. In this context it makes sense that Chaucer's tomb in Westminster Abbey was enlarged and monumentalized (his remains probably being moved as well) in 1556, shortly after the accession of Henry's daughter Mary. Chaucer's bones must have provided an irresistible occasion for the reclamation of the old religion and a pre-Henrician, more whole country. The changes to the burial site could well have been a gesture of Mary's "taking"—a taking back—of the world of which her father had so regularly despoiled her. See Lethaby, "Chaucer's Tomb," and Pearsall, *Life*, 295–96.

17. Hammond, *Fleeting Things*, 234.

18. There are many studies of the complex relationship of Spenser to Chaucer. In 1762 there was Thomas Warton's *Observations*, sect. V ("Of Spenser's imitations from Chaucer"). See also, besides those cited elsewhere in this book, Crampton, *Condition of Creatures*; Bennett, *Evolution of "The Faerie Queene"*; Anderson, "'Nat worth a boterflye'"; Berry, "Borrowed Armor"; Bloomfield, "Chaucer's Squire's Tale and the Renaissance"; Esolen, "Disingenuous Poet Laureate"; Giamatti, *Play of Double Senses*; Johnson, "*The Shepheardes Calender*"; Lasater, "Chaucerian Narrator"; Nadal, "Spenser's 'Muiopotmos'"; Watkins, *Specter of Dido*.

19. The broad spectrum of tones of irony and humor more generally emanating from the Spenserian narrator has been increasingly recognized in scholarship. See, e.g., Nelson, "Spenser *ludens*"; Martz, "The *Amoretti*." Harry Berger argues repeatedly and forcefully for a Spenserian narrator whose relation to his stories can include out-and-out hilarity; see *Spenserian Dynamics*, "'Kidnapped Romance,'" and "Narrative as Rhetoric."

20. Bruns, *Heidegger's Estrangements*, 7–8.

21. Ruskin, *Love's Meinie*, 13.

PART I

Forming Canons

CHAPTER 2

"Wrastling for this world"

Wyatt and the Tudor Canonization of Chaucer

JOHN WATKINS

For more than four hundred years, critics have honored Wyatt as the first representative of an English Renaissance conceived as an absolute break with the Middle Ages. Surrey eulogized him as the "hand . . . / That reft Chaucer the glory of his wit," and Puttenham later canonized him with Surrey as one of the "two chieftains" of a new poetic generation that "greatly pollished our rude & homely maner of vulgar Poesie from that it had been before."[1] Twentieth-century American critics have taken up this once nationalistically driven championship of Wyatt's originality. Thomas Greene hails him as the first English poet to respond fully to the Petrarchan "anguish of temporality" and historical distance.[2] Stephen Greenblatt ranks Wyatt with More, Spenser, Marlowe, and Shakespeare as a quintessentially Renaissance intellectual who exemplifies "an increased self-consciousness about the fashioning of human identity as a manipulable, artful process."[3] Yet in the years following the publication of Greene's *Light in Troy* and Greenblatt's *Renaissance Self-Fashioning,* British critics have taken a more skeptical view of Wyatt's alleged turn against the medieval past. As Dennis Kay, Helen Cooper, and A. C. Spearing have argued, Wyatt's vocabulary and thematic concerns arise from direct intertextual dialogue with Chaucer.[4] *Troilus and Criseyde,* for instance, explored the conflict between "truth" and "newfangledness" well over a century before Wyatt's complaints about a world devoid of "steadfastness."

While I want to build on Kay, Cooper, and Spearing's case against the Renaissance as an absolute departure from the medieval past, I also want to resist an aspect of their work that relies on the same humanist hermeneutics that authorized the myth of a European Renaissance in the first place. All three critics present Wyatt's relationship to Chaucer as an encounter between two autonomous personalities presiding over a fixed canon of texts. I will argue instead that Wyatt's poetry engages Chaucer's through factional conditions in which such autonomy was not an option. Neither Wyatt nor the Chaucer whom he reveres achieved the steadfastness of a stable, fully integrated subjectivity isolated from historical process. Since the acts of reading, collecting, excerpting, imitating, echoing, and above all editing Chaucer's texts were politically driven, Henry VIII's court confronted Wyatt with not one model of Chaucerian authority but several. Instead of providing the basis for one stable, poetic identity, this factionalization of Chaucer amplified Wyatt's characteristic restlessness and self-division.

As the son of a Yorkshireman knighted for service to Henry VII, Wyatt owed his fortune, lands, and title to the Tudors.[5] Throughout his career, however, alliances with courtiers destined to fall from Tudor favor threatened to sever him from the king, the source of his aristocratic identity. Wyatt's predicament was that of many Tudor new creations: his entire social standing depended on his unswerving loyalty to a notoriously fickle and unpredictable regime. When Wyatt's career seemed shakiest, his writing turned nostalgically toward the steadfastness of the Chaucerian past. But during the 1530s and 1540s, when Wyatt produced most of his lyric poetry, Chaucer was less steadfast than he seemed. Tudor readers confronted Chaucer in everything from isolated lines embedded in poems by other people to manuscripts and miscellanies of dubious textual reliability, to Caxton's printed editions of individual works, and to William Thynne's 1532 edition of Chaucer's complete *Works*, an edition notorious for its canonization of works written long after Chaucer's death.[6] By embodying divergent notions of what an author was, each of these formats carried a different political valence: the more they contributed to a laureate identity for Chaucer as a spokesman for transhistorical English values, the more they contributed to Henrician nationalism.

Before I analyze Wyatt's recreations of Chaucer, I want to inspect these rival disseminations of Chaucer's works throughout the early Tudor literary system. Two volumes, William Thynne's *Works* and the Devonshire manuscript, a handwritten miscellany by various authors that circulated among Henry VIII's courtiers, represent strikingly antithetical poles in Chaucer's cultural reception.[7] In producing a standardized Chaucer, Thynne supported the same Tudor drift toward centralization and autocracy that manifested itself in the suppression of feudal rights, the dissolution of the monasteries, the anathematization of the papacy, and other repudiations of the medieval past. According to Thynne's son Francis, editing Chaucer was central to Henry VIII's imperialism: "[M]y father hadde to have Chaucers Woorkes rightlye to be published. For the performance whereof, my father . . . had comissione to serche all the liberaries of England for Chaucers Workes, so that oute of all the Abbies of this Realme (whiche reserved anye monumentes thereof) he was fully furnished with a multitude of Bookes."[8]

Taken at face value as a response to Henry's love for Chaucer, Thynne's antiquarianism might suggest a purely nostalgic retreat from contemporary politics. But his tour of abbey libraries strikingly resembles another instance of state-financed scholarship, undertaken at almost the same time, whose goals were explicitly political. Twice during the crisis over the royal divorce, Henry commissioned scholars to examine both national and foreign libraries, bookshops, and monasteries for evidence proving first the invalidity of his marriage to Catherine of Aragon and later his sovereignty over English ecclesiastical matters.[9]

At our historical distance, the tales, ballades, dream visions, and romances that were the objects of Thynne's search might seem unrelated to the patristic, scholastic, and rabbinical commentaries, decretals, and law texts examined by the commissioners. But the dedication of Thynne's 1532 edition by Sir Brian Tuke to Henry VIII underscores the political nature of Thynne's project. Thynne was first moved to edit Chaucer "by a certayne inclynacion & zele / whiche I haue to here of any thyng soundyng to the laude and honour of this your noble realme."[10] Editing Chaucer becomes part of what Richard Helgerson calls the "writing of England," the creation of a distinctly English cultural identity.[11] Modeled on European editions of Virgil's *Opera,* Thynne's massive folio volume endowed Chaucer with a canonical identity as a native, Gothic laureate.

For later writers like Camden and Drayton, antiquarian enterprises like Thynne's often had a distinctly counter-monarchical implication, the establishment of an English national identity apart from the Crown.[12] Thynne's project, by contrast, contributed directly to the centralization of the Tudor state by casting Chaucer as a champion of the King against the conflicting claims of Church and nobility. Although the 1532 edition appeared two years before the proclamation of the royal supremacy and the suspension of annate payments decisively ended Henry's subordination to Rome, the Tudors had been restricting baronial prerogatives since the late fifteenth century.[13] Thynne reinforced this power shift away from a potentially rebellious aristocracy by including poems like "To the King's Most Noble Grace" and "To the Lordes and Knightes of the Garter," which seem to have been written by Hoccleve to support Henry V's suppression of the Oldcastle rebellion.[14] By attributing these expressions of stridently Lancastrian royalism to Chaucer, Thynne established a Chaucerian, laureate sanction for Henry VIII's campaigns against heresy and rebellion.

By dismissing the apocryphal additions to the Chaucerian canon as typical expressions of sixteenth-century Protestantism, literary historians have overlooked the political context in which they came to be identified as Chaucer's. With works like the "Plowman's Tale" and "Jack Upland," the 1542 Thynne and other post-Reformation editions of Chaucer reject Catholicism not just for doctrinal errors but for its usurpation of royal prerogatives:

> Kings and lordes shuld lordship han . . .
> Christ, for us that shedde his blood,
> Bad his preestes no maystership have.
> ("Plowman's Tale," 1119–21)[15]

The Chaucer produced by sixteenth-century editors as the fountain of all subsequent English poetry championed the royal supremacy in the larger context of Tudor centralization.

Inspired by a commitment to the realm as the King's absolute possession, Thynne's editions of Chaucer erased crucial aspects of England's medieval past. They do so not only by canonizing anticlerical satires but also by altering the means of textual production. While works like the "Plowman's Tale" reinforced the efforts of Henrician antiquarians to discover precedents for the King's struggle against Rome, the printed format of Thynne's editions eliminated the haphazardness of medieval manuscript transmission.[16] Collection, collation, and authorized publication became the textual correlatives of bureaucratic centralization. In a very literal way, Thynne's project challenged medieval property rights. Thynne's commission to ransack the abbey libraries anticipates the abbeys' dissolution less than ten years later. Appropriating manuscripts that might bolster an Erastian religious policy marked an early stage of the Crown's complete appropriation of monastic wealth. By 1532, Chaucer was no longer the possession of aristocrats and religious houses fortunate enough to own an individual manuscript. Under royal authorization, his collected corpus was now the property of a national readership.

Yet Thynne's version of Chaucer and the absolutist politics in which it participated were not uncontested. In 1536, Lord Thomas Howard defied the Tudor ambition to control aristocratic bloodlines by marrying Henry's niece, Lady Margaret Douglas, without his permission.[17] After Henry imprisoned the couple in the tower, they exchanged several lyrics still preserved in the Devonshire manuscript, a collection of miscellaneous poems by several court authors. The exchange culminates in Howard's rime royal complaint against the cruelty of their fate:

O very lord, O loue, O god, alas!
        That knowest best myn hert + al my thowght,
What shall my sorowful lyfe donne in thys case
        Iff I forgo that I so dere haue bought
                Syns ye and me haue fully brought
        Into your grace and both our hertes sealed
        Howe may ye suffer, alas, yt be repealed[18]

As scholars have often noted, this lyric is Howard's best poem because he stole it from Troilus's lament to fortune in Book IV, lines 288–329, of Chaucer's *Troilus and Criseyde*. The blank spaces indicate deletions of Criseyde's name, and a later stanza updates Chaucer's original grammar by substituting "Why wyld thow not" for the by then archaic phrase "Why nyltow fleen." With such editing, Howard appropriated Troilus's fictional complaint as an expression of his own suffering under a tyrannical king. For members of his class, the transformation of Chaucerian narrative into anonymous lyrics could serve as a code for expressing aristocratic resistance to Henry.[19]

Scholars have dismissed these transformations of Chaucerian narratives into Tudor lyrics as testimony to an insufficiently developed understanding of linguistic and stylistic anachronism.[20] Yet the appearance of the same poem—or parts of the same poem—in Thynne's editions and in the Devonshire manuscript signals a conflict between two constructions of Chaucer. The magisterial Chaucer of the printed editions bolstered the Henrician notion of England as an empire grounded in the king's authority. By contrast, the unacknowledged Chaucer excerpted in the manuscript miscellanies spoke for an aristocracy whose prerogatives diminished in direct proportion to the Crown's aggregation of power. The "facts" of Chaucer's biography as it evolved throughout the fifteenth and sixteenth centuries could corroborate either authorial identity. By establishing a precedent for England's opposition to Rome, the common view of Chaucer as "a right Wicleuian" abetted Henry's nationalization of the Church.[21] But the equally common view of him as a knight who had spent time in the Tower—a view enhanced by the attribution to him of Thomas Usk's *Testament of Love*—linked him to disenfranchised and imprisoned aristocrats like Thomas Howard and Thomas Wyatt.[22]

Scholars have long acknowledged the Devonshire manuscript as one of the more authoritative sources for over eighty poems in Wyatt's canon.[23]

But in addressing the question of Chaucer's influence on Wyatt, scholars have overlooked what the poets' proximity in the same manuscript suggests about their relationship. As I will argue, it indicates an ambivalence toward the Tudor dissemination of Chaucer that complements Wyatt's ambivalence toward the dissemination of power throughout Tudor society. Certain biographical evidence might suggest Wyatt's predisposition to embrace the pro-royal, proto-Protestant Chaucer canonized by Thynne. Unlike the Howards, Wyatt's family were members of a newly arrived Tudor aristocracy. Thomas Wyatt himself was a committed partisan of Thomas Cromwell, the man who most embodied the drive toward government centralization that curtailed the power of the older, feudal nobility.[24] Wyatt had several direct connections with those responsible for the Tudor "centralization" of Chaucer. His early translation of Plutarch's *De remediis utriusque fortunae* was published around 1527 by Richard Pynson, a printer whose three-part edition of Chaucer published the previous year anticipated Thynne's attempt to establish and codify the canon.

But despite these circumstances that would seem to encourage Wyatt's loyalty to Henry VIII and to the Tudor Chaucer, he was repeatedly at odds with Henry's government. In 1536, he was imprisoned with several other men implicated in Anne Boleyn's fall and escaped execution largely through Cromwell's intervention.[25] Cromwell's own fall in 1540 led Wyatt into even graver danger. The more Wyatt found himself on the margins of royal favor, the more he joined aristocratic writers like Thomas Howard in appropriating Chaucer as an oppositional voice. Rather than favoring the anticlerical works that Thynne foregrounded in support of Henry VIII's struggle against the Church, Wyatt turned to *Troilus and Criseyde,* the Knight's Tale, and such Boethian lyrics as "Fortune," "Truth," and "Lak of Stedfastnesse." By adopting this Chaucer's Boethian complaints about humanity's plight before an inscrutable destiny, Wyatt identified himself with the other Devonshire manuscript writers in their coded resistance to Henry. Yet as I will argue, as much as Wyatt strove to incorporate this Chaucer's Boethian vision into his own poetry, the social structures that might once have supported an actual abandonment of worldly commitments no longer existed. Instead of withdrawing from the frenzy of political careerism, Wyatt embraced it with renewed, though often desperate, confidence. As a Tudor new creation, he had no other place to turn. This lack contrasts markedly with what we know of Chaucer himself. Chaucer could espouse a policy of Boethian withdrawal because he had multiple social identities: as the son of a vintner, member of the royal household, and controller of the customs on wool, he resisted exclusive identity with any single social class or political faction. When his association with the King's party became a liability in the 1380s, for instance, he distanced himself from the court and retreated into the comparative safety of county politics as a justice with the commission of the peace for Kent.[26] As the scion of a well-established English family, Thomas Howard enjoyed a membership in the provincial aristocracy that was independent of his status as a Henrician courtier. By contrast, Wyatt owed everything to the Tudors. He might affect the *contemptus mundi* stance of more established aristocrats, but he could hardly renounce the court on which his identity depended.

Probably around the time of the Boleyn crisis, Wyatt modeled his poem "If thou wilt mighty be" on Chaucer's "Truth," or "Balade de Bon Conseyl." Both Wyatt's poem and its Chaucerian precedent consist of three rime royal stanzas paraphrasing passages from Boethius's *Consolatio* about the instability of human affairs. The envoy appended to Chaucer's poem in one manuscript suggests that he wrote it to console his friend Philip de la Vache for losses suffered during the Appellant crisis. Throughout the poem, Chaucer urges his auditor to renounce the world's vain pursuits and rest in a redemptive, ultimately transcendent truth:

> Flee fro the prees and dwelle with sothfastnesse;
> Suffyce unto thy thing, though it be smal,
> For hord hath hate, and climbing tikelnesse,
> Prees hath envye, and wele blent overal.
> Savour no more than thee bihove shal,
> Reule wel thyself that other folk canst rede,
> And trouthe thee shal delivere, it is no drede. (1–7)[27]

The insistent imperatives and the final refrain suggest a confidence in the gospel of withdrawal and self-sufficiency supported by experience as well as by Boethian authority. As Paul Strohm has argued, withdrawal was Chaucer's central survival strategy during the factional crises of the 1380s.[28] Just when his once advantageous association with the King's affinity might have led him to a disaster like Thomas Usk's, he severed his London ties to Richard II by leaving his position at the Custom House and his house over Aldgate and by strengthening his more neutral county associations with Kent.

Although Wyatt repeatedly echoed Chaucer's Boethian counsels, he never fully heeded them. Throughout his career, he broke his resolutions to flee from the press of courtly preoccupations almost as soon as he made them.[29] Immediately after his release from prison in 1536, he reenacted Chaucer's Kentish retreat by returning to his family seat at Allington and becoming the Knight of the Shire of Kent.[30] But within six months, he accepted an appointment as ambassador to the imperial court of Charles V. He returned to Kent and to his estranged wife once more after the disaster of 1541.[31] But by the middle of 1542, rumors circulated that he was about to become vice admiral of a fleet sailing against France. In October of that year, Henry dispatched him to escort the imperial ambassador from Cornwall to London. By riding in such haste that he contracted a fever and died en route, Wyatt gave his life in service to the King.

The inability to separate himself definitively from the court that defeated Wyatt's biographical attempts at Boethian resignation manifests itself even in his most conspicuously Chaucerian literary imitations. His revision of Chaucer's ballade narrows the call to absolute withdrawal from the world to less comprehensive counsels against lasciviousness and greed:

> If thou wilt mighty be, flee from the rage
> Of cruell wyll, and see thou kepe thee free
> From the foule yoke of sensuall bondage . . . (1–3)[32]

Wyatt replaces Chaucer's opening imperatives with conditional verbs signaling persistent enthusiasm for secular advancement. Whereas Chaucer's imagined audience consisted of courtiers longing for centers of stability set apart from the "tikelnesse" of courtly ambition, Wyatt addresses those longing to be "mighty." In the course of his poem, he reverses Chaucer's argument by urging his readers to abandon lust precisely to advance their careers.

At a point of particularly close intertextual contact, both poets urge their readers to contemplate humanity's divine origins:

> Her is non hoom, her nis but wildernesse:
> Forth, pilgrim, forth! Forth, beste, out of thy stal!
> Know thy contree, look up, thank God of al;
> Hold the heye wey, and lat thy gost thee lede,
> And trouthe thee shal delivere, it is no drede.
> ("Truth," 17–21)

> If to be noble and high thy minde be meued
> Consider well thy grounde and thy beginnyng,
> For he that hath eche starre in heauen fixed,
> And geues the Moone her hornes and her eclipsyng:
> Alike hath made the noble in his workyng,

So that wretched no way thou may bee
Except foule lust and vice do conquere thee.
("If thou wilt mighty be," 8–14)

For Chaucer, the recollection of a heavenly "hoom" discounts this world as a "wildernesse" to be escaped. But for Wyatt, the knowledge of one's "grounde and . . . beginnyng" in God leads to an antithetical conclusion: the belief that one's innate nobility underwrites the hope of "noble and high" rewards. In Chaucer's cosmos, nothing stands between the miserable uncertainties of this life and God's liberating "trouthe." Wyatt complicates this model by identifying God as the maker not only of the fixed stars but also of "the Moone her hornes and her eclipsyng." If his God provides the ground of a static, transcendent truth, he also creates a mutable universe. Instead of liberating one from the "tikelnesse" of court, He ordains the waning, waxing, and eclipsing that typifies the courtier's daily experience.

Wyatt's First Satire, "Myne owne John Poyntz," links his inability to withdraw from worldly pursuits directly to his unstable social position as a second-generation aristocrat dependent on Tudor favor. Probably written shortly after Anne Boleyn's death and during his rustication at Allington, the poem ostensibly transforms the courtier's disgrace into the provincial aristocrat's self-sufficiency: although Henry banished Wyatt from his presence, Wyatt writes as if he has rejected the court and embraced the countryside in an act of defiant, unconstrained choice.[33] Hunting and hawking on his family estate, he affects the independence of the older, feudal nobility who owed nothing to the Tudors. Yet the poem's setting alone exposes this pretense, since Henry Wyatt had purchased Allington less than fifty years before in his first flush of favor with the newly crowned Henry VII. As Greenblatt notes, "the estate to which the poet retreats from power is the reward for royal service and . . . the pleasant acres are swelled with confiscated monastic lands."[34] Throughout the poem, Wyatt's persistent fascination with the court reveals the futility of his efforts to imagine a life for himself that is not finally indebted to Tudor influence.

The First Satire stages this confrontation between the independence of the feudal nobility and the servility of the Tudor new creations against a patently Chaucerian backdrop. Although the poem paraphrases a stoic verse epistle that Luigi Alamanni had recently written, its conspicuous recollections of Chaucer's antifactional complaints ground its politics in an English, aristocratic tradition.[35] By echoing Chaucer's exhortation to "Flee fro the prees, and dwelle with sothfastnesse," for example, its opening lines identify Wyatt as one who has heeded Chaucer's Boethian counsels and renounced worldly corruption:

> Myne owne John Poyntz, since ye delight to know
> The cause why that homeward I me drawe,
> And fle the presse of courtes . . . (1–3)

Like Chaucer, Wyatt opposes truth to political intrigue. Boasting of his own incapacity to "torne the worde that from [his] mouthe is gone" (30), he locates the "tikelnesse" that Chaucer associated with political life in general with the specific unreliability of courtly discourse. At the end of the poem, he associates his verbal and moral integrity with the same county where Chaucer himself once fled the court's duplicity. Here "in Kent and Christendome" (100), he can commit himself fully to the Chaucerian values of "treuth" and "sothfastenesse."

Wyatt's determination to preserve aristocratic integrity leads to a direct citation of Chaucer as the defender of the social order threatened by Henry's centralizing programs. In denying his ability to lie, Wyatt comments explicitly on the relationship between two Canterbury tales:

> I am not he suche eloquence to boste,
> To make the crow singing as the swanne . . .
> Praysse Syr Thopas for a noble tale
> And skorne the story that the knyght tolld. (43–44, 50–51)

Yet another Chaucerian figure intrudes implicitly on the passage, since the lines echo the Miller's announcement, in the *Canterbury Tales,* that he knows "a noble tale for the nones, / With which [he] wol now quite the Knyghtes tale" (3126–27). These Chaucerian echoes transform Wyatt's general complaint about flattery and dependence into a more pointed critique of *arriviste* culture. Both recollected moments, Chaucer the Pilgrim's parody of quest romance in the Tale of Sir Thopas and the Miller's boast that he can match the Knight's performance with an equally "noble tale," constitute affronts to aristocratic tastes and conventions. Reading the *Canterbury Tales* as an aristocratic text, Wyatt assumes that Chaucer shows the absurdity of such presumptuous gestures in order to reaffirm traditional social distinctions. Presenting himself as a member of the older nobility, he defends this proper reading of Chaucer against the new aesthetic of the Henrician court. In the presence of a king who regularly imprisoned aristocrats like Howard while advancing base-born men like Cromwell, one loses the ability to make sound aesthetic judgments. Praising *Sir Thopas* for a "noble tale" becomes the aesthetic correlative of raising the son of a Putney blacksmith to the chancellorship of England.

Thus far, I have examined the First Satire as an unambivalent statement of Wyatt's determination to follow his master Chaucer both in a literal flight from court to Kent and in a metaphorical flight back into the stable class distinctions of the medieval past. But the poem itself never achieves the decisive break from the court that it proclaims. Since Wyatt's own family experienced the class mobility that he decries in the appropriated voice of a more established aristocracy, the secure class standing that underwrites his independence from the Crown is a pretense. As Alistair Fox has noted, Wyatt's passing complaint about the "clogg" that "doeth hang yet at [his] hele" (86) threatens to expose his Kentish retreat as house arrest rather than a freely chosen withdrawal from politics.[36] At such moments, Wyatt's apparently heartfelt assertions of the country's moral superiority to the court start looking like conventions cloaking the fact of an imposed rustication that he hopes will soon be reversed. Despite the poem's advocacy of hunting and hawking, the court remains its central preoccupation. Paradoxically, Wyatt's persistent fascination with the court invites an antithetical interpretation of his satire as an advertisement for further royal service. Unlike the flatterers whom he satirizes, Wyatt can be trusted to speak his mind and to advise the king or carry out his commands in all honesty.

Wyatt grounds the ambivalences of a poem that both renounces the court and hints at reembracing it in a confrontation between divergent Chaucerian subtexts. Whereas the social stratification of *The Canterbury Tales* and the Christian stoicism of the Boethian lyrics support his retreat into aristocratic self-sufficiency, *Troilus and Criseyde* questions its feasibility. In boasting of his Kentish independence, Wyatt echoes one of Criseyde's internal monologues that foregrounds anxieties about the irresistibility of overmastering social and political circumstances:

> I am myn owene womman, wel at ese—
> I thank it God—as after myn estat,
> Right yong, and stonde unteyd in lusty leese.
> (*Troilus and Criseyde*, II.750–52)

> No man doeth marke where so I ride or goo;
> In lusty lees at libertie I walke.
> ("Myne owne John Poyntz," 83–84)

Criseyde speaks the first passage in deciding whether she should consider Troilus's overtures. As a widow, she enjoys a social and emotional independence that she would surrender in binding herself to another man. Editors do not agree on what Chaucer meant by the phrase "in lusty leese." While some gloss it as a description of Criseyde walking "freely in pleasant meadows," others read it as an assurance that she was "not tied in love's leash."[37] On the surface, Wyatt seems to take it in the first sense, as an image of rustic independence free from the corruptions of courtly convention. Walking unmarked by any man on his own ancestral estate, he identifies himself with Criseyde in a moment of proud, almost defiant autonomy. His apparent rejection of the alternative meaning of the phrase might even be biographically overdetermined: having renounced both the court and its pervasive sexual politics, he walks emphatically not in "lusty lees" defined as erotic subservience.

Yet in achieving this cross-gendered intertextual identification with Criseyde, Wyatt signals his eventual surrender to Henrician authority. Although many fourteenth-century widows enjoyed lasting social and economic independence, Criseyde does not. For her as for the Wife of Bath, widowhood turns out to be a transitional phase before an eventual resubmission to patriarchy. As her failure to remain her "owene womman, wel at ese" and living apart from men becomes a prototype of Wyatt's failure to live apart from Tudor favor, the social dynamics of gender and patronage intersect in a master narrative of emasculation. Wyatt's return to the Kentish lands that are his by patrimonial right might be read as a gesture of hypermasculine, aristocratic autonomy. But his dependence on the Crown renders him a second Criseyde who betrays his avowed convictions: he is no more capable of living without the King than she is capable of living without a Troilus or a Diomedes. Women under patriarchy and courtiers under tyranny are equally "sliding of corage." Both suffer the irresolution for which Chaucer explicitly condemns Criseyde and for which Wyatt implicitly condemns himself in poems like "Who so list to hounte."

Witnessing Henry VIII's treatment of Margaret Douglas and other unfortunate ladies of court may have heightened Wyatt's identification with female characters incapable of resisting destiny. Critics have often noted how recollections of Anne Boleyn's tragedy in particular figure in his most bitter attacks on the court.[38] In my final section, I want to examine how her death contributes to Wyatt's sense of alienation from a feudal past that is tragically irrecoverable. One of the Chaucerian texts that most haunts his poetry emphasizes the power of certain privileged women to assuage rather than to suffer tyrannical wrath. The Knight's Tale joins the Prologue to *The Legend of Good Women* and the Wife of Bath's Tale in depicting queens or other high-ranking women who successfully intercede for men under royal sentence. As Paul Strohm and David Wallace have argued, this *topos* of queenly intercession figured as significantly in late medieval courtly practice as in Chaucerian fiction.[39] In actual historical experience, queenly intercession might have been part of an elaborate ruse that ultimately heightened the king's power; a king who pardoned offenders too quickly would merit less awe than one who accorded mercy only when pressed by his queen's willingness to humiliate herself in pleading for a subject's life. But from the perspective of the subject in question, it mattered little whether the queen's pleading was grounded in genuine concern for his life or in absolutist theatrics. In either event, he owed his escape to a convention of queenly intercession.

By the time Wyatt turned to Chaucer's poetry for consolation in his struggle against tyranny, the Tudor aggregation of political authority would deprive the queen of her time-honored right to question the Crown's judgments. The last instance of queenly intercession along medieval lines that I know of occurs in a letter from Francesco Chieregato, the papal nuncio at the court of the twenty-five-year-old Henry VIII, to Vigo de Campo San Pietro. Following a riot against London's foreign population on May 1, 1517, Henry set out to punish the participants as severely and conspicuously as possible. But in pleasing the ambassadors and other foreigners whom the mob had outraged, he risked appearing as a tyrant to his own people. Catherine of Aragon solved his dilemma by taking on the role of intercessor for four hundred rioters sentenced to die:

> There remained some 400 prisoners whom the King had destined in like manner for the gallows, but whom our most serene and most compassionate Queen with tears in her eyes and on her bended knees, obtained their pardon from his Majesty, the act of grace being performed with great ceremony.[40]

Since Catherine was herself a foreigner, she could plead for the rioters without seeming sympathetic to their xenophobia. As a Spaniard living in London, she could pose as a representative of the outraged "strangers" themselves, in proclaiming that justice had been fulfilled and that it was now time for pardon and reconciliation.

Shortly over a decade later, such a scene would have been impossible. In the drive toward Tudor absolutism, the Crown could no longer accept so much as the fiction of a challenge to its authority, even from someone as close as to the monarch as a spouse. During Catherine's last months as queen, Henry's dynastic and imperial ambitions placed her in the unprecedented position of having to plead for herself. With Anne Boleyn's subsequent tragedy, the woman who held the traditional office of intercessor suffered herself the ultimate demonstration of royal justice. In an earlier period, a gentleman like Sir Thomas Wyatt might have found a refuge from the king's wrath in the queen's intercession. But in 1536, his intimacy with a queen suspected of multiple adulteries was the source of his danger. Significantly, the intercessor who saved him was Thomas Cromwell—a man who owed his position entirely to the King's favor—rather than a queen who derived her authority in part from her own noble blood. Yet in the vortex of Henrician politics, no intercessor held a very secure tenure. When Cromwell's own fall led to Wyatt's second disgrace in 1541, Catherine Howard stepped in to save him in a surprise return to the older model of queenly intercession. Yet less than a year later, Catherine herself died on the block and Wyatt received several offices that had belonged to her paramour Thomas Culpepper.[41]

A sonnet that Wyatt wrote sometime after the disasters of 1536 measures the contemporary collapse of the queen's intercessory office against memories of the medieval, Chaucerian past epitomized by the Knight's Tale:

> You that in love finde lucke and habundance
> And live in lust and joyful jolitie,
> Arrise for shame! do away your sluggardie!
> Arise, I say, do May some obseruance!
> Let me in bed lye dreming in mischaunce;
> Let me remembre the happs most vnhappy
> That me betide in May most commonly,
> As oon whome love list litil to avaunce. (1–8)

Wyatt constructs this poem, which overtly thematizes the act of recollection, around recollections of several Chaucerian passages. As R. A. Rebholz has noted, the sonnet echoes "The Complaint unto Pity," *Troilus and Criseyde,* and *The Canterbury Tales.*[42] Yet this general allusiveness coalesces in a conspicuous imitation of the passage immediately preceding Palamon and Arcite's first glimpse of Emilye one May morning in the Knight's Tale:

> She was arisen and al redy dight,
> For May wole have no slogardie anyght.
> The sesoun priketh every gentil herte,

And maketh it out of his slep to sterte,
And seith "Arys, and do thyn observaunce."
(Knight's Tale, 1041–45)

The subtext offers Wyatt a compelling image of erotic and political alienation. He identifies with Palamon and Arcite, confined in a tyrant's tower and condemned to watch others enjoying the May rites from which they are excluded. Despite May's proscriptions of "slogardie anyght," neither Wyatt nor the Theban heroes can obey her summons. Just as the Thebans' imprisonment separates them from Emilye, political circumstances precluded a relationship with Anne Boleyn and would later separate Wyatt from Elizabeth Darrell.[43]

The Knight's Tale provides Wyatt a principle for organizing his "happs most vnhappy" into a coherent pattern, the belief that his "natiuitie / Mischaunced was with the ruler of the May." Every major event in Palamon and Arcite's lives occurs in May. Wyatt's May experiences, like Arcite's, are unambiguously hostile. In May 1534, he found himself imprisoned in the Fleet for brawling. While imprisoned in the Tower in May 1536, he seems to have watched Anne Boleyn's execution from his cell.[44] In his Maytide sonnet, the spectacle of her execution takes the place of Palamon and Arcite's first glimpse of Emilye. When Wyatt looked out from what Chaucer had called the "grete tour, that was so thikke and stroong, / Which of the castel was the chief dongeoun" (Knight's Tale, 1056–57), he did not fall in love at first sight but witnessed the final agony of the woman he probably loved. Although we can only speculate about the intensity of his feelings for Anne as a private person, his dominant Chaucerian subtext underscores the significance to him of her death as a public figure. When Palamon and Arcite look "thurgh a wyndow, thikke of many a barre / Of iren greet" (Knight's Tale, 1075–76), they see not only a private woman whom they will love but also the Duke's sister-in-law who will join Hippolyta in interceding for their lives when Theseus sentences them to death. By the time Wyatt was imprisoned on suspicion of capital crimes, Henry VIII had stripped Anne Boleyn of her public dignities. In her last moments, she provided Wyatt not hope in the possibility of royal lenience but a witness to the severity of royal vengeance.[45]

No editor has ever detected a Chaucerian source for the most plaintive poem that Wyatt seems to have written in response to Anne's death, "Who lyst his welthe and eas Retayne." With its counsels against social and political ambition, the poem's opening stanza loosely imitates Seneca's *Phaedra,* which also provides the ominous Latin refrain, *circa Regna tonat.*[46] But despite this primary debt to Seneca, Wyatt recalls the Boethianism of such conspicuously Chaucerian works as "If thou wilt mighty be" and "Myne owne John Poyntz." Wyatt draws closer to Chaucer's counsel against the "press" of temporal concerns here than anywhere else in his canon. Finding no comfort on earth, he follows Chaucer's Boethian precedent in resorting instead to the transcendent virtues of fidelity and truth.

The penultimate stanza locates Wyatt's overwhelming alienation from the world in the execution of the one person who might have protected him against factional conspiracy:

> The bell towre showed me suche syght
> That in my hed stekys day and nyght;
> Ther dyd I lerne out of a grate,
> Ffor all vaoure, glory or myght,
> That yet *circa Regna tonat.* (16–20)

Nowhere else does Wyatt so openly recall the circumstances of Anne's death. Probably written at the same time as the sonnet on May's "happs most vnhappy," this stanza grounds its contempt for the world in yet another cankered recollection of the Knight's Tale. Palamon and Arcite's window "thikke of many a barre / Of iren greet" (Knight's Tale, 1075–76) becomes the "grate" through which Wyatt witnesses the degradation of chivalry itself. Tudor despotism has deprived the world of its ideals. What sticks in the nobleman's mind is not the idealization of a princess as a goddess but the condemnation of a queen for treason, adultery, and incest. As the Chaucerian fiction of queenly intercession yields to the Senecan reality of judicial murder, the only Chaucerian texts that retain their authority are those relegating innocence, truth, and faithfulness to a divine order apart from political experience.

Bitterness, disillusion, cynicism, and anxiety have become the qualities that most typify Wyatt's poetry for twentieth-century readers. In our more hermeneutically self-conscious moments, we attribute these apparently psychologized traits to a social environment that transcends and ultimately produces individual consciousness. Wyatt's restlessness becomes an illusion of interiority, a cultural superstructure arising on the base of Tudor despotism. Yet the base on which Wyatt's tortured interiority arises consists not only of immediate social and political circumstances but of mediating literary artifacts that bear the traces of past as well as present social and political conflict. The fragmentation of Chaucer's sixteenth-century cultural authority among divergent interests provided the channels through which Wyatt gave his internal struggles poetic expression.

Notes

1. Surrey, "W. resteth here, that quick could never rest," in Howard, *Poems*, ed. Jones, 27; Puttenham, *The Arte of English Poesie*, in Smith, *Elizabethan Critical Essays* 2:62–63. Subsequent references to Puttenham are noted by page number within the text.

2. See Greene, *Light in Troy*, 244.

3. Greenblatt's chapter on Wyatt in *Renaissance Self-Fashioning*, 2.

4. See Kay, "Wyatt and Chaucer"; Cooper, "Wyatt and Chaucer"; Spearing, *Medieval to Renaissance*, 278–310. For earlier discussion of Wyatt's debt to Chaucer, see Mason, *Humanism*, and Southall, *The Courtly Maker.*

5. Muir, *Life and Letters*, 1–3. Even though the Wyatts had been prominent in West Riding affairs since the reign of Edward III, they were squarely members of the upper gentry rather than the aristocracy. Henry Wyatt was the first Wyatt to achieve prominence, and he owed his elevation entirely to the Tudors.

Wyatt's *arriviste* status continued as a handicap even after his death. The longstanding use of Wyatt as a foil for the more refined Earl of Surrey, the scion of an ancient aristocratic family, reflects class biases against a newly created nobility. See Sessions, "Surrey's Wyatt."

6. For a comprehensive account of Chaucer's Renaissance reception, see Miskimin's *Renaissance Chaucer.*

7. For an account of Chaucer's editorial history from Caxton to Robinson, see the essays in *Editing Chaucer*, ed. Ruggiers.

8. Francis Thynne, *Animadversions*, 6.

9. See Scarisbrick, "Henry VIII and the Vatican Library."

10. Quoted in Spurgeon, *Five Hundred Years of Chaucer Criticism*, 79–80.

11. See Helgerson, *Forms of Nationhood*, 12–13.

12. See Helgerson, *Forms of Nationhood*, 125–31.

13. See Stone, *Crisis of the Aristocracy*, 199–204; Miller, *Henry VIII and the English Nobility.*

14. See Skeat's introduction to *Chaucerian and Other Pieces*, 7:xl–xli.

15. *Ploughman's Tale*, in Skeat, *Chaucerian and Other Pieces*, 7:147–90. Line references are cited in the text. For further discussion of tale's aesthetic and political significance as an addition to the Chaucerian canon, see Wawn, "Genesis of 'The Plowman's Tale'," and "Chaucer, 'The Plowman's Tale,' and Reformation Propaganda."

16. For further discussion of the transition from manuscript to print culture, see Lerer, *Chaucer and His Readers*, 143–46.

17. I am indebted to Southall's account of the Howard-Douglas affair in "The Devonshire Manuscript."

18. I include in the text my own transcription of the Devonshire Manuscript, British Museum Additional MS 17492, folio 29.

19. The Devonshire manuscript suggests that such unacknowledged appropriation of Chaucerian materials occurred frequently among Henry's courtiers.

See Seaton, "Medieval Poem in the Devonshire Manuscript," 55–56. Other Tudor manuscripts also incorporate generous amounts of Chaucer. See Kay's discussion of Bodley MS Rawlinson C. 813 in "Wyatt and Chaucer," 244n.16.

20. See Mason, *Humanism*, 143–78.

21. John Foxe, *Actes and Monumentes* (1570), quoted in *Chaucer: The Critical Heritage*, ed. Brewer, 1:108.

22. See John Bale, *Illustrium Maioris Britanniae Scriptorum . . . Summarium*, 198; John Leland, *Commentarii de Scriptoribus Britannicis*, 419–26.

23. See Harrier, *The Canon*; Southall, *The Courtly Maker.*

24. Muir, *Life and Letters*, 25–37.

25. Muir, *Life and Letters*, 27–36.

26. See Strohm, "Politics and Poetics," 90–97, 106–12; Strohm, *Social Chaucer*, 10–23; Patterson, *Chaucer and the Subject of History*, 32–39.

27. All references to Chaucer's poetry are to *The Riverside Chaucer.* Line numbers are cited in the text.

28. Strohm, *Social Chaucer*, 24–46.

29. Zagorin links Wyatt's professional resilience to his culture's endemic ambivalence toward the court. See "Sir Thomas Wyatt and the Court of Henry VIII."

30. For discussion of Wyatt's final months, see Muir, *Life and Letters*, 211–13; Zagorin, "Sir Thomas Wyatt and the Court of Henry VIII," 135.

31. Wyatt had been charged with treason in connection with Cromwell's fall; Catherine Howard had interceded on his behalf, with the result that Henry pardoned him. Although Wyatt maintained his innocence, he was not legally acquitted of the charges.

32. All references to Wyatt's poetry are to Muir and Thomson's edition of *Collected Poems*. Line numbers are cited in the text.

33. For discussion of the poem's date, see Muir, *Life and Letters*, 251; Rebholz, ed., *Complete Poems*, 437–39.

34. Greenblatt, *Renaissance Self-Fashioning*, 132. Although I am indebted to Greenblatt's analysis of the poem's concern with steadfastness as a response to the turbulence of Henrician politics, I emphasize its Chaucerian underpinnings to resist his insistence that "there is in the early modern period a change in the intellectual, social, psychological, and aesthetic structures that govern the generation of identities" (1). Several medievalists have challenged this canonization of the Renaissance as an originary moment in the history of subjectivity. See especially Patterson, *Chaucer and the Subject of History* and Aers, "A Whisper in the Ear of Early Modernists."

35. See Fox's discussion of Wyatt's relationship to Alamanni in *Poetry and Politics*, 270–72.

36. Fox, *Politics and Literature*, 272.

37. Donaldson opts for "in love's leash" (*Chaucer's Poetry*, 614); Shoaf prefers "in pleasant pasture" (*Troilus and Criseyde*, 74). After noting that editors have traditionally preferred "in pleasant pasture," *Riverside Chaucer* concedes that Donaldson has a better case (1034).

38. See Fox, *Politics and Literature*, 267–68; Zagorin, "Sir Thomas Wyatt and the Court of Henry VIII," 130–32.

39. See Strohm, *Hochon's Arrow*, 95–119; Wallace, *Chaucerian Polity*, 363–76.

40. Brown, ed., *Calendar of State Papers*, 2:887.

41. See Muir, *Life and Letters*, 211.

42. See Rebholz's edition of *Complete Poems*, 361–62.

43. See Muir's discussion of Wyatt's separations from Elizabeth Darrell in *Life and Letters*, 84–87; see also Fox, *Poetry and Politics*, 273–77; 281.

44. See Fox, *Politics and Literature*, 267.

45. Spearing, *Medieval to Renaissance*, offers a complementary discussion of the poem's elegiac relationship to the medieval past and concludes that for Wyatt, "the Chaucerian tradition, well though he obviously knows it, is no longer valid" (281–82).

46. Rebholz notes the Senecan source in *Complete Poems*, 424.

CHAPTER 3

Authority and the Defense of Fiction

Renaissance Poetics and Chaucer's *House of Fame*

CAROL A. N. MARTIN

The decentered, sometimes anarchic poetics of Geoffrey Chaucer's *House of Fame* has vexed its readers at least since William Caxton composed a conclusion for it, and modern treatments agree upon little more than that the poem comments upon or investigates problems of language Chaucer faced as a poet.[1] Renaissance editors of the poem constitute no exception to the rule, despite their closer proximity in time and culture. Standard Renaissance editions of Chaucer's works handle the *House of Fame* gingerly, for the *House of Fame* resolves neither itself nor the questions it raises about speaking truly. For editors who regarded Chaucer not only as the English Homer who legitimated literary production in English but also as an author whose work was especially compatible with the religio-political aims and authority of Henry VIII, the *House of Fame* posed a particularly awkward problem, as Thomas Speght's influential edition makes clear. In this paper I posit that Renaissance uneasiness with the *House of Fame* reflects a fundamental hermeneutical discord between the indeterminacy of Chaucer's paradox-oriented dialectics, rooted in the discipline of rhetoric, and the truth claims of the more usually employed dialectics of scholastic philosophy.

A comparison of Chaucer's poetics with those exemplified in other Renaissance defenders of poetry such as Boccaccio and Sidney clarifies where and how the two traditions of dialectics diverge.[2] Chaucer in his *House of Fame* no less than Giovanni Boccaccio in his *Genealogie deorum gentilium libri* and Sir Philip Sidney in his *Apologie for Poetrie* insisted upon investigating the truth content possible to poetrie. However, he showed less confidence than Boccaccio in his own (and the general human) capacity for apprehending an absolute and complete truth. His philosophical reserve did not represent an isolated eccentricity but resembled the skeptical fideism described at length by Sheila Delany and Gordon Leff.[3] By incorporating this philosophical stance into his poem, Chaucer engages readers in a process by which they come to understand limitations and functions of poetry and of their own intellectual habits. This location of the *House of Fame* in a debate between scholastic and rhetorical dialectics defines Chaucer's *ars poetria* as more intelligently and deliberately engaged in the dispute between philosophy and rhetoric than some critics are willing to concede, but I do believe that the contents and debate format of the conversation between the protagonist Geffrey and his scholastic raptor bear the weight of such a reading. As a practitioner of an ancient rhetorical dialectics, Chaucer would represent a tradition fast disappearing from a culture so increasingly committed to philosophical certainty that it could justify heresy trials and, ultimately, ecclesial and political schism on the basis of philosophically grounded truth claims.

Despite so fundamental a hermeneutical shift, Chaucer and Sidney show surprising similarities in thought and method, even in rhetorical strategy. Yet Chaucer's poetic, rhetorical dialectics allowed the hermeneutical impetus of his argument to remain open to readerly and editorial interpolation in ways that Sidney's scholastic treatise could not. Both Boccaccio's and Sidney's formal arguments result in claims to authority, whether by successful persuasion or by virtue of rank. Their hermeneutics prove analogous to Speght's reliance upon a Protestant vision of truth and its concomitant reliance upon secular authority to establish its political preeminence. Analogous priorities emerge from analysis of Thynne's and Speght's editions of Chaucer's works.

Speght's treatment of the piece serves as the latest, most developed example of editorial uneasiness with the *House of Fame* among the major Renaissance editions. He certainly did little to foster the work's popularity or prominence. In his reserve toward the *House of Fame* he may not have intended deliberate effacement, but its effect was to mute the work's presence and status. Three factors diminish its presence: the work's placement in relation to other pieces; the entire absence of mention of the *House of Fame* in the "Life," which guided perceptions of Chaucer's career until the 1840s; and the misleading evasiveness of Speght's summary of the argument in the *House of Fame.* Combined, these three circumstances effectively diminish the presence of the *House of Fame* in the Chaucer canon; Speght's summary of the argument suggests that he deliberately muted Chaucer's testing of authority.

The order in which Speght presented Chaucer's works may have supported only coincidentally Speght's own inclination to neglect the work, for Speght followed Stowe's 1561 order, which in turn followed William Thynne's (1532). Thynne's edition significantly departed from Pynson's 1526 treatment of the *House of Fame,* where it followed *Troilus and Criseyde* and preceded the *Parlement of Foules.* Pynson had ratified its full status as a major component of the Chaucer canon not only by its placement but also by adorning it with an introductory woodcut. In the Thynne-Stowe-Speght sequence, works seem arranged according to a hierarchy of importance. It places *The Canterbury Tales* first, followed by *The Romaunt of the Rose, Troilus and Criseyde, The Legend of Good Women,* and the *Boece,* works chosen, it would seem, for their length and for their combined courtly and moral reputations.

Deliberate or not, Speght's positioning of *The House of Fame* buried it in a sequence of shorter "Works by themselves": "The Dream of Chaucer called the Duchess," "The Assembly of Foules," "The Floure of Courtesie," "How Pity is dead, etc.," "La belle dame sans mercy" (acknowledged as non-Chaucerian), "Annelida and false Arcite," "The Assembly of Ladies," "The Conclusion of the Astrolaby," "The Complaint of the Black Knight," "A Praise of Women," *The House of Fame, The Testament of Love,* a spate of short lyrics (some clearly identified as non-Chaucerian), "Chaucer's Dream," "The Floure and the Leafe," "The ABC, called la priere de nostre dame," "Jack Upland," "Chaucer's Words to Adam his own Scrivener," and the *Siege of Thebes* (correctly attributed to Lydgate). Thus *The House of Fame* follows upon a miscellaneous assortment of Chaucer's early and/or unfinished work, works of Chaucerian imitators, and even the technical treatise of instruction on use of the astrolabe; it directly precedes *The Testament of Love,* which by length alone appears more "major." Moreover, the advertisement of the edition and Speght's dedication to Cecil explicitly drew attention to "The Death of Blanch, called his Dream," "The Flower and the Leaf," "The Treatise of Jack Upland Against Fryars," and "ABC Commonly Called La Priere de Nostre Dame." These works lead off and close the section of Chaucerian pieces, occupying the positions of emphasis. Against these, a work purporting to show "how the Deeds of all Men and Women, be they good or bad, are carried by Report to Posterity"—Speght's summary of the work's "argument"—suffers from faint praise.

When, after marginalizing the poem's position, Speght also omits it from his comprehensive description of Chaucer's life, he creates circumstances which on the most generous reading appear inexplicably careless. In their practical effects, they create conditions that make it easy for readers to overlook the presence of the *House of Fame* in the Chaucerian canon. The misleading character of his summary of the argument in the *House of Fame* suggests that Speght may have followed a deliberate strategy to suppress the potential disruptiveness of Chaucer's poem.

Speght composed introductory summaries of "the arguments" of each work, which Derek Pearsall has described as "short, pithy, and accurate for the most part."[4] The commentary on the *House of Fame* stands out as remarkable for both its unusual brevity and its misleading generalization.[5] It consists of a single terse statement: "In this Book is shewed how the Deeds of all Men and Women, be they good or bad, are carried by Report to Posterity."[6] Speght's remarks on other works reveal his broad interests in plot summary, dramatic and stylistic decorum, source relationships, genre, narrative voice, historical atmosphere, and moral aphorism,[7] out of which he easily could have composed a more expansive description of the *House of Fame*—if, as I argue here, the relationship of this work to its sources, to truth, and to its readers were not problematized as part of Chaucer's larger investigation of poetic authority.

Moreover, the generality of Speght's statement sidesteps the question, so insistently raised by Chaucer, of whether the reports of fame to posterity be true. In fact, the bland assertion that the good and bad deeds of men and women are carried to posterity carries the unproblematized presumption that the reports are accurate. Speght can hardly have missed Chaucer's doubts on this subject: A substantial portion of the poem (ll. 1520–1868) describes Fame's arbitrary judgments, and the narrator himself finds them so inexplicable that he identifies Fame as the sister of notoriously blind Fortune (1542–48). The version of the poem Speght knew included a conclusion added by Caxton and Thynne, to mitigate its nonconclusive terminus, but while the new ending alleviated the abruptness with which Chaucer broke off, the closure at which it arrived was purely narrative. Chaucer's concluding lines are:

> At the last I saw a man,
> Which that I nought ne can,
> But he seemed for to be
> A man of great auctorite. (Chaucer, 2155–58)

After this the Caxton/Thynne edition continued:

> And therewithall I abraide
> Out of my slepe halfe afraide.
> Remembring well what I had sene
> And how hie and ferre I had bene

In my goost, and had great wonder
Of that the god of thonder
Had let me knowen and began to write
Like as ye have herd me endite,
Wherefore to study and rede alway
I purpose to do day by day.
Thus in dreaming and in game
Endeth this litell booke of Fame.[8]

Despite its prolixity, the Caxton/Thynne ending merely adds the narrative detail of the narrator's awakening and suggests the moral consequence that the poet determines to return to his daily studies; it does not compensate for the omission of the man of authority. So although Speght might not have been shocked by the abruptness that startles modern readers, he still would have had to struggle with the absence of authority from the poem. The noncommittal formulation of Speght's summary of the argument evades one of the poem's most insistent themes.

His brief introduction to the *House of Fame* actually does little but express his own wish that poetic fame distribute and enforce poetic justice, that it establish for men and women the reputation of their deeds. The usual course, following the lead of such defenders of poetry as Petrarch and Boccaccio, was to laud the fame of the poet; even Sidney paid court to poets of reputation. Chaucer's double inversion, first his investigation of the truthfulness of the fame a poet bestows, then his own declared disregard for his own fame (ll. 1871–72), broke with established precedent and must have been disorienting or at least inconvenient to editors who wished to reinforce the precedent.[9]

Speght's praise of Chaucer's "rare Conceit" and "great Reading," combined with Chaucer's putative portrayal of his contemporaries "given to devotion, rather of custom than of zeal" (1), issue in an expectation of leadership. That Speght himself presumed that learning, wit, and religious perspicacity ought to lead to cultured authority is suggested by the fact that he reproduced Thynne's dedication to Henry VIII. The dedication reconfirms not only the proper role of fame as a reward for poetic achievement but also the presupposition that poetry is engaged in an intellectual battle for truth, fueled by religious controversy. Thynne, moreover, had justified publication of Chaucer's work as a strategic move in the intellectual battle over truth waged by English Protestants against Roman influence. He hoped the king would

> toke in good part my poor study and desirous mind, in reducing unto light this so precious and necessary an ornament of the tongue

> in this your Realm, over pitous to have been in any point lost, falsified, or neglected. So that under the shield of your most royal Protection and Defence, it may go forth in publick, and prevail over those [who] would blemish, deface, and in many things clearly abolish the laud, renoume, and glory heretofore compared, and meritoriously adquired [*sic*] by divers Princes, and other of this said most noble Isle, whereunto not only Straungers under pretext of high learning and knowledge of their malicious and perverse minds, but also some of your own subjects, blinded in folly and ignoraunce, do with great study contend. (xxxi)

The dedication of Chaucer's works to Henry, Thynne further makes clear, is entirely proper to one in whom "is renued the glorious Title of Defensor of the Christen Faith, which by your noble Progenitour, the Great Constantine, sometime king of this Realm, and Emperour of Rome, was next God and his Apostles, cheefly maintained, corroborate, and defended" (xxxi). One could hardly imagine a more complete association of poetry with both unquestionable truth and political power. Speght's edition appends itself to this constellation of national political, religious, and literary interests first by printing Thynne's dedication, then by presenting the "Plowman's Tale," "Jack Upland," and the record of Chaucer's fine for beating a Franciscan friar as additions to the Chaucer canon; the religio-political interests behind Speght's inclusion of "Jack Upland" are clear, for Speght took his text not from a manuscript but from John Foxe's radical Protestant martyrology, the *Actes and Monuments*.[10] Renaissance justifications of poetry found value in poetry in precisely this nexus of concerns.

Boccaccio's impassioned defense of poetry in the fourteenth book of his *Genealogie deorum gentilium libri* provides an appropriate foil for comparison with Chaucer and Sidney because of its combination of contemporaneity with Chaucer and cultural continuity as both heir to and progenitor of Renaissance critical theory. For my purposes, whether Chaucer actually parodied Boccaccio's treatise directly or whether he merely parodied other traditional portrayals of poetic inspiration and fame is a moot point;[11] the contrast in their positions still stands. Against attacks launched by philosophers, theologians, lawyers, and generally envious or ignorant readers, Boccaccio articulates a defense of poetry's validity, based upon its access to divine truth. The question of poetry's truth value compared to that of philosophical logic is precisely the question both Chaucer and Sidney would also engage. I am arguing that Chaucer's nonresolution of the question, a stance made possible by his poetic form, helps to explain the depth of Renaissance discomfort with Chaucer's *House of Fame*.

Boccaccio's defense of poetry permits no such irresolution, regardless of what private anxieties he harbored. In justifying his own lifelong interpretive study of pagan lore, he utilizes sharp tones which suggest that his imagined accusers might live as much in his own anxieties as in time and space, a suggestion corroborated by his correspondence with Petrarch. To his critics, Boccaccio's decades-long research in pagan philosophy, literature, and astrological astronomy and his role as a sympathetic interpreter and curator of pagan religion rendered Boccaccio vulnerable to contamination. Anxious to counter potential accusations against his theology and perhaps anxious to reassure himself, in his first thirteen books he sporadically ridicules instances of pagan superstition or points out remnants of pagan religion neutralized in medieval folklore.[12] To guarantee his orthodoxy absolutely, he writes out an elaborated version of his Creed (124–27, 195n.5). He counters both external critics and internal anxieties by anchoring his vulnerable points in an authority to which he and his critics both assign certitude.

The very choice to argue the point of poetry's truth content from within a scholastic treatise betrays a perhaps subconscious concession on Boccaccio's part that the claims of philosophy lead to more certain forms of truth than does poetry. His defense, and especially his attacks upon opponents as "ignorant" (16), "incompetent" (17), "garrulous and detestably arrogant" cattle (18) bear the earmarks of "a certain tendency to reductive theorizing . . . [a tendency] to reduce differences among persons and stress their common ground (and common weaknesses)" observed by Margaret Ferguson.[13]

Boccaccio concentrates his defense in a detailed analysis of poetic inspiration which assimilates to itself increasingly sacred associations, although he begins with relative moderation. He defines poetry as "a sort of fervid and exquisite invention, with fervid expression, in speech or writing, of that which the mind has invented" (39). Poetic fervor "is sublime in effects: it impels the soul to a longing for utterance; it brings forth strange and unheard-of creations of the mind, it arranges these meditations in a fixed order, adorns the whole with unusual interweaving of words and thoughts; and thus it veils truth in a fair and fitting garment of fiction" (39). Its fictive veil distinguishes poetry from more practical expressions of rhetoric (42) and delights both learned and unlearned readers simultaneously: "The power of fiction . . . pleases the unlearned by its external appearance, and exercises the minds of the learned with its hidden truth; and thus both are edified and delighted with one and the same perusal" (51). Moreover, "Poetry, like other studies, is derived from God, Author of all wisdom" (37). This definition seems moderate enough, as long as Boccaccio perceives poetry as the invention of a poet's mind, derived from God apparently on the same footing as other modes of wisdom, and directing readers toward knowledge. Eventually, however, the sort of truth Boccaccio attributes to poetic fervor asserts preeminent authority for poets by emphasizing the divine source of their inspiration.

Following an argument made by Cicero in *De natura deorum* (3.53), one of his most important sources, Boccaccio moves poetry to a privileged status when he claims the essential unity of poetry, theology, and philosophy. He does so when he locates the origin of poetry in religious worship (42–44), arguing that poets are speakers of divine truth, whether of prophecy or of philosophy.[14] Even pagan poets have at least partial access to God's truth, if not to Christian revelation: Virgil had glimpses of God's truth, while "our own poet Dante . . . often unties with amazingly skilful demonstration the hard knots of holy theology; will such a one be so insensible as not to perceive that Dante was a great theologian as well as philosopher?" (53). By this shrewd choice of examples, he virtually silences potential counterarguments, for he positions himself behind Dante's authority. Dante had chosen Virgil as his spiritual guide, and who in fourteenth-century Italy would have dared question Dante's stature? Boccaccio cements the claim to poetic authority by declaring the immutable nature of the truth poets represent. It "constitutes a stable and fixed science founded upon things eternal, and confirmed by original principles; in all times and places this knowledge is the same, unshaken by any possible change" (25).

Boccaccio validates the probity of poets by defining their activity as belonging to the contemplative rather than active life, thus silently appropriating the monastic claim to a more perfect way of life than the active life could achieve.[15] This position constitutes a major departure from classical rhetoric, which conceived of itself as the foundation of public life. Boccaccio launches his case by contrasting an abstract poet's eremitical life of heroic virtue with the avarice and luxury of lawyers. By doing so, he defuses an accusation of asocial incivility against poets and establishes the secular (and by implication, inferior) values of his opponents. He then develops his own distinction between classes of rhetoricians, lawyers, and poets, by describing poetic isolation as a necessary condition for inspiration, analogous to monastic claustration, voluntary poverty, and the ascetic discipline of solitary study ("plain living and little sleep" [57]). Not merely a matter of practical concentration, sacrifices made by poets in the service of their art gradually take on a valence of religious devotion.

> Contemplation of things divine is utterly impossible [in places of active life]; unless such contemplation is practically uninterrupted, the poet can neither conceive his works, nor complete them. . . . The reason why poets seek to dwell in sylvan spots is clear. We read also that Paul the Hermit did this, and Antonius, Macharius, Arsenius, and many other reverend and holy men, not from want of sophistication, but to serve God with a freer mind. (55–56)

Although withdrawal from the active life seems at first merely a necessary working condition, Boccaccio finally appropriates the eremitical analogy by naming the Desert Fathers as examples of poetic experience. By way of contrast, the scholastic eagle who literally "raptures" the poet Geffrey in the *House of Fame* would curb any pretense that Geffrey's solitude shares the character of monastic contemplation: "[Thou] lyvest thus as an heremyte, / Although thyn abstinence ys lite" (659–60). Geffrey's solitude produces not sacred contemplation but a disabling daze.

Boccaccio does finally fully equate poetic inspiration with mystical vision.

> Poetry devotes herself to something greater; for while she dwells in heaven, and mingles with the divine counsels, she moves the minds of a few men from on high to a yearning for the eternal, lifting them by her loveliness to high revery, drawing them away into the discovery of strange wonders, and pouring forth most exquisite discourse from her exalted mind. . . . Poets have chosen a science or pursuit of knowledge which by constant meditation draws them away into the region of stars, among the divinely adorned dwellings of the gods and their heavenly splendors. (24, 25)

In this mode, the poet first contemplates poetry, and so opens himself to its influence; but from there on, the process is one in which the poet is largely passive, drawn by poetry into a "yearning for the eternal," into a reception of "exquisite discourse." Poetry itself, not an individual poet, speaks of philosophy, theology, truth. Nonetheless, the poet inherits through fame a long survival, almost the equivalent of eternal life: "the songs of poets, like the name of the composer, are almost immortal" (26). Ironically, however, Boccaccio's rapturous contemplation of poetry's virtues has been argued in the prose form of a scholastic treatise, and its aim has been to achieve certainty; his whole appeal for validation he directs on a mundane level to his royal patron, King Hugo IV of Cyprus and Jerusalem (3), much as Thynne directed his appeal to Henry VIII.[16]

Chaucer's *House of Fame* presents a very different self-justification. Like Boccaccio, Chaucer uses Dante's authority, for he juxtaposes a first-person narrator with an aquiline raptor borrowed from Dante, but he then stages an argument between that authority and himself.[17] In the course of that argument, Chaucer reduces the dignity first of the poet, then of his raptor, of fame itself, and finally of the truth status of poetry. Chaucer's parody of poetic rapture does not capitulate to the accusations of philosophy against poetry, however, for he also parodies scholastic dialectics, and he couches both in poetic fiction. By depicting limitations of both rhetoric and philosophy, he develops by means of his fiction a subtler analysis of the methods and institutions governing the search for truth than either scholastic demonstration or direct inspiration theories had yet provided. Fame, too, proves no more solid than a memorial engraved in a "roche of yse" (1138, cf. 1128–64), and Chaucer's narrator declares his independence of fame (1871–72). The last phase of the poem features a flimsy discursive world from which emerge only "soth and fals compouned" (2108). When he concludes the poem before the arrival of the "man of gret auctoritee," Chaucer resigns closure of the poem and of its meaning to readers. That he does so fulfills his earlier invocation on his readers' interpretive acuity (81, 90–93).

The defense of poetry based upon the supposed divine madness, poetic frenzy, or inspiration of the poet was a commonplace of humanist poetics, passed on through Horace, Ovid, Pliny, Claudian, Statius, Cicero, and Isidore, repeated in Scipionic dream visions and commonplaces in the Middle Ages, maintained in Dante and Petrarch, presumed by Politian, Ficino, Tasso, and Scaliger; it made for humanists the central legitimation of poetry.[18] Whether or not Chaucer knew Boccaccio's treatise, he could legitimately parody the same conventions Boccaccio praised, in the expectation that a reasonable proportion of his audience would be familiar with them. Chaucer's depiction of poetic rapture in the *House of Fame,* the first step of his poetics, radically departs, then, from a central orthodoxy of his own ideological allies against philosophical attack.

In the image of the poet in the grip of philosophy, Chaucer posits a more complex relationship between poetry and philosophy than mere opposition. The poet is literally "raptured" by a figure representing philosophical dialectics, yet although his raptor quite literally moves Geffrey, he cannot control Geffrey's will and imagination. The *House of Fame* eagle purportedly comes to remove Geffrey from his books and to move him to a place where he might find "tydyngs of love" about which he might write; more simply put, Jove sends his eagle to provide poetic inspiration. So much Chaucer reveals at the eagle's first appearance; as the fiction unfolds, the same eagle takes on attributes of scholastic philosophy, complicating the original image.[19] The figure of the raptured narrator accumulates associations as well. Rather than figuring merely as an abstract poet, Geffrey preserves an individuality and an independence of opinion appropriate not to the certitudes of philosophical dialectics but to the pedagogy of old-fashioned Boethian rhetorical dialectics.

Ironically, Chaucer presents the initial stages of Geffrey's scholastic rapture as relatively uninspiring. The eagle "demonstrates" the theoretical possibility of collecting all speech uttered on earth in a house fixed between heaven and earth and sea. His difficult matter and logic (853–64) as well as his would-be function as a teacher identify him as a scholastic logician; that is, as an expert in what the university curriculum loosely termed *dialectic.* He lectures on the science of speech (765–852) and tries hard to teach astronomy (935–49, 991–1017).

As befits a representative of philosophy, the eagle takes pride in the plainness of his language, in the fact that he has successfully demonstrated his scientific point without recourse to poetic figures, rhetorical colors, philosophic jargon, or other subtle diversions of speech. He demands,

> Have y not preved thus symply,
> Withoute any subtilite
> Of speche, or gret prolixite
> Of termes of philosophie,
> Of figures of poetrie,
> Or colours of rethorike? (854–59)

Yet his clarity and certitude elicit little more than bare assent from Geffrey, who responds merely "y answered and seyde, 'Yis'" (864). The answer fulfills to the letter the yes or no answer required by debate, and Geffrey does not even rise to the aggressive challenge, "And whoso seyth of trouthe I varye, / Bid him proven the contrarye" (807–8). The eagle's defiance is deliberate provocation—hardly sound logical practice, for in formal academic debate, dialecticians were responsible for making their point stick, respondents merely for preventing a successful conclusion.[20] Geffrey, despite the emphatic form of his assent, stymies further discussion. Even when the eagle coaxes him to amplify his answer, he dampens rather than encourages further discussion. "'A good persuasion,' / Quod

I, 'hyt is, and lyk to be / Ryght so as thou has preved me'" (872–74). Regardless of how proven the philosopher's position, this poet declines debate. Since the pedantic eagle has already proved his point and Geffrey has neither further information nor questions, additional elaboration by the eagle would be merely redundant. Scholastic demonstration may have led to a proof, but it has not given any reason why its captive audience should care about its facts.

Closer attention to the eagle's argument, however, qualifies even the factual certitude he would claim, for the eagle's avoidance of poetic figures does not preserve his own logic from confusion. He fails to distinguish adequately between the terms *speech* and *sound* and thereby conflates three distinct arguments. That all natural things incline by nature to their natural places, that sound is nothing other in substance than broken air, and that speech, noise, and sound multiply and move like waves in concentric circles are all venerable inherited opinions which no scholar of that time would dispute,[21] but to superimpose the arguments and thereby to equate speech with sound confuses genus and species.[22] The eagle builds a fallacious syllogism that, because "soun ys noght but eyr ybroken" (765), and "speche . . . In his substaunce ys but air" (766, 768), therefore, when air is broken, speech is the result. Speech is a species of the genus sound, but not all valid arguments that can be made about sound will necessarily apply equally well to speech, for not all sound is speech. More fundamentally, the eagle's discrediting of speech would preempt the eagle's own argument, for if he destroys the validity of speech, he also destroys the validity of any argument made by means of speech, including his own.

Chaucer scores two strikes against philosophical dialectics in his depiction of the eagle's demonstration. Most obviously, the argument fails to evoke a response from its audience, to "move" Geffrey to emulation or application of its truths; Sidney was to make a similar point in his *Apologie*. Thus the philosopher fails in the primary goal of rhetoric. Chaucer, however, makes a second, more devastating point by introducing the eagle's own fallacious reasoning: Even on its own terms, logic can lead to error rather than to the certitude it claimed because its vehicle, human reason, is finite.

The eagle's regard for logic and disregard for poetic figures literalize the disjunction between rhetorical and scholastic uses of the term *dialectics* in intellectual discourse of Chaucer's day. Dialectic in the discipline of rhetoric and in major classical logic texts such as Aristotle's *Topics*,

Cicero's *Topica,* and Boethius's *De Topicis differentiis* was an investigative, speculative methodology still available in Chaucer's day to anyone engaged in advanced study. Scholastic philosophy, asserting itself in the twelfth-century rise of the University of Paris, diverged in purpose and methodology from rhetoric, and the former liberal art Dialectica was subsumed into scholastic logic, in which demonstration was the preferred methodology for seeking philosophical truth.[23] What had been a speculative methodology in rhetoric was reconceived in university circles as the usual logical strategy for proving a truth already posited.

The old rhetorical concept of dialectics as a speculative methodology survived in scholarly consciousness, although it lost popularity. The development of scholastic demonstration had conflicted with rhetorical, monastic traditions of learning almost from its first introduction, and the coexistence of two traditions remained uneasy.[24] In the thirteenth century, scholars such as Robert Kilwardby (ca. 1215–79) clarified distinctions between dialectic, posited as a method of rhetorical investigation, and demonstration, perceived as the more rigorous methodology of scholastic philosophy. According to Kilwardby, the scholastic preference for demonstration was based on the principle that demonstration did not argue on both sides of a question but only on the "true" side: opinion (the conclusion of rhetoric) can change; knowledge cannot. Rhetorical dialectic might still have a proper function, he conceded, because demonstration may not be possible in ethical philosophy, the division of philosophy proper to rhetoric.[25] Thus the rhetorical version of dialectics, although discredited, remained a live element in English intellectual life.

The scholastic preference for "knowledge," however, encouraged devaluation of poetry. On methodological grounds, scholastics denied the value of poetry as a source of truth; some went so far as to deny any truth value to poetry and to argue against the propriety of using allegorical interpretive methods on secular literature.[26] When Chaucer balances his scholastic dialectician against a poet, then, he is not merely mischievous; he is taking up an already existing debate among English philosophers. His dialectic of dialectics, posing a philosophical dialectician against a rhetorical dialectician, cancels neither of the two disciplines but arrives at a tension that preserves the individuality of each.

After the philosophical eagle has his chance of arriving at truth, the debate between philosopher and poet tilts toward symbolic and aesthetic perceptions of imagination. The eagle, still trying to capture Geffrey's mind as well as his body, carries him to the Macrobian/Ciceronian perspective from which "al the world . . . / No more semed than a prikke"

(906–7). This point of reference is clearly more than a scientific or geospatial location, for Geffrey cannot make out any recognizable details (911–12), yet he perceives "ayerissh bestes," varieties of weather, and "th'engendrynge in hir kyndes" (965, 966–67, 968), which awaken associations with Martianus' *Marriage of Mercury and Philology* and the *Anticlaudianus* of Alan of Lille, philosophical allegories in poetic form. Since Geffrey cannot distinguish any form on earth, we must suspect that his bookish memories suggest his very perceptions through his *imaginatio* or *fantasia,* that faculty of image making theorized in the Middle Ages as mediating between sensory experience and intellection.[27]

This point in the poem marks an important transition, for here Geffrey begins, awkwardly at first, to synthesize poetry and philosophy in his own way. The first strategy Geffrey attempts begins with simplistic elements of both disciplines.

> And than thoughte y on Marcian,
> And eke on Anteclaudian,
> That sooth was her descripsion
> Of alle the hevenes region,
> As fer as that y sey the preve;
> Therfore y kan hem now beleve. (985–90)

Geffrey's fusion of apparently empirical, scholastic "proof" with "belief" marks him as exaggeratedly naïve. These allegorical celestial journeys require a different sort of interpretation and understanding than simple belief in the sense of assenting to their literal probability. Yet he knows, apparently intuitively, that he is more likely to find his proper mode of intellection in imaginative forms of thought. When the eagle offers to teach Geffrey the names and locations of the stars and zodiacal signs, knowledge he is sure (correctly) would be useful to a poet (998), Geffrey declines the offer, since the eagle would require him to give up his "fantasye" (992) in exchange.[28]

Although Geffrey rejects the eagle's offer of factual truth, we should be wary of assuming that Chaucer therefore rejects scholastic logic entirely; as Paul Strohm has observed, Chaucer in his *Astrolabe* articulates a pedagogical stance toward Lewis very near to the eagle's.[29] As an oblique testament to the usefulness of logic, Geffrey himself at first regards the eagle's proposal as an "impossible" (702), a scholastic category indicating philosophical invalidity. Geffrey's own use of scholastic categories to refute the eagle confounds the apparently absolute polarity between imaginative poet and factual philosopher. Furthermore, when Chaucer invents the eagle's fallacious demonstration, he of course gives evidence of his own logical acumen.

Chaucer ultimately ridicules as preposterous the exclusionary dichotomy of approaches to knowledge. If the scholastic approach busies itself with facts and definitions, the lay poet is hopelessly naïve and vague. The inadequacy of both extremes hints that Geffrey's intuitive response to the eagle's beauty and his enthusiasm for the fantasies of the universe mark a very plausible third possibility. Chaucer's poem dramatizes for readers the unarticulated problem inherent in dichotomy itself. In this particular instance, to posit a binary opposition between poetry and fact is pointless; even if poems were empirically and scientifically accurate, their "truth" lies in a different direction. The choice between logical demonstration and simple belief, like the opposition between philosophy and poetry, misses the real issue of understanding by its presentation of a false dichotomy.

Because both poles of the debate serve a branch of learning, Chaucer's dialectic can afford to be less polarized than Boccaccio's, for he can accept that both methodologies serve truth in their own proper sphere, a model of codependence of the two disciplines which recognizes their differences yet denies their ultimate contradiction. The scholastic eagle's insistence upon finding the right place does not ultimately conflict with Geffrey's tenacious search for the right tidings, the right story-vehicle, to suit his theme, his search for the *causes* and origins of poetry. Chaucer buries their mutual goal beneath a dialectic of wordplay: The Greek word *topic,* a rhetorical *terminus technicus* for the investigative tropes of dialectic, is translated into Latin logical terminology as *locus,* literally, "place."[30] Geffrey's rhetorical search for a topic and the eagle's philosophical search for a locus inevitably bring them to the same destination, for topic and locus both function as vehicles of invention within their respective disciplines. When the eagle successfully lands them both at the same place, Geffrey also has the topic he has been seeking. Chaucer makes his point not by a linear philosophical logic but by the imaginative logic of poetry.

Sir Philip Sidney matches Chaucer's dialectical sophistication, and although Sidney, like Chaucer, rejects Boccaccio's analogy between poetry and contemplation, Sidney's position reclaims for poetry something of the exalted status assigned it by Boccaccio. Both Chaucer and Sidney embrace a poetics of the active life, Sidney overtly, Chaucer by describing Geffrey's urban vigil after a day of work. Both Sidney and Chaucer acknowledge intellectual and spiritual limitations on poets and readers in poetic inspiration. Consequently, they both deflate the level of truth to which poets have access, locate the primary milieu of the poet in the imagination, and portray the inadequacy of philosophy in its inability to affect the will, to move anyone to desire the virtues described and defined by the philosopher. Yet while Sidney praises Chaucer for his ability to "drawe with [his] charming sweetnes the wild vntamed wits to an admiration of knowledge,"[31] an elegant encomium in agreement with Speght's praise of Chaucer's learning and sweetness, Sidney and Speght presume a dignity of decorum in which Chaucer had little interest. Because Chaucer and Sidney investigate parallel concerns, and because Sidney's dialectics represent the dominant tradition of dialectics, the differences between them help to identify characteristics of Chaucer's poetics that might have been problematic to Renaissance editors.

Writing as a Protestant in the English Reformation, Sidney could hardly have adopted Boccaccio's eremitical model of monastic contemplation. Instead, Sidney presents a model of the poet based on the active life. The activity of Sidney's poet surpasses that of Chaucer's Geffrey, for it carries a moral imperative Geffrey apparently had not felt; Geffrey happened to be engaged in the active life because it suited his personal talents and social circumstances—his mode of career is personal rather than normative. The pressure to compose comes from personal choice or from the philosophical eagle rather than from a duty to reform either society or poetry. Sidney's Calvinist convictions contributed to his depiction of the poet as zealously engaged in social responsibility,[32] and his rigorous humanist training in Ciceronian and Senecan rhetoric, his belief in reason (if qualified), and his courtly, aristocratic status reinforced his senses of political and social obligation. His emphasis that poetry inspires valor in warriors, wisdom in kings, confirms his interest in the practical social effects of poetry for moral and political education. Sidney's praise of the poet's active authority aims also at vindication of his own urgent involvement in political affairs, since the composition and defense of poetry had been the primary outlet for his frustrated desire to take an active statesman's part in the political events of his time.[33] He was especially committed to advocacy of the continental Protestant league, but he had not persuaded Elizabeth I to the wholehearted allegiance to which he so aspired.[34]

Sidney's apology, like those of Boccaccio and Chaucer, centers on the topic of poetic inspiration, although it is difficult to ascertain the status he would assign it. He first projects strong claims for the poet's authority as Boccaccio had done, but then he hedges those claims with distinctions and qualifications, establishing within his treatise an internal dialectic similar to Chaucer's. He associates poets with scriptural and pagan prophets *(vates)* (154), lending an aura of universal authority to the poet-vates, but when he examines a particular instance of pagan vates, he disclaims the particular application. Like Boccaccio, he praises Virgil's stature among the ancients, then qualifies his approval, remarking that using Virgil's poetry for fortune-telling was "a very vaine and godles superstition" (154). Later, he would distinguish that the pagan poets did not teach theology but imitated the theology of the culture about them (191), placing them in a clearly subservient position; but in his opening pages, he uses the archetypal association of poets with divine truth to summon readers to respect. A page after chiding Virgil for his readers' excesses, he restores the pagan term *vates* to honor, applying it to David (154–55). Sidney describes an ideal, then acknowledges that no particular poet fills that ideal.[35] What remains is the ambience of ancient authority.

His division of poetry into three classes, divine (that is, scripture), philosophical (the nonfictive poetry the ancients called "didactic"), and fictive (158–59), would seem to relieve him of the need to maintain the same standards of truth for fiction as he would for scripture. He could discuss the value of poetry not in a metaphysical context but from "ethic and politic consideration," as a human institution. True, a poet must have natural genius ("a Poet no industrie can make," 195), but poetry is practiced within the scope of human gift and wit. In his discussion of Plato's objection to poets, Sidney insists on the relative modesty of his own claims when he protests, "[Plato] attributeth vnto Poesie more then my selfe doe, namely, to be a very inspiring of a diuine force, farre aboue mans wit" (192). He makes explicit the fact that his use of Plato is a use of Plato's authority ("Plato . . . whose authoritie I had much rather iustly conster then uniustly resist" [191]; "I had much rather . . . show their mistaking of Plato . . . then go about to ouerthrow his authority" [192]), then he positions himself as making even more limited claims for poetry than does Plato.

Yet Sidney also claims a good deal of power for poets, including pagan poets, and it is by no means clear that the limitations he would impose later in the argument apply properly to Sidney's Christian poet: what he qualifies in one context, he reinstates in another. Having bracketed off scriptural poetry from his discussion in order to emphasize the human origins of poetry, he reintroduces later examples of scriptural uses of poetry, citing Christ's parables (166–67), Nathan's prophecy (174), Christ's quotations from scriptural poetry (181), and Paul's quotation of pagan poets (191). Furthermore, although poetry might be confined to the realm of human wit, the poet transcends nature as we know it, making another and better nature, "disdayning to be tied to any such subiection [as astronomy, geometry, music, natural philosophy, law, grammar, rhetoric, medicine, history, or philosophy], lifted vp with the vigor of his owne inuention," making a new nature from his own wit (156).

Sidney's understanding of the poet's powers of invention may represent a descent from Boccaccio's mystical vision concept, yet it certainly aspires to a philosophical vision of the ideal well beyond the aspirations of Chaucer's Geffrey. Poetry may be limited to human wit but not to the realm of the natural, not even to the metaphysical, for, as Sidney explains, the metaphysical extrapolates from a foundation in nature, a basis he denies as applicable to poetry (155–56). The potential for hubris in a view of this sort is strong enough that Sidney immediately reminds readers to "giue right honor to the heauenly Maker of that maker" (157); then he balances the absolute rightness which appears to be implicit by recalling that, even if human minds can conceive of perfection, human wills prevent achievement of it (157). Still, the claim that "our erected wit maketh vs know what perfection is" constitutes a considerable stake to the authority of truth; if the errors of the ancients have been corrected by Christian revelation, the intelligence of a Christian poet can conceive truth to an extent that commands obedience.

As is the case for Chaucer, poetry's advantage over philosophy resides for Sidney not solely in the mind but also in poetry's power to create desire and arouse the will, a capacity which would have a particular attraction for Calvinist thinkers. The power to arouse a desire to reach perfection is, for Calvin (and through him, for many English Protestants), to hold a key to the constant process of religious conversion. For Calvin, sustained dependence upon God is motivated by consciousness of failure in the attempt even to desire to reach perfection, so that the power to reignite that aspiration would materially assist one in the struggle toward salvation.[36] To the extent that Calvin was rearticulating an orthodox concept of sin, one could say that, broadly speaking, the principle is generally Christian, but Calvin's doctrine of total human depravity, the utter incapacity of human will even to desire salvation, placed new emphasis on agents that could aid the will. For Sidney, poetic ideals arouse precisely such desire for virtue. "For as the image of each action styrreth and instructeth the mind, so the loftie image of such Worthies most inflameth the mind with desire to be worthy, and informes with counsel how to be worthy" (179). The poet's encouragement to desire worthiness could, then, potentially contribute to religious conversion as much as to public virtue.[37]

If Sidney acknowledges limits to the perfection a human being can achieve, he leaves no doubt of the apprehensible standard beyond the particulars of individual experience. In strong contrast, Chaucer's Geffrey, content to observe passively his entire vision in Fame's house, suddenly leaps into participation when he enters the labyrinth of Rumor. He knows the house is made only of "twigges" (1936) and that its inhabitants favor "lesinges, / Entremedled with tydinges, / And eek allone be hemselve" (2123–25), but here for the first time, Geffrey fits in and, more importantly, wills his activity as a poet. The strange house literally spins out a continuous supply of "tydynges," as both Geffrey and the eagle notice (1924–30, 2004–6, 2025), yet as soon as Geffrey enters the house, he adjusts and the rotation seems to him to stop ("therwithalle, me thoughte hit stente, / And nothing hyt aboute wente—," 2031–32). Since rumors continue to fly out the windows, it seems clear that the spinning continues. The difference lies in Geffrey's parallel actions. The house "swyft as thought, / . . . aboute wente" (1924–25), and Geffrey, too, "alther-faste wente / About, and dide al myn *entente* / Me for to pleyen and for to lere" (2131–33; italics mine). From his now-comfortable perspective in this world of decidedly mixed truths, he *sees* someone who *seems* a "man of gret auctoritee," but authority never arrives in the poem. Chaucer was content, as Sidney was not, to count himself among the throng who know only partial truths.

Like Chaucer, Sidney demonstrates the power to move readers in his own figurative analogies and winning descriptions; in fact, in a strategy similar to Chaucer's fictional demonstration, Sidney at key points in his argument practices his own theory. Instead of explaining discursively how a poet is to delight readers, Sidney moves rather than reasons with them. One of Sidney's most effective strategies is typological prosopopoeia, as evidenced in his personification of moral philosophers. By accusing them of personal inconsistency, obscurity, and pedantry, he parodies the circularity of their reasoning.[38]

> I see [moral philosophers] comming towards mee with a sullen grauity, as though they could not abide vice by day light, rudely clothed for to witnes outwardly their contempt of outward things, with bookes in their hands agaynst glory, whereto they sett theyr names, sophistically speaking against subtlety, and angry with any man in whom they see the foule fault of anger. (161–62)

In this one sentence Sidney parodies more than the exaggerated self-contradictions of people for whom the principle of noncontradiction was fundamental. More sly, and more important to his argument, is the inconsistency between their abstractly reasoned contempt of outward things and their witness-bearing clothing. The very fact that their clothing "witnesses" testifies to the persistence of metaphor, despite the philosophers' stated ideal of plainness of speech. The sentence structure of this and the following sentence mock in their tortuous form the demand for "a playn setting downe" (162) of virtue;[39] in this sentence alone, the main clause is augmented by seven assorted subordinate clauses and adjectival or adverbial phrases. Sidney's imagination supplies in the image of moral philosophers the palpable example Chaucer so recommended in the *House of Fame,* and Sidney, like Chaucer, turns the philosophers' own discourse back upon themselves. But Sidney's pace and tone discourage readers from establishing a critical distance from his arguments. The passage engages readers by a familiar and comic idea, then reinforces engagement by the pithy rhythm of aphorism in the clause "as though they could not abide vice by day light." Finally, its humor discourages rebuttal; to object that not all philosophers are hypocrites or pedants would seem both overly literal-minded and, in the face of such persuasive good humor, rather churlish.

Such a practice might serve well for the purposes of a poet committed to a particular known truth, for direct appeal to the imagination offers the poet a high level of control over the impression the text makes on readers. Markedly absent from Sidney's treatise is any discussion of readerly engagement in an interpretive process; here we find nothing comparable to Chaucer's invocation to "[hym] that mover ys of al" (81) on behalf of his readers.[40] For Chaucer's readers, mind, will, and experience supplement the images entering their minds; in Sidney, the poet controls what images enter the minds of his readers, over whom he then has particular power because images work directly upon their wills.

Sidney's devices resort, like Boccaccio's, to the typically reductive counterattack of defensive discourse. The strategy operates all the more effectively in Sidney than in Boccaccio for Sidney's controlled and amused rather than angry tone. In places, he pits his opponents against each other rather than expend his own energy, then he invites his readers to eavesdrop. He uses his opponents as weapons against each other: he appeals to Aristotle's "plain determin[ation]" that poetry is "more Philosophicall and more studiously serious then history" (167), then to the historians who recorded that, when he went to battle, Alexander left his philosopher-teacher behind but "tooke deade *Homer* with him" (189). Again, he draws attention to the fact that Plato had so little real power against a tyrant that he was himself enslaved (190).

Sidney thus preserves a privileged position for himself: he encourages readers to laugh at his opponents' foolishness without seeming to implicate himself in the argument. His opponents' own discourses seem to condemn themselves without seeming to call upon Sidney to exercise authority. It could be said that, in the *Apologie*, dialectics is a game Sidney plays primarily when he controls both voices, so that even imagined debate issues in a conclusion favorable to Sidney's interests. His poet's motives are (ideally) unselfish; since he derives his authority from his vision of virtue and uses it only to inspire desire for that virtue in readers, poet and reader theoretically serve the same vision. Still, the poet as teacher and motivator retains strong control over what readers apprehend, and the vision, after all, is the poet's.

Part of Sidney's willingness to assume authority may respond to a significant shift in the social composition of the English reading public. The readers Sidney imagines for poets are hardly the same audience imagined by either Boccaccio or Chaucer; the invention of the printing press had admitted a socially wider audience than earlier writers had been able to address. Sidney's model sketches an educated, right-thinking poet who has insights of genuine value to a less educated or less morally inspired readership. Yet the change in readership does not fully account for the authority Sidney claimed for his hypothetical poet. Remarkably, Sidney never portrays his poet as a puzzled reader, Geffrey's constant role. Sidney himself takes a superior critical stance toward what he himself has read. In other words, Sidney's poet takes on the function of philosophy.[41]

Sidney's choice of form reinforces this function. Although he imitates juridical rhetoric, the treatise operates much of the time on philosophical logic. Unification of philosophy and poetry has been said to be Sidney's major contribution to Renaissance poetics;[42] he himself describes the poet as a "moderator" (163). Yet this moderator, as Margaret Ferguson remarks, "eventually steals the prize from the original contenders" (142). In spite of his intended mediation, the overriding irony of Sidney's *Apologie* remains that Sidney tacitly concedes the superior effectiveness of a philosophical genre for communicating truth. He might scoff at "Schoolemen [preoccupied with] *Genus* and difference" (165), but he also claims very early in his treatise to be "a peece of a Logician" (150) himself—and that in a context which suggests to readers that they, too, ought to be logicians if they wish to resist the interested arguments of self-love. He establishes his discourse, then, as an argument; he proceeds by "schoolmen's" categories of classification, definition, and determination of differences. In allowing philosophers to set the terms and the methods of discussion, he actually restricts the proper realm of poetry within narrower limits than either Boccaccio or Chaucer. Rhetoric controls Sidney's style, the part of literature which pertains to "words," but philosophy and its distinctions predominate when Sidney assesses the "matter" of English literature (196), its content.

Sidney's discovery of "great wants" in Chaucer (196) seems to belong to the realm of matter. Although he does not explain what he means, his treatment of Chaucer otherwise suggests that Chaucer's comic vision may explain Sidney's unease. The only Chaucerian work Sidney praises explicitly is *Troilus and Criseyde* (166, 196), and even Chaucer's effective characterization of Pandarus Sidney classifies as satire, which he couples with Terence as a "lower" expression of truth than epic heroism (166). That Sidney associates Chaucer with comedy is clear, for he uses Chaucer's expression to articulate his own charge that "Comedies giue the largest field [of sinful fancies] to erre, as *Chaucer* sayth" (183). Chaucer says no such thing, in fact; he merely likens literary production to harvest. Comic laughter to Sidney issues not from delight but from "a scornful tickling," and comic authors too frequently "styrre laughter in sinfull things, which are rather execrable then ridiculous: or in miserable, which are rather to be pittied then scorned" (200).

The sense of decorum and order behind these reflections is the same sensibility as that with which he tries to resolve the conflict between poetry and philosophy by means of relatively linear, certainly hierarchical, argument. A good poet should write of higher things. Chaucer chose instead to adjust discord through a multivalent fiction, permitting each voice its own proper validity, laughing at human intellectual ineptitude. By insisting upon writing in poetry, Chaucer retained a major persuasive advantage.[43] He could layer several ideas, images, and associations; the same strategy that might confuse linear argument enriches fictive poetry. By writing his defense in poetry, Chaucer forces philosophically minded readers to take up the argument on his terms, to meet him in his own mode of figural language, where he can best depict his own ideas of the relationships of poetry to philosophy and of both disciplines to truth. Chaucer makes no jealous claim for absolute, scientific truth status for poetry; he merely declines his opponents' definition of the terms of the problem, which excludes the value of poetry as a vehicle of truth.

Although Chaucer's dialectics need not imply despair of meaning in their avoidance of narrative and hermeneutical closure, they could certainly look dangerous to a Renaissance editor (such as Speght) with a heavy investment in political, religious, and poetic authority. The clash between Chaucer's moderated claims to an authority of truth and those of his Renaissance editors may account for Speght's treatment of the *House of Fame.* At the least, a work that mocks the evanescence and dubious reliability of fame fits awkwardly with Speght's presentation of Chaucer as "our Antient and Learned English Poet," equivalent in stature with classical authors.[44] The presence of so fractious a work might even challenge the proper importance of poetic fame presumed by Thynne's dedication to Henry VIII in such phrasings, reprinted and thereby reaffirmed in Speght's edition, as "Many great Poets and Orators have highly employed their studies and courages, leaving thereby notable Renoume of themselves, and example perpetual to their posterity" (xxx). Understandably enough, Chaucer's *House of Fame* was one example set by Chaucer that his Renaissance editors ironically declined to follow.

Notes

1. Jordan, "Lost in the Funhouse," 100; see also 100–115, esp. 114n.1; Shook, "*The House of Fame*," 418; Allen, "Recurring Motif."

2. In choosing Boccaccio and Sidney for comparison with Chaucer, I opt for the clear divergences they offer; Spenser's "October" eclogue would represent a poetic discussion of the same problem, but inclusion of it in this argument seems an unnecessary complication of the present investigation. I am interested in lines of divergence between two traditions of dialectic as a way of explaining why Renaissance editors such as Speght, who was not operating with Chaucer's double dialectics, might have been uncomfortable with *The House of Fame.* Cheney's *Spenser's Famous Flight* investigates in far more detail than I could here how Spenser works with the same tradition.

3. See Delany, *Chaucer's "House of Fame"* and her *The Naked Text*, esp. 48–56; Leff, *Dissolution of the Medieval Outlook*.

4. Pearsall, "Thomas Speght," 76.

5. None of Speght's notes is extensive, but he supplied at least three full lines of introduction for most works, fuller paragraphs for the *Canterbury Tales* (fourteen lines), *The Book of the Duchess* (eight to nine lines), the apocryphal *The Flower and the Leaf* (eight and a half lines), and *The Testament of Love* (twelve lines); even individual Canterbury tales feature introductions longer than that to *The House of Fame*.

6. *Works of Geoffrey Chaucer*, ed. Speght, from *English Books 1641–1700*, 467. All references to Speght's edition are to this microfilm of the 1687 reprint of the 1602 edition; for publication data, see Pearsall, "Thomas Speght," 91.

7. So interested was Speght in moral closure that his relatively brief commentary on Chaucer's *Troilus and Criseyde* described (258) the miserable end Henryson had invented for her in his *Testament of Cresseid* (which immediately followed upon Chaucer's *Troilus*) as though Henryson's moral were Chaucer's.

8. Speght edition, 484. See Fyler, Textual Notes to *House of Fame*, 1142, and Explanatory Notes to *House of Fame*, 990, both in *Riverside Chaucer.* Caxton's edition of the poem broke off Chaucer's version at line 1095, where "tales" begin to crowd upon one another, well before Chaucer mentioned the "man of great auctorite," and Caxton identified the conclusion as his own work. Thynne reinserted the remaining Chaucerian lines; tacked on Caxton's ending, amended for meter; and omitted Caxton's identification of himself as author of the conclusion. Speght thus may never have realized that the conclusion he read was non-Chaucerian.

9. See Cheney, *Spenser's Famous Flight*, 8–10, for a compact discussion of the line of tradition and of Chaucer's aberration from it.

10. For further detail on Speght's, Thynne's, and Pynson's editions, see Pearsall, "Thomas Speght," 76–78, 83, 88; Blodgett, "William Thynne," 39; Hammond, *Chaucer*, 114.

11. Boccaccio's treatise was under revision while Chaucer was in Florence in 1373 and Chaucer could easily have read in Galeazzo Visconti's copy (Howard, *Chaucer*, 194, 229–30); although critics are of divided opinion as to whether Chaucer knew the *Genealogie*, his contemporary Gower certainly made use of it. Its influential circulation among English literati—John Gower, Humphrey Duke of Gloucester, John Lydgate, William Caxton, Erasmus, Thomas Lodge, Greene, Spenser, "E.K.," Jonson, Milton, and possibly even Sidney, to name only the best known—is beyond question. See Coulter, "Genealogy of the Gods," 340–41; Wright, *Boccaccio in England*, 36–43, passim; Smith, *Elizabethan Critical Essays*, I:lxxviii–lxxix, 402n.206; Seznec, *Survival*, 312; Lewis, *English Literature*, 396. As a convenient point of orientation, use of the figure of the Demogorgon is regarded as evidence of knowledge of Boccaccio's treatise.

12. Giovanni Boccaccio, *Genealogie*, 79 (2.7). English quotations in the following paragraphs are all taken from Osgood, translator, *Boccaccio on Poetry.*

13. Ferguson, *Trials of Desire*, 168.

14. To sharpen the religious point of this argument, Boccaccio speculated that God would not have bestowed so precious a gift first upon pagans rather than upon his own people, the Hebrews (42), repudiating opinions (although he presents them as possibilities) that poetry originated among the Assyrians or Greeks (43, 46).

15. On the history of the separation of the active life from the contemplative, see Constable, *Three Studies*, esp. 93–141.

16. Nobody seems to know why Boccaccio not only preserved the dedication to Hugo but also continued throughout the work to address him, when Hugo died in 1359 and Boccaccio was still revising in the 1360s and thought of it as unfinished in 1371 (Osgood, Introduction, *Boccaccio on Poetry*, xiii n.2).

17. Dante, *Purgatorio* 1.19–24, 28–30 and *Paradiso* 1.62f.; see Schless, *Chaucer and Dante*, 46–50; Taylor, *Chaucer Reads "The Divine Comedy,"* 21–23.

18. Greenfield, *Humanist and Scholastic Poetics*, 25, 57–61, 102, 116–17; Lewis, *English Literature*, 322; Morrison, *History as a Visual Art*, 37; Russell, *English Dream Vision*, 89–94, 101–2.

19. Chaucer concretizes Boethius's metaphor of eagle for thought when he remarks,

> And thoo thoughte y upon Boece,
> That writ, "A thought may flee so hye
> Wyth fetheres of Philosophye,
> To passen everych element. . . ." (*HF* 2.972–75)

(Cf. *Bo* 4.M1; see also Leyerle, "Chaucer's Windy Eagle," 263n.). All Chaucer quotations are taken from *Riverside Chaucer.*

20. Stump, ed. and trans., *Boethius's "De topicis differentiis,"* 165.

21. Fyler, Explanatory Notes (983nn. 734, 765–81, 788–821): Aristotle, Augustine, Boethius, and Dante all used the doctrine of "natural inclination," and the theory of sound appears in Boethius's *De musica*, Macrobius's *Somnium Scipionis*, Vincent of Beauvais's *Speculum naturale*, and even earlier in Plato's *Timaeus*.

22. Stump, *Boethius*, 174, point 3; Fyler's note to ll. 765–81 acknowledges that the eagle's frequent pairing of *spech* and *soun* "blur[s] the distinction between them."

23. Stump, *Boethius*, 15, 17, 24–25; Kenny and Pinborg, "Medieval Philosophical Literature," 25, 30.

24. For lucid comparisons of monastic rhetorical methodology with scholastic dialectical methodology, see Anderson, "Enthymeme and Dialectic," and Renna, "Idea of Jerusalem."

25. Kretzman and Stump, *Cambridge Translations*, I:278–82; Stump, *Boethius*, 19–20; Marrone, "Kilwardby, Robert," 7:253.

26. See Colish, *Mirror of Language*, 160–61; Smalley, *English Friars*, 299–300.

27. For more thorough discussion of the functions of memory and imagination, see Carruthers, *Book of Memory*, 51–60, passim, 169–70; Clanchy, *From Memory to Written Record*, 172–75.

28. Frese stresses that Geffrey's refusal of astronomical instruction is a refusal to "limit his imaginative freedom to deploy these traditional names in poetically appropriate recontextualizations" (175), in *"Ars Legendi,"* 175–77.

29. Strohm, *Social Chaucer*, 48.

30. For more elaborate explication of the disciplinary crossover, see Stump, *Boethius*, 16; Carruthers, *Book of Memory*, 33–38, 43–45, 174, 308n.122, 314n.90.

31. Sidney, *Apologie for Poetrie*, in Smith, *Elizabethan Critical Essays*, 1:151. All subsequent references to the *Apologie* are to this edition.

32. Sinfield, "Cultural Politics," 130–31; Weiner, *Sir Philip Sidney*, 6–8, 24–25.

33. Duncan-Jones has suggested further that the *Apologie* may have been timed to substitute his literary engagement for the more usual accomplishments of a courtier in the eyes of Elizabeth's First Secretary, Francis Walsingham, Sidney's prospective father-in-law (*Sir Philip Sidney*, 233–36).

34. Sinfield, "Cultural Politics," 132.

35. On this pattern in Renaissance aspiration, see Kinney, *Humanist Poetics*, 126, 132.

36. Weiner, *Sir Philip Sidney*, 15.

37. Weiner, *Sir Philip Sidney*, 50.

38. Sidney, *Apologie*, 161–63; cf. Levao, "Sidney's Feigned *Apology*," 133; cf. Ferguson, *Trials of Desire*, 138.

39. For further discussion of this same passage, see Ferguson, *Trials of Desire*, 142.

40. Chaucer's invocation on behalf of readers follows immediately his invocation of the assistance from the god of sleep for his own compositional activity and is immediately succeeded by a curse on maliciously intentioned readers. I would not deny the comic tone of the passage (ll. 66–108), but its very existence acknowledges readers as active participants in poetic composition, for better or for worse.

41. Sidney writes in the *Apologie* as though the moral significance of poetic characters were clear, a clarity he admires, for instance, in Chaucer's depiction of Pandarus (166). This clarity may be achieved primarily for the occasion: his own characters in the *Arcadia* develop in more complex ways than the *Apologie* might seem to suggest. What he actually asks for is a rhetoric which combines clarity with natural depiction ("all virtues, vices, and passions so in their own *natural* seats *laid to the view*"), so that readers might forget the poets who present the image and think they are apprehending directly ("we seem not to hear of them, but clearly to see through them," 166). As Kinney notes, "humanist rhetoric for Sidney steadfastly continues to serve, direct, and advise us (as readers) on judging actions" (*Humanist Poetics*, 231). His restraint is the restraint of a teacher waiting for a pupil to arrive at realization.

A further study of how allegory functions in Sidney's characters seems called for but exceeds the scope of this chapter; Sidney's fiction enters into a different discourse and entertains a different audience than does the *Apologie*.

42. Kinney, *Humanist Poetics*, 132, 230.

43. See Roney's more extensive argument to this effect in her introduction to *Chaucer's "Knight's Tale,"* 1–41.

44. Pearsall, "Thomas Speght," 75.

CHAPTER 4

Thomas Speght's Renaissance Chaucer and the *solaas* of *sentence* in *Troilus and Criseyde*

CLARE R. KINNEY

In a letter "To the Readers" prefacing his 1598 edition of *The Workes of our Antient and Learned English Poet, Geffrey Chavcer,* Thomas Speght regrets that, in the haste of readying the text for publication, he has not completed various editorial tasks "which might more fully haue bene performed, if warning and conuenient leisure had bene giuen."[1] At the end of the list of corrections that concludes the 1598 text, he returns to this theme: "Sentences . . . which are many and excellent in this Poet, might have been noted in the margent with some marke, which now must be left to the search of the Reader." Speght was able to remedy this and other omissions in his second edition of 1602, in which he announces on the title page that the reader will not only find the "whole worke by old Copies reformed," the "signification of the old and obscure words prooued: also Caracters shewing from what Tongue or Dialect they be deriued," and the "Latine and French, not Englished by Chaucer, translated" but also "Sentences and Prouerbes noted." In his dedicatory letter to Sir Robert Cecil in the 1602 text, Speght reasserts that he has "reformed the whole Worke, whereby Chaucer for the most part is restored to his owne Antiquitie; and noted withall most of his Sentences and Prouerbes."[2] His provision of a glossary and rudimentary notes to Chaucer's text places his project—the last of six editions of Chaucer that appeared between 1532 and 1602—at the beginning of the modern editorial tradition. Indeed, the 1602 edition—reprinted in 1687 with no significant modifications—remained the definitive text of Chaucer well into the eighteenth century: this was the version of Chaucer that Milton, Pepys, Dryden, and Pope knew and owned.[3]

My intention here is to explore that "noting" of sentences and proverbs which Speght added to the text of 1598. In the 1602 *Works,* senten-

Than he, ne more desired worthinesse.

What cas (qd. Troilus) or what auenture
Hath guided thee to seen my languishing,
That am refuse of euerie creature?
But for the loue of God, at me praying
Goe hence away, for certes my dying,
Woll thee disease, and I mote needs deie,
Therefore goe way, there nis no more to seie.

But if thou wene, I be thus sicke for drede,
It is not so, and therefore scorne nought:
There is an other thing I take of hede,
Wel more thā ought ẏ grekes han yet wrouzt
Which cause is of my deth for sorow ⁊ thouzt:
But though that I now tell it thee ne lest,
Be thou not wroth, I hide it for the best.

This Pandare, that nigh malt for wo ⁊ routh
Full often sayed alas, what may this be?
Now friend (qd. he) if euer loue or trouth
Hath been er this betwixen thee and me,
Ne doe thou neuer such a crueltе,
To hiden fro thy friend so great a care,
Wost thou not well that I am Pandare?

I woll parten with thee all thy paine,
If it so be I doe thee no comfort
☞ As it is friends right, sooth for to saine,
To enterparten woe, as glad disport
I haue and shall, for true or false report
In wrong and right loued thee all my liue,
Hide not thy woe fro me, but tell it bliue.

Then gan this sorrowfull Troilus to sike,
And sayd him thus, God leue it be my best
To tellen thee, for sith it may thee like,
Yet woll I tell it, though my heart brest,
And well wote I, thou maiest doe me no rest,
But least thou deeme I trust not to thee
Now harke friend, for thus it stant with me.

Loue, ayenst the which who so defendeth
Himseluen most, him alderlest auaileth,
With dispaire so sorrowfully me offendeth
That straight vnto the death my hart faileth:
Therto desire, so brenningly me assaileth,
That to been slaine, it were a greater ioy
To me, than king of Greece be and of Troy.

Suffiseth this, my full friend Pandare,
That I haue said, for now wotest thou my wo:
And for the loue of God my cold care
So hide it well, I told it neuer to mo:
For harmes mighten followen mo than two
If it were wist, but be thou in gladnesse,
And let me sterue vnknowne of my distresse.

How hast thou thus vnkindly and long
Hid this fro me, thou foole? (qd. Pandarus)
Perauenture thou mayst after such one long,
That mine auise anone may helpen vs:
This were a wonder thing (qd. Troilus)
Thou couldest neuer in loue thy selfen wisse,
How diuell maiest thou bringen me to blisse,

Ye Troilus, now hearken (qd. Pandare)
Though I be nice, it happeth often so,
That one that of axes doeth full euill fare,
By good counsaile can keep his frend therefro:
I haue my selfe seen a blinde man go
There as he fell, that could looken wide,
A foole may eke a wise man oft guide. ☜

A whetstone is no caruing instrument, ☜
But yet it maketh sharpe keruing tolis,
And after thou wost ẏ I haue aught miswent,
Eschue thou that, for such thing to schole is,
Thus often wise men bewaren by foolis: ☜
If thou so doe, thy wit is well bewared,
By his contrarie is euerie thing declared. ☜

For how might euer swetnesse haue be know
To him, that neuer tasted bitternesse?
No man wot what gladnesse is I trow,
That neuer was in sorrow, or some distresse:
Eke white by blacke, by shame eke worthines
Each set by other, more for other seemeth,
As men may seen, and so the wise it deemeth.

Sith thus of two contraries is o lore, ☜
I that haue in Loue so oft assayed,
Greuaunces ought connen well the more
Counsailen thee, of that thou art dismayed,
And eke thee ne ought not been euill apaied,
Though I desire with thee for to beare
Thine heauie charge, it shall thee lasse deare.

I wote well that it fared thus by me,
As to thy brother Paris, an hierdesse,
Which that icleped was Oenone,
Wrote in a complaint of her heauinesse:
Ye saw the letter that she wrote I gesse:
Nay neuer yet iwis (qd. Troilus)
Now (qd Pandare) hearkeneth it was thus.

Phebus, that first found art of medicine,
(Qd. she) and coud in euerie wightes care
Remedie and rede, by herbes he knew fine,
Yet to himselfe his cunning was full bare,
For loue had him so bounden in a snare,
All for the daughter of king Admete,
That all his craft ne coud his sorrow bete.

Right so fare I, vnhappie for me,
I loue one best, and that me smerteth sore:

Page from Thomas Speght's 1602 edition of Chaucer, showing maniples found in *Troilus and Criseyde*. Reprinted by permission of the University of Virginia Library.

tious or proverbial material is quite literally "indexed" by the pointing finger of a little fist or maniple in the margin of the page (see figure).[4] Rather than being "left to the search of the reader," the author's *sententiae* are now clearly marked by the editor. Speght's interpretive acts, the choices he made in isolating these aphoristic "micro-texts," intervene graphically between reader and poems. The pointing hands on the printed page do not simply draw one's attention to the "sententious" moments in a given work; they also construct a digest of Chaucer for the reader's consumption.

Speght's practice, to be sure, is in accordance with that well-established tendency among fifteenth- and sixteenth-century commentators to single out Chaucer for praise not only as "worshipful fader & first foundeur & embelissher of ornate eloquence in our englissh" but also as a quintessentially serious and sententious poet.[5] William Caxton's insistence (in an afterword to his edition of Chaucer's *House of Fame*) that Chaucer "wrytteth no voyde wordes / but alle hys mater is ful of hye and quycke sentence" is echoed more than a hundred years later in the letter from Speght's friend Francis Beaumont, which is printed at the beginning of the 1598 and 1602 editions: "[Chaucer] is in his Troylus so sententious, as there be few staues in those bokes, which include not some principall sentence; most excellentlie imitating Homer and Virgill, and borowing often of them, and of Horace also, and other the rarest both Oratours and Poets that haue written."[6] Beaumont's rather exaggerated encomium (one does not usually think of Chaucer as being a reader of Homer), which locates Chaucerian sententiousness within a tradition stretching back to ancient Greece, reinforces Speght's own hint that in simultaneously restoring the poet "to his owne Antiquitie" and in providing the apparatus that will make his work fully comprehensible to contemporary readers, he is granting Chaucer the status and authority of a Greek or Latin poet. The editor's noting of sentences in the Chaucerian text may be compared with the ubiquitous humanist interest in quarrying the classical authors for fragments of detachable wisdom: Speght is, as it were, pre-selecting the Chaucerian entries for a Renaissance commonplace book.[7]

In considering the "Renaissance Chaucer" constructed by Speght's selective indexing of sentence and proverb, I have chosen to concentrate on his annotations to *Troilus and Criseyde,* the poem Beaumont found supremely rich in Chaucerian sententiae.[8] Geoffrey Bennington, in his study of sententiousness in the French eighteenth-century novel, remarks that the utterances we classify as sententiae "seem to want to transcend the contingency of the diegetical universe."[9] It is thus particularly interesting to ask what happens when Speght attempts to extract discrete monitory or moral statements from the larger (and emphatically "diegetical") narrative in which they are actually articulated, a narrative which notoriously bears witness to the contingency and instability of all human speech acts.

It may first be useful to establish what an Elizabethan scholar would have understood by the terms *proverb* and *sentence*. In the 1593 edition of his rhetorical handbook *The Garden of Eloquence*, Henry Peacham defines them as follows:

> *Paroemia,* called of us a Prouerbe, is a sentence or forme of speech much used, and commonly knowen, and also excellent for the similitude and signification: to which two things are necessarily required, the one that it be renowned, and much spoken off, as a sentence in euerie mans mouth. The other, that it be witty, and well proportioned, whereby it may be discerned by some speciall marke and note from common speech, and be commended by antiquitie and learning. . . .
>
> *Gnome,* otherwise called *Sententia,* is a saying pertaining to the maners and common practices of men, which declareth by an apt breuitie, what in this our life ought to be done, or left undone. First it is to be obserued, that euerie sentence is not a figure, but that only which is notable, worthie of memorie, and approued by the iudgement and consent of all men, which being such a one, maketh by the excellency thereof the Oration not onely beautifull and comely, but also graue, puissant, and full of maiestie.[10]

For Peacham, proverbs are characterized by their use of "similitude" and by their presence "in euerie mans mouth." Sententiae, however, do not necessarily employ figurative language and have a broader monitory scope in teaching "what in this our life ought to be done, or left undone." Although their wisdom is approved by common "iudgement and consent," they are not exactly maxims which are on everyone's lips since they express elevated sentiments in language which is "graue, puissant, and full of maiestie." At the same time, we should note that the distinction between the two terms can be somewhat blurred; Peacham actually begins his definition of *Paroemia* by suggesting that proverbs are a particular kind of "sentence."[11]

Speght's selections generally conform pretty accurately to Peacham's representative definitions. The 221 little fists dotting the 1602 *Troilus* at first glance offer few surprises, and there is, furthermore, a considerable overlap between the sentences and proverbs marked by Speght and the proverbs, proverbial phrases, and sententious sayings identified in the *Troilus* by more recent commentators upon the poem.[12] To give a clearer sense of Speght's actual practice, I reproduce below fifteen consecutive "indexes" from Book 3 (beginning at the moment when Pandarus, having persuaded Criseyde to stay overnight at his palace, starts to put in motion his plans for the consummation of the lovers' affair). The verse lines are exactly as they appear in the 1602 text (with the addition of book and line numbers, and with asterisks marking the position of Speght's marginal fists); I have numbered them for easier reference and named the speaker in each case.

1. But Pandarus, that wel couth ech adele*
   The olde daunce . . . [3.694–95: Narrator]
2. So thriue I, this night shall I make it wele,
   Or casten all the gruel in the fire.* [3.711: Pandarus]
3. It is nat god a sleping hound to wake* [3.764: Pandarus]
4. That for to holde in loue a man in honde,*
   And him her lefe and dere hart to call [3.773–74: Pandarus]
5. O god (qd. she) so worldly selinesse,*
   Which clerkes callen false felicite,
   Ymedled is with many a bitternesse [3.813–15: Criseyde]
6. For either ioyes comen nat ifere,*
   Or els no wight hath hem alway here. [3.817–18: Criseyde]
7. Now if he wote that ioy is transitory*
   As euery ioy of worldly thing mote flee [3.827–28: Criseyde]
8. Nece, al thing hath time I dare avow,* [3.855: Pandarus]
   For when a chambre a fire is, or an hall
   Well more nede is, it sodainly rescow
   Then to disputen and aske amongs all,
   How the candle in the straw is falle
   Ah benedicite, for al among that fare,
9. The harme is done, and farwel feldefare.* [3.861: Pandarus]
10. A ring (qd. he) ye hazel wodes shaken* [3.890: Pandarus]
11. O time ilost, wel maist thou cursen slouth* [3.896: Pandarus]
12. I am, till God me better minde send,
    At Dulcarnoun, right at my wittes end.* [3.930–31: Criseyde]
13. Eke al me wo is thus, that foke now blen
    To saine right thus: ye, jalousie is loue* [3.1024: Criseyde]
14. For I haue sene of a ful misty morow*
    Folowen ful oft a mery somers day [3.1060–61: Narrator]

15. Ye nece, woll ye pullen out the thorne*
That sticketh in his hart (qd. Pandare) [3.1104: Pandarus]

Ten of Speght's selections (examples 1–4, 8–12, and 14) correspond to instances of proverbs or proverbial phrases cited in Bartlett J. Whiting's catalogue of proverbs, proverbial phrases, and sententious remarks in Chaucer's *oeuvre.* Whiting does not classify example 15 as a proverbial phrase, but it is hardly surprising that Speght deems its well-worn metaphor proverbial (he also indexes it at 2.1272). Whiting classifies example 5 as sententious material; he does not mention examples 6 and 7, but their variations on the theme Criseyde has already advanced at 3.813 supports Speght's decision to index these lines as well.

The only other passage not mentioned by Whiting is Criseyde's remark about people's tendency to misrepresent jealousy as love (example 13). Speght's annotation of these lines bears witness to his special predilection for indexing generalizations about the nature and lore of love. Throughout the poem, he is particularly assiduous in indexing Pandarus's comments and advice to both Troilus and Criseyde on the *ars amatoria,* and he also promotes to the status of sentence a couple of oxymoronic verses from Troilus's version of #132 of Petrarch's *Canzoniere,* "S'amor non è" (1.400–20)—"For aie thurst I the more that iche it drinke" (1.406) and "For heat of cold, for cold of heat I die" (1.420).[13] Overall, Speght's annotations suggest that he is more concerned with noting the sorrows of love than with affirming its higher worth or putatively transcendent power (significantly, there are no little fists in the margins of Troilus's Boethian hymn to universal love [3.1744–71]). He does, however, index several lines in Criseyde's Book 2 consideration of the pros and cons of taking a lover, lines insisting upon the particular woes women suffer through love (2.755, 2.777, 2.784, 2.791, 2.798, 2.804). If, as at least one scholar has argued, our editor was the father of that Rachel Speght who in 1617 published a response to a viciously antifeminist pamphlet by Joseph Swetnam, we should not, perhaps, be astonished by his willingness to elevate to the level of "sentence" a female character's remarks on the sufferings of her sex.[14]

I have already suggested that there are few surprises in the lines Speght includes in his indexed material (his *omissions* are another matter, and I address some of these later in this chapter). Among his 221 selections only three gave this reader pause, and I reproduce them below:

What, who wol demen though he see a man*
to temple gone, that he the images eateth:

> . . . to her self she said, who yaue me drinke?*
> God haue thy soule, for broght haue I thy bere* (2.372, 2.651, 2.1638)

My first example is taken from a speech in which Pandarus insists that even if Criseyde shows kindness to Troilus and permits him to visit her, her good name will not necessarily be sullied; the second is Criseyde's spontaneous response to the spectacle of Troilus riding through Troy in triumph after a skirmish with the Greeks; the third is whispered by Pandarus to Troilus just before he brings the lovers together for their first private interview. All three employ striking—in the first and third instances even shocking—metaphors that hardly constitute proverbs or sentences as Speght's contemporaries would have understood these terms. While these verses have certain features in common with Peacham's representative definitions, being "excellent for [. . .] similitude and signification," "witty," "well proportioned," of an "apt breuitie," "notable," and "worthie of memorie," there is no evidence that they are (like proverbs) "renowned and much spoken of" and "commended by antiquitie or learning" or (like sententiae) moral and monitory remarks concerning the "maners and common practices of men" which are "graue, puissant, and full of maiestie." Speght seems in these instances to have whimsically conferred upon original and arresting figurative phrases (embedded in very specific narrative contexts) the status of detachable, context-transcending proverbs or sentences.

Yet however surprising it is to find Criseyde's intoxicated reaction to her first sight of Troilus or Pandarus's irreverent conflations of sacred and profane images highlighted by Speght, these verses nevertheless have something in common with the more conventionally proverbial or sententious material the editor usually chooses to index. Of the 221 little fists decorating the poem, 177 (just over 80 percent) point to speeches of characters in the *Troilus*—most of them, that is, mark the poetic narrative's quotation of other people's words.[15] (Indeed such indexings often embrace an additional level of reported speech—as, for example, when a speaker prefixes a proverbial or sententious remark with the phrase "men say," or concludes it with the words "As writen clerkes wise.")[16] A considerable portion of *Troilus and Criseyde* is given over to the representation of different discourses: the many utterances in which the opinions and desires of its characters are made manifest produce a radically heteroglot universe in which the vision of no speaking subject is absolute or unchallenged.[17] And the fact that so much of the material Speght indexes is drawn from this plurality of utterances casts an interesting light on the congeries of sentences and proverbs his maniples emphasize.

In a suggestive article examining the monitory speech acts of *Troilus and Criseyde,* Karla Taylor argues that the proverbs so frequently invoked by characters in the poem repeatedly "betray the expectations of stability they arouse" and take on ironically different resonances according to the context in which they are uttered.[18] Pandarus and Diomede, she notes, both use versions of the proverb "Nothing ventured, nothing gained": "Unknow unkist, and lost that is unsought" (1.809), remarks the former, prodding Troilus into action; "For he that naught assaieth, naught atcheueth" (5.784), says the latter before attempting to woo Criseyde.[19] Speght dutifully indexes both of these lines, despite the fact that the very words that Pandarus uses to encourage Troilus are eventually turned against him by the opportunistic Diomede. His incorporation of these decontextualized utterances into his own gathering of isolatable maxims privileges the *solaas* of the sententious moment at the expense of the larger *sentence* (and more complex ironic pleasures) offered by the narrative whole.

In refusing to recognize the contingency of these individual speech acts as he collects his Chaucerian sententiae, Speght ends up embracing contradictions. In Book 4, he indexes a line from Pandarus's speech advising Troilus to seize the occasion and abduct Criseyde before she can be handed over to the Greeks:

> But manly set the world on fire and leuen*
> And if thou die a martir go to heauen. (4.622–23)

Later on in the same book, he indexes a verse from Criseyde's response to Troilus's suggestion that they elope together, a verse presenting an opposite point of view:

> Beth nat too hastie in this hote fare,*
> For hastie man ne wanteth neuer care. (4.1567–68)

Nor is such inconsistency the only consequence of Speght's separation of utterance from narrative context. In Book 1, for example, he marks out the following verses, culled from one of Pandarus's speeches:

> . . . for thou were wõt to chace
> At loue in scorne, and for dispite him call
> Sainte Idiote, lord of these fooles all.*
>
> And saied, that loues seruaunts euerichone
> Of nicete, ben verie Goddes Apes* (1.908–10, 1.912–13)

These lines offer a striking instance of double heteroglossia: the narrator represents the discourse of Pandarus as the latter chastises the now penitent Troilus by representing the blasphemies he used to utter against Cupid. The trenchant phrases deriding love and lovers are not offered as proverbs or sententiae which carry truth claims *within* the narrative moment: they are examples of the hero's past folly. Speght's decontextualizing indexing, however, quite ignores this fact.

A simple reexamination of certain Speghtian selections within their original narrative frame tends to complicate—or undercut—their putatively exemplary or sententious status. At the end of Book 3, Speght indexes the verses in which Pandarus warns Troilus:

> The worst kind of infortune is this,
> A man that hath been in prosperite,*
> And it remember, when it passed is. (3.1626–28)

Early in Book 4, after learning that Criseyde must be surrendered to the Greeks, Pandarus attempts to cheer up Troilus by asserting that there are more fish in the sea:

> What God forbid alway that ech plesaunce*
> In o thing were, and in none other wight[.] (4.407–8)

Troilus frankly rebukes him for this unchivalrous sentiment:

> But canst thou plaien raket to and fro,*
> Nettle in dock out, now this, now y[t] Pandare?* (4.460–61)

He continues,

> Why gabbest thou, that saidest unto me,
> That him is wors that is fro wele ithrow*
> Than he had erst none of that wele know. (4.480–82)

Speght's marginal fists silently reduce all the above phrases to a single level of general sententiousness. Read in context, however, Pandarus's words at 4.407–8 redefine the implicit and local definition of "prosperite" (that is, the continuing enjoyment of a single beloved) that made the first maxim applicable to Troilus's condition. And the "double heteroglossia" informing Troilus's replies complicates matters even further. At 4.460–61 Troilus invokes two down to earth proverbial phrases ironically: he is not reaffirming Pandarus's revisionary sentiments but re-citing them in Pandaric language in order to attack them. He then paraphrases Pandarus's original statement about fortune, not to reassert its truth value but to say to his friend, "If, as you have suggested, this is a statement of truth, how can you possibly claim that I should abandon my woe and concede that 'wele' is more likely to be found in a variety of erotic objects?" In the dialogic world of the poem, it is impossible to grant all four statements equal claims to sententious or proverbial wisdom.[20] Its Renaissance editor's interest in identifying isolated phrases which are "notable, worthie of memorie, and approued by the iudgement and consent of all men" forces upon *Troilus and Criseyde* a univocality which its very narrative practice perpetually puts in question.[21]

Speght's indexing of Pandarus's mutually exclusive sentences at 3.1626–28 and 4.407–8 brings me to another issue. I have already mentioned that 80 percent of the editor's marginal fists point to speeches made by characters within the poem; over half of these utterances (a total of 93) belong to the loquacious go-between. A significant proportion of the sententious material Speght indexes is thus not so much Chaucerian as Pandaric wisdom. If we think of Speght's selections as constituting an interpretive digest of the poem (a guidebook to its local beauties of *sentence*), what are the implications of that digest's containing more of Pandarus's remarks than anybody else's (including the narrator's)? In the heteroglot universe of the *Troilus*, the urbane Pandarus has a pithy generalization to suit every circumstance—but his energetic yet commonplace wisdom is ultimately defeated by the slipperiness of experience: faced with Criseyde's betrayal of Troilus, her uncle can only "stant, astonied . . . / As still as ston; o word ne coud he sey" (5.1728–29). Bent on cataloguing Pandaric sententiousness, Speght ignores the attempts of the poem that *contains* Pandarus to disrupt conventional (that is, Pandaric) efforts to fix experience in vacuum-sealed apothegms.

In considering the ironic consequences of Speght's practice of isolating sententious moments in a poem so preoccupied with the instability of human utterances, we might recall the well-known words of Chaucer's Nun's Priest to his audience at the conclusion of his tale of Chauntecleer: "Taketh the frute, and let the chaffe be still" (a line duly indexed by Speght in the 1602 edition). Speght, it seems, is doing our sifting for us. He is also, if we invoke a previous commentator upon Chaucer, being over-selective: according to William Caxton there is *no* unfruitful content in the verse of a poet who "eschew[s] prolyxete / castyng away the chaf of superfluyte / and shewying the pyked grayn of sentence."[22] Even if we ignore Caxton's hyperbole, we must recognize that the business of separating fruit from chaff—or of sorting out and/or hierarchizing the different kinds of fruit that may be present in one narrative—is often a tricky task for Chaucer's reader (the Nun's Priest himself offers his audience at least three different "official" morals from which to choose).[23] *Troilus and Criseyde*, a poem already thoroughly resistant to easy moralization because of its dialogic narrative structure (which is further complicated by the ambiguous relationship between the understanding of its narrator and that of its controlling creator and by the ontological shifts of its final stanzas), is all the more slippery because utterances that look like fruit in one narrative context turn into chaff in another. Because Speght's indexings overwhelmingly point to representations (or even representations of representations) of speech acts whose claims to authority and stability are being undercut rather than reaffirmed by the narrative containing them, his practice tends to undo the poem's sly interrogation of the conventional discourses in which we seek to generalize—and fix—experience.

In her recent study of the sixteenth-century humanist practice of gathering and "framing" (that is, forming, arranging and assimilating) fragments drawn from the works of classical antiquity in commonplace books, Mary Thomas Crane notes that "[P]edagogical focus on the extraction of fragments undermines attention to narrative sequence. . . . Indeed, the very concept of framing, with its emphasis on closure and control, suggests that [the English humanists'] tendency to collapse narrative anecdotes and myths into a shortened maxim or exemplum . . . reflects ideological as well as rhetorical motives."[24] She goes on to suggest that narrative "was too dangerously errant, too free from constraints, to be valued or even enjoyed for anything other than the moral fragments it might contain."[25] It seems to me that the decontextualizing interventions I have identified in Speght's editorial noting of Chaucerian sententiae exhibit a similar interest in resisting the "errancies" of a narrative strikingly preoccupied with the wanderings of desire and with the instability of the words that seek to represent or contain desire. The very fact, furthermore, that the large majority of Speght's citations point to utterances that are not represented as the "original" formulations of Chaucer-the-poet, but rather as invocations of commonplace or conventionally sententious wisdom by his characters, suggests that the Renaissance Chaucer Speght constructs through his selective digest of the *Troilus* is not so much a maker of new wisdom as the re-citer of maxims which are always already in intellectual circulation.

To assert, however, that Speght has constructed a "Chaucer" divorced from the ambiguities of his own narrative by no means exhausts the implications of Speght's selective indexing of the *Troilus*. One of the more surprising features of his practice is that although he carefully marks dozens of sentences and maxims uttered by its characters that manifestly fail to "transcend the contingency" of the poem's "diegetical" narrative universe, he nevertheless seems oddly uninterested in indexing the *Troilus*'s final stanzas—stanzas in which the voice of Chaucer-the-poet seems to fuse with that of his narrator as the latter strives to articulate a moral vision transcending all earthly vicissitudes.[26] If Speght has seemed to display a "Pandaric" sensibility in the kind of material he marks for his readers, he certainly does not seem to share Pandarus's (ultimately rather double-edged) conviction that "the end is euery tales strength" (2.260)—a sentence he somewhat conspicuously fails to decorate with a marginal pointing finger. Indeed, Speght finds only twenty-two verses worth noting in the entirety of the *last* book of the poem, as opposed to forty-seven lines in Book 1, sixty-six in Book 2, forty in Book 3, and forty-six in Book 4.

Let us inspect the material Speght indexes after Criseyde's surrender to Diomede, the narrative point of no return in Book 5 (I have indicated the speaker of the lines in each case):

> [Women] woll saine, in as much as in me is,
> I haue hem doen dishonour welaway
> All be I not the first that did amis.* (5.1065–67: Criseyde)
>
> From hazell wood, there iolly Robin plaied,*
> Shall come all that thou abidest here,
> Ye, farwell all the snow of ferne yere. (5.1174–76: Pandarus)
>
> But who may bet beguile, if him list,*
> Than he on whom men wenen best to trist. (5.1266–67: Troilus)
>
> But Troilus thou maiest now East and West
> Pipe in an Iuie leafe, if that thee lest* (5.1431–32: Narrator)
>
> Eke great effect, men write in place lite,*
> Thentent is all, and nat the letters space (5.1629–30: Criseyde)
>
> The gods shewene both ioy and tene*
> In slepe, and by my dreme it is now sene (5.1714–15: Troilus)
>
> In eche estate is little harts rest*
> God leue us to take it for the best. (5.1749–50: Narrator)
>
> And for there is so great diursite*
> In English, and in writing of our tong,
> So pray I to God, that none miswrite thee,
> Ne thee misse metre for defaut of tong (5.1793–96: Narrator)
>
> Lo here of painems cursed old rites,*
> Lo here what all her gods may auaile,
> Lo here this wretched worlds appetites,
> Lo here the fine and guerdon for trauaile,

Of Joue, Apollo, of Mars, and such raskaile,
Lo here the forme of old clerkes speech
In poetrie, if ye her bookes seech. (5.1849–55: Narrator)

As a group, these indexings seem pretty haphazard and unilluminating as final sentences of and on the poem. In some characteristically pithy proverbial phrases, Pandarus expresses his doubts that Criseyde will ever return to Troy.[27] Criseyde's fairly complicated meditation on the moral consequences of her action (5.1059–85) is reduced to a feeble assertion that she is not the only woman who has proven untrue; the final indexing of her words at 5.1629–30 (drawn from her last letter to Troilus) is hardly an instructive *exemplum* since it is so bitterly ironical in context. Troilus's assertion of the validity of prophetic dreams (5.1714–15) and his not particularly surprising observation that we are most likely to be deceived by those we most trust (5.1266–67) offer no very conclusive insights into his experience.

This leaves us with four indexed remarks belonging to the poem's narrative voice. One of these (5.1431–32) simply reiterates the sentiments expressed by Pandarus at 5.1174–76; another (5.1793–96) records the poet's worries about the accurate transcription and transmission of his work.[28] Yet another begins a stanza (5.1849–55) that distances the maker from his pagan subject matter in a manner somewhat beside the point (given that Chaucer's own moralization of his narrative in the preceding stanzas suggests that Troilus's error is not that he worships Jove, Apollo, and Mars but rather that he has elevated his earthly passion for Criseyde above all other things, a transgression over which pagans hold no monopoly). There remains the narrative judgment following the poem's last description of Troilus's impotent misery and Fortune's fickle favoring of Diomede: "In eche estate is little harts rest / God leue us to take it for the best" (5.1749–50). The indexed (first) line simply reiterates the universal nature of human vicissitude; the line following asks that we may have the patience to "take [destructive flux] for the best" but at this stage holds out no hope that we may transcend our unhappy subjection to the uncertainty of human affairs.

These four lines, then, offer the only remarks of the poem's narrator that Speght indexes in the last eight hundred lines or so of Book 5. It seems to me remarkable that although Speght annotates 5.1749, he practically ignores the sixty-three lines usually considered to constitute Chaucer's Epilogue to *Troilus and Criseyde* (5.1807–69; beginning with the ascent of Troilus's spirit to the eighth sphere)—lines which considerably complicate both the "solaas" and the "sentence" offered by the work as a whole. In particular, he shows no interest in indexing the stanzas in which Troilus's ghost acquires a philosophical distance on earthly attachments (5.1814–34), and Troilus's creator goes on to declare:

> O young fresh folkes, he or she,
> In which y^t^ loue upgroweth with your age,
> Repaireth home from worldly vanite,
> And of your harts up casteth the visage
> To thilke God, that after his image
> You made, and thinketh al nis but a faire,
> This world that passeth sone, as floures faire.
>
> And loueth him, the which y^t^ right for loue,
> Upon a crosse, our soules for to bey,
> First starfe, and rose, and sit in heuen aboue,
> For he nill falsen no wight dare I sey
> That woll his hart al wholly on him ley,
> And sens he best to loue is, and most meeke,
> What nedeeth fained loues for to seeke? (5.1835–48)

Speght's indifference to lines 1840–41 is particularly curious, since "al nis but a faire" does seem to have been a proverbial phrase in quite common circulation.[29] At any rate, in choosing not to index any of these lines, the editor also refuses to grant any special authority to Chaucer's own (explicitly Christian) sentence—a sentence which significantly supplements the stoic acceptance of vicissitude described in lines 1749–50. The careful collator of the speech acts that sought to fix the significance of experience within a narrative that has born witness to the power of contingency and flux ignores, at the last, his poet's exaltation of a faith and a love that transcend both the uncertainties of earthly desire and the ambiguities of all earthly histories.

Speght's lack of interest in indexing any of these lines seems of a piece with his choice not to mark any sentences in Troilus's Boethian Hymn in Book 3, "Love, that of erthe and see hath governaunce . . ." (3.1744–71), a song which celebrates (for the reader, if not for the unenlightened Troilus) the power of *caritas,* of Divine Love. Might it be that his project of providing Chaucer's text with the kind of critical machinery more generally associated with the editing of a classical author actually prevents Speght from engaging with the Christian moralizing of this narrative of pagan lovers? Mary Thomas Crane notes that the technique of "framing and gathering" allowed humanist scholars "a way to choose out only those fragments [of classical texts] in which the cultural codes of pagan antiquity and Christian Europe intersected."[30] If "our antient and learned English poet Geffrey Chaucer" is to become an honorary classical authority, might an inversion of this procedure be taking place? At the end of his "Life" of Chaucer in the 1602 *Works,* Speght cites a remark of Roger Ascham calling Chaucer the "English Homer" and granting him an authority equal to that of "Sophocles or Euripides in Greeke";[31] we might recall here as well Beaumont's insistence that Chaucer's *Troilus* is full of sentence[s], "most excellentlie imitating Homer and Virgill, and borowing often of them, and of Horace also, and other the rarest both Oratours and Poets that haue written." Is Speght (perhaps unconsciously) downplaying his author's cultural belatedness as he indexes a work which he himself believed to have been translated out of Latin, ignoring Chaucer's explicitly Christian maxims so that his "sentences" can be detached from their historical moment and placed within a hypertext of timeless and universalized wisdom?

In making these suggestions, I am not trying to claim that Speght refuses throughout the *Works* to index explicitly Christian sententiae: the fists in the margins of *The Canterbury Tales,* for example, mark many Christian maxims. But while Chaucer's frame tale of a contemporary pilgrimage to Canterbury inescapably marks that work's historical moment, Speght was unaware that the source of the *Troilus* was Boccaccio's *Il Filostrato:* a passing remark in his "Life" of Chaucer shows that he believed its narrator's claim (2.14) that it was a translation of a Latin work. Viewed in this light, the very last indexed line in *Troilus and Criseyde,* "Lo here of painems cursed old rites" (5.1859), gestures as much toward historical antiquarianism as toward moral judgment. Lo here is our most ancient and learned English poet participating in an admirable kind of *translatio studii,* at once mediating the world of pagan antiquity for us and imitating the best it has to offer, all the while showing us his own connectedness with "the rarest both Oratours and Poets that haue written."

Speght's tacit separation of Chaucer from his proper historical moment by his exclusion of the Christian palinode of the *Troilus* from the material he indexes means that he can also ignore the sentiments of the poem's concluding stanza of prayer:

> Thou one, two, and three, eterne on liue,
> That raignest aie in three, two, and one,
> Uncircumscript, and all maist circumscriue,
> Us from visible and inuisible fone
> Defend, and to thy mercy euerichone,

So make us Jesus to thy mercy digne,
For loue of maide, and mother thine benigne. (5.1863–69)

The Dantean subtext of the first three lines, and the privileged position of the Virgin in the final verse of the poem, emphatically remind the reader that Chaucer is writing before the Reformation: from the point of view of a Protestant editor, these verses make the poet not nearly timeless enough. But the final stanza also and ironically (given the implications of Speght's strategies of selection in his aphoristic digest of the poem) presents us with a poet who has finally given up the task of circumscribing the significance of his own work. Chaucer has surrendered both himself and his poem into the care of One who is "Uncircumscript, and all maist circumscriue." Speght attempts to circumscribe Chaucer's "sentence" by a selective highlighting of discourse in which his omissions are as significant as his inclusions. Chaucer himself, however, constructs a narrative in which all attempts to fix significance that do not concede the contingency of our earthly and imperfect utterances are likely to be viewed ironically; the poet himself may gesture toward a condition that transcends "the contingency of the diegetical universe" but the final lines of his poem relocate even that gesture within the realm of the merely contingent. Only the God who is uncircumscript and all may circumscribe gets to frame the final sentence.

Notes

An avatar of this chapter was presented at the 29th International Congress on Medieval Studies at Kalamazoo in 1994; the finished version has benefited from suggestions from its audience on that occasion, as well as from the bibliographical expertise and advice on early modern matters typographical of my colleague David Vander Meulen.

1. *The Workes of our Antient . . . Chavcer*, ed. Speght, 1598, sig. a1^{v}.

2. *The Workes of Our Ancient . . . Chaucer*, 1602, sig. a1^{r}.

3. For a general description of both the 1598 and the 1602 editions, see Pearsall, "Thomas Speght," 71–92.

4. As far as I am aware, no scholars have discussed this feature of Speght's work at any length. Pearsall glances briefly at Speght's indexings of The Wife of Bath's Tale ("Thomas Speght," 86). See also Muscatine, *Book of Geoffrey Chaucer*, 33. The most striking previous use of the marginal hand in a sixteenth-century English text may be seen in Coverdale's *Great Bible* of 1539; for a discussion of the (very different) purpose of these maniples see Tribble, *Margins and Marginality*, 24–26. Speght's selective indexings do not, incidentally, offer any significant or sustained correlation with the marginal glosses to be found in any

one of the *manuscripts* of the poem, which are catalogued by Benson and Windeatt in "Manuscript Glosses," 31–53.

5. Quotation is from Caxton, Epilogue of *Boethius de Consolacione Philosophie* (1479), cited in Spurgeon, *Five Hundred Years of Chaucer Criticism*, 1:58. On Chaucer's reputation as a moralist, see also Pearsall, "Thomas Speght," 86, and Windeatt, "Chaucer Traditions," especially 5–9.

6. Caxton, Epilogue to his edition of *The Book of Fame* (c. 1483), reprinted in Spurgeon, *Five Hundred Years*, 61. Caxton is himself echoing the passage in John Lydgate's *Siege of Thebes* (1420–1422) which celebrates Chaucer's

> . . . Sugrid mouth,
> Of eche thyng / kepyng in substaunce
> The sentence hool / with-oute variance,
> Voyding the Chaf / sothly for to seyn,
> Enlumynyng / þe trewe piked greyn
> Be crafty writinge / of his sawes swete. (Spurgeon, 28)

The Francis Beaumont mentioned is neither the Jacobean dramatist nor his father; see Pearsall, "Thomas Speght," 266n.6. Beaumont's letter discloses that he read Chaucer with Speght when they were Cambridge undergraduates; see Speght, *Workes* (1602), sig. a3^{v}. The 1602 edition slightly alters the 1598 text's version of Beaumont's comment, which originally read: "and in his Troylus is so sententious, as there bee few staues in that Booke, which are not concluded with some principall sentence: most excellently imitating Homer and Virgil, and borrowing often of them, and of Horace also, and other the rarest both Oratours and Poets that haue written." Given that Speght's maniples often do *not* mark the final lines of the rhyme royal stanzas, one can understand why the letter was subsequently modified.

7. The 1687 reprinting of the 1602 text continues to "note" proverbs and sentences, but in it each marginal hand is replaced by a more discreet asterisk. (This may reflect a declining interest among educated readers in the excerpting of sententiae.) The asterisks are not set in the margins but become the very last characters of the verse lines. One index in the 1687 printing shifts a line, from 1.645 to 1.646 (presumably through a compositor's error), and several particularly long lines, where there seems to have been no room to include an extra character, lose their markers completely (see 1.839, 2.651, 3.1634, 4.659, 4.1584, 4.1611, 5.327, 5.547).

8. Speght's fists occur at the following lines in *Troilus and Criseyde* (since Speght does not number Chaucer's lines, my line numbers are based on *Riverside Chaucer*): 1.12, 1.91, 1.194, 1.210, 1.214, 1.217, 1.218, 1.237, 1.257, 1.300, 1.384, 1.406, 1.420, 1.449, 1.509, 1.517, 1.591, 1.630, 1.631, 1.635, 1.637, 1.645, 1.685, 1.694, 1.708, 1.740, 1.747, 1.762, 1.784, 1.807, 1.809, 1.839, 1.857, 1.889, 1.895, 1.903, 1.910, 1.913, 1.944, 1.946, 1.950, 1.956, 1.961, 1.964, 1.969, 1.1024, 1.1065, 2.21, 2.27, 2.36, 2.42, 2.47, 2.117, 2.164, 2.167, 2.271, 2.281, 2.343, 2.344, 2.372, 2.384, 2.392, 2.398, 2.402, 2.470, 2.483,

2.538, 2.585, 2.607, 2.622, 2.636, 2.651, 2.671, 2.715, 2.755, 2.777, 2.784, 2.791, 2.798, 2.804, 2.861, 2.866, 2.888, 2.894, 2.985, 2.1028, 2.1030, 2.1041, 2.1109, 2.1149, 2.1178, 2.1234, 2.1238, 2.1245, 2.1272, 2.1276, 2.1332, 2.1368, 2.1371, 2.1378, 2.1380, 2.1385, 2.1391, 2.1501, 2.1523, 2.1533, 2.1535, 2.1553, 2.1615, 2.1639, 2.1739, 2.1741, 2.1745, 3.13, 3.35, 3.38, 3.87, 3.115, 3.181, 3.188, 3.294, 3.306, 3.321, 3.329, 3.398, 3.405, 3.530, 3.638, 3.641, 3.642, 3.694, 3.711, 3.764, 3.773, 3.813, 3.817, 3.827, 3.855, 3.890, 3.896, 3.931, 3.1024, 3.1060, 3.1104, 3.1147, 3.1213, 3.1219, 3.1256, 3.1379, 3.1496, 3.1627, 3.1630, 3.1634, 4.6, 4.314, 4.391, 4.407, 4.415, 4.421, 4.460, 4.461, 4.481, 4.504, 4.587, 4.600, 4.622, 4.659, 4.727, 4.765, 4.770, 4.834, 4.927, 4.931, 4.958, 4.963, 4.972, 4.974, 4.980, 4.985, 4.990, 4.997, 4.1006, 4.1011, 4.1099, 4.1105, 4.1255, 4.1283, 4.1305, 4.1374, 4.1406, 4.1408, 4.1453, 4.1456, 4.1457, 4.1563, 4.1567, 4.1584, 4.1611, 4.1645, 5.97, 5.327, 5.342, 5.350, 5.363, 5.384, 5.547, 5.553, 5.741, 5.755, 5.757, 5.784, 5.790, 5.1067, 5.1174, 5.1266, 5.1432, 5.1629, 5.1714, 5.1749, 5.1793, 5.1849.

9. Bennington, *Sententiousness in the Novel*, 5.

10. Peacham, *The Garden of Eloquence*, 29–30, 189.

11. One can see a similar blurring of distinctions in Sir John Harington's 1591 translation of Ariosto's *Orlando Furioso*, which, like Speght's edition of Chaucer, supplements the work of a vernacular poet with a critical apparatus more often associated with classical authors. Harington, like Speght, notes his author's "sentences" in the margins of his text; one such "sentence" reads: "It is a *proverbe* used long ago, / We soone beleeue the thing we would haue so" (emphasis added). *Orlando Furioso*, Book 1, stanza 56.

12. See, e.g., the chapter on *Troilus and Criseyde* in Whiting, *Chaucer's Use of Proverbs*.

13. Speght indexes Pandarus's love advice at 1.685, 1.808, 1.809, 1.857, 1.895, 1.903, 1.910, 1.913, 1.944, 1.950, 1.956, 1.960, 1.964, 1.969, 2.344, 2.372, 2.384, 2.392, 2.398, 2.402, 2.585, 2.1028, 2.1030, 2.1149, 2.1234, 2.1238, 2.1245, 2.1368, 2.1371, 2.1380, 2.1385, 2.1391, 2.1501, 2.1503, 2.1535, 2.1739, 3.294, 3.306, 3.321, 3.773, 3.1104, 3.1630, 3.1634, 4.407, 4.415, 4.600, 4.622, 4.927, 4.931, 4.1099, 5.342, 5.350.

14. For the Thomas/Rachel Speght connection, see Wright, *Middle Class Culture in Elizabethan England*, 488. For more on the Joseph Swetnam-Rachel Speght interchange, see Henderson and McManus, *Half Humankind*, 15–17.

15. The reader will note that of the fifteen consecutive examples of indexing from Book 3 cited earlier, thirteen mark speeches of Pandarus or Criseyde.

16. Versions of phrases in which a speaker directly invokes other authorities occur in the following lines indexed by Speght: 1.694, 1.708, 1.740, 1.960–61, 2.1328, 2.1368–69, 3.292–94, 3.813–14, 4.414–15, 4.974, 4.980, 4.997, 4.1006, 4.1374, 4.1453, 4.1584, 5.97–98, 5.790–91.

17. In describing *Troilus and Criseyde* as a "heteroglot" text I am appropriating the critical terminology of Bakhtin; see *Dialogic Imagination*, 70. I have argued elsewhere that Bakhtin's claim that the multiple re-presentation of compet-

ing discourses is a constitutive characteristic of the novel ignores the heteroglossia of certain sophisticated verse narratives; see my *Strategies of Poetic Narrative*, 29.

18. Taylor, "Proverbs"; see in particular 281, 286–87.

19. Taylor, "Proverbs," 288.

20. The poem itself complicates even further the status of Pandarus's remark at 4.407–8; at the end of Pandarus's attempt to hearten Troilus, the narrator comments, "These words saied he for the nones all / To help his friend, Least he for sorow deide, / For doubtlesse to doen his wo to fall, / He raught nat what unthrift that he seide" (4.428–31).

21. Perhaps the most ironic local instance of this phenomenon is seen in Speght's indexing of Troilus's words: "O welaway, so sligh arne clerkes old, / That I nat whose opinion I may hold" (4.972*–73).

22. Proem to Caxton's 2d edition of *Canterbury Tales* (c. 1483); see Spurgeon, *Five Hundred Years*, 62. See also the quotation from Lydgate's *Siege of Thebes* in note 7.

23. See lines 3431–32, 3433–35, 3436. Speght indexes only line 3431.

24. Crane, *Framing Authority*, 163. For her gloss on "framing" see 4.

25. Crane, *Framing Authority*, 163.

26. For a discussion of who *speaks* the epilogue, see, e.g., Manning, "*Troilus*, Book V."

27. See Whiting, *Chaucer's Use of Proverbs*, 201n. 12.

28. This particular notation seems to reflect an editorial preoccupation already visible in Speght's prefatory letter to his readers, in which he argues that apparent flaws in Chaucer's meter are due to scribal errors in the copying of his text, and quotes 5.1793–96 in full to demonstrate Chaucer's own anxieties about proper transmission (Speght, *Workes* [1602], a2^{r}).

29. See the note on lines 1840–41 in *Riverside Chaucer*, 1057.

30. Crane, *Framing Authority*, 52.

31. Speght, *Workes* (1602), sig. c3^{v}.

PART II

Claims for Narrative Poetry

Chauncer and Spenser

CHAPTER 5

Narrative Reflections

Re-envisaging the Poet in *The Canterbury Tales* and *The Faerie Queene*

JUDITH H. ANDERSON

For some time now, reports of the "death of the author" have been greatly exaggerated. His presumed demise, to be sure, has been strategically useful, not merely in renewing the formalist critique of the "intentional fallacy" but also in laying to rest the naïve assumption of a unified, autonomous self essentially apart from history and in rational control of the unconscious. Arguably, however, it has also been misleading and even dangerous, since it has tended to trivialize agency, accountability, and any responsibility to history that really matters. In its stead, I prefer to conceive of the *withdrawal* of (not necessarily by) the author as a *moving* term whose distance from the text varies and shifts, both predictably and unpredictably, and is subject to localized textual evidence, whether literary, historical, or both. Here, it is my intention (for which I may or may not be responsible) to pursue this conception by relating Spenser to Chaucer. I do so first because a narrative voice or narrator is one of the most conspicuous features of Chaucer's writing and one that has dominated much interpretation of it in the past half-century; and second because of Spenser's assertion of poetic affinity with what he termed Chaucer's "owne spirit."[1]

Chaucer's Tales of Sir Thopas and Melibee are the only two Canterbury tales told by a figure representing the poet himself. Together, these tales afford disparate reflections on the poet's craft and the kind of poetry he writes and thus on his identity as a poet: *Sir Thopas* suggests "elvyssh" pleasures, careless play, and a faerie escape from ideological duties; *Melibee* responds to history, responsibility, and prudential care; the one offers recreation, and the other engages the pressures of social reality.[2] Spenser wove memories of the Tale of Sir Thopas through the first four books of

The Faerie Queene and then made the *Melibee* a pretext for the first of the pastoral cantos of Book VI, the crucial canto that precedes and enables the Acidalian vision. Spenser's memories of *Sir Thopas* occur in eroticized contexts: for example, Redcrosse's allusive pricking into the initiation of narrative in Book I and later his reunion with Duessa to consummate his lust, Arthur's dream of the faerie queen and his subsequent desire for Florimell, and Scudamour's account in Book IV of his quest for Amoret. Spenser's complementary memories of Chaucer's *Melibee* directly juxtapose imprudent indulgence with its vulnerability to hostile worldly forces. Although explicit memories of *Melibee* are concentrated in the ninth canto of Book VI, their roots reach back to earlier books, notably to the soothing words of Despair in the ninth canto of Book I, and they reach forward to Melibee's capture and death after the Acidalian vision, which Melibee, of course, does not see. Spenser appears to have understood Chaucer's self-representations in terms of the large, symbolic patterns of *The Faerie Queene*, aligning *Sir Thopas* consistently with the pleasure principle and the *Melibee* more specifically, although not exclusively, with its harsh price.[3]

Like Chaucer himself, Spenser also deployed these symbolic valences in connection with his own identity as a poet. For example, the faerie queen of Arthur's dream, whose literary origin lies in Chaucer's *Sir Thopas*, affords an ever elusive alternative to the real Tudor Queen available to direct address in the proems; the faerie of the dream therefore suggests both a more inaccessible ideal and a fantasized liberation from courtly service on Elizabeth I, including the poetics of courtship. Melibee, the contrasting example, is a pastoral singer who has withdrawn in disillusionment from the court, only to be destroyed by forces alien to his song; his fate suggests that time and history, realities outside the poet's wishes, will nevertheless exact their ruthless due, and it casts a long shadow over the similar withdrawal from court in the 1590s by Colin Clout, Spenser's pastoral speaker.[4]

Spenser's memories of *Sir Thopas* and *Melibee* provide background and motivation for the relation of his poetic identity to the other major locus of self-depiction, hence artistic self-definition, in *The Canterbury Tales*, namely, the General Prologue. Along with the tales of Sir Thopas and Melibee and the Retraction, this Prologue is the only sustained instance of Chaucerian self-representation in the Canterbury collection, a Chaucerian text that Spenser's often recalls. On the face of things, the conspicuous narrator of Chaucer's Prologue, who is at once personally allusive and fictive, offers another clarifying reference and likely antecedent for Spenser's. Indeed, if Spenserian narration is a representation of storytelling and the Spenserian narrator represents the conventional storyteller, as Harry Berger has argued, strikingly similar claims have been made for Spenser's Chaucerian antecedent.[5] On conceptual grounds, which might appeal to an allegorist, they imply a significant relation between the fully dramatized Chaucerian narrator and his narration and the more openly rhetorical and abstractive Spenserian forms.

A number of characteristics of the General Prologue invite comparison with *The Faerie Queene,* among them its movement from seemingly assured categories and symbols to an increasingly uncertain and self-reflexive awareness of its own construction, an awareness figured first in the narrator's unsteady valuations of the pilgrims and then in his anxiety as he approaches his rendering of the tales themselves:

> But firste I pray you, of youre curtesy
> That ye ne arette it nat my folly
> Thogh that I playnly speke in this matere
> To tellen you her wordes and eke her chere[,]
> Ne thogh I speke her wordes properly[;]
> For this ye knowen as wel as I[:]
> Who shal tellen a tale after a manne
> He mote reherce as nye as euere he canne
> Euerych word, if it be in his charge[,]
> Al speke he neuer so rudely ne large[,]
> Or els he mote tellen his tale vntrewe
> Or feyne thynges, or fynde wordes newe[—]
> He may nat spare al tho he were his brother[;]
> He mote as wel saye o worde as another.[6]

Surely, this narrator protests too much. Again and again, and then yet again, he signals a conclusion, only to continue spinning his apologetic wheels—in fact, for several lines more than I've cited. In order to account for his behavior, we can posit a poet genuinely uncertain about the acceptability of the tales he is about to report; or, recalling the persistence of irony in the General Prologue, we can envision a poet who really isn't worried at all but still wants to cover himself in case others are, poking fun, while he's about it, at the convention of the willing reporter's dubiously sincere apology; or we can combine these two figures into a poet who communicates duplicitously through the guise of a narrative persona and therefore both gets to have his worry and to distance himself from it; or, in a final poststructural maneuver, we can forget about the poet altogether and, taking a further plunge into textuality, describe the text as the site of awareness, a self-reflexive construct figured in an ironized speaker, the text in this case effectually becoming the conscious subject.[7] On numerous occasions, the same interpretive choices play themselves out in *The Faerie Queene,* memorable instances occurring in the proem to Book V, where the narrator soliloquizes anxiously and at length about the "state of present time," and in the egregiously overwritten description in Book I of Una's plight when Sans Loy assaults her: so penetrating are her "shriekes, and shrieking cryes, . . . That molten starres do drop like weeping eyes; / And *Phoebus* flying so most shamefull sight, / His blushing face in foggy cloud implyes" (vi.6).[8] The occurrences of such obvious candidates for irony are all the more conspicuous in Spenser's writing precisely because they are fewer and farther between than in the General Prologue; this a problematical fact in itself inviting interpretation and likely related to the generally less fully dramatized form of Spenser's narrative and narrator.

Whether considered book by book or altogether, the general progress of *The Faerie Queene* conceptually resembles Chaucer's Prologue, moving from assurance to self-reflexive doubts. With each book, initial assumptions about symbolism are quickly questioned: the bloody cross, the Palmer's rationalizing, Britomart's armor, the merely nominal heroes—that is, the 'mond brothers—of Book IV, the relation of myth and symbol to history in Book V and of pastoral to violence in Book VI. The overall movement from Books I to III, the first installment, to Books IV to VI, the second, is also a progression from relative assurance to more pronounced worry and doubt. Although I am not suggesting that the whole movement of Spenser's expansive poem derives from Chaucer's Prologue, I think we can observe in the two some similarity of perspective regarding poetic materials, intentions, and achievements and thus again regarding elements of a poetic identity.

The concrete particularity and fictive complexity of portraits in Chaucer's Prologue resist consistent allegorical interpretation, but in broad terms these portraits also invite it, since they range from the physical, moral, and spiritual ideality of the Knight at the outset to the equally comprehensive and obvious degeneracy of the Pardoner at the end.[9] Moreover, the notoriously ironic non sequiturs of this Prologue (for example, "But for to speke of her conseyence") constitute a form of duplicity, or "other-speech," and they tantalizingly suggest the disruptions of expectation and disjunctions of form associated with allegory proper.[10] If Spenser looked for meaning in Chaucer's Prologue, and on the evidence of his writings I imagine he did, the message he found was indirection, the endlessly ironic techniques of which were to decenter and define his own doubled and redoubled representations, including his own as a poet.

In a classic two-pronged consideration of allegory and irony, Paul de Man characterizes "the notion of *dédoublement,* or dividing in two," in a way highly suggestive of the doubled narrative voices of Chaucer and Spenser. Dédoublement, which is essential for irony, "sets apart a reflective activity, such as that of the philosopher [or the poet], from the activity of the ordinary self caught in everyday concerns." Reflective activity and the ordinary self are, perhaps, not quite *Sir Thopas* and *Melibee,* eroticized pleasure and harsh reality, but they do not constitute an entirely unlike pair, and de Man's development of their valences is further relevant.[11] "The notion of self-duplication or self-multiplication"—*se dédoubler*—de Man continues, is the ironic "relationship, within consciousness, between two selves"; it is an intra- rather than an intersubjective relationship that realizes "the *distance* constitutive of all acts of reflection" (194–95). The dédoublement that is available in a fictive "world constituted out of, and in, language" enables the subject both to differentiate itself from, and to remain within, the [everyday] world (196).

Subsequently, Gordon Teskey makes explicit the connection between allegory and irony that de Man does not fully exploit. He describes irony as allegory's own Other; it underlies and enables allegory in much the same way, I would add, that Hate precedes and enables Love in the cosmic allegory of Spenser's Temple of Venus.[12] As irony underlies allegory, so difference underlies unity, and doubleness precedes the perception of oneness, as Una's doubling in the false Una initiates her naming, or cognitive form (I.i.45). In an extension of the relationship between irony and allegory, the irony that pervades Chaucer's self-representations might thus be seen to invite, rather than exclude, the allegory that more overtly characterizes Spenser's.

To decenter self-representation through dédoublement, however, is not the same as to avoid it entirely. Both Spenser and Chaucer give their narrators a tantalizingly persona(l) dimension that exceeds, but includes, simple use of the first person pronoun. Even before the narrator of the tales of Sir Thopas and Melibee emerges, Chaucer's representative is the more fully (not to say plumply) mimetic figure, an active participant in the pilgrimage and a thoroughly embodied voice, a figure who eats, drinks, and interacts socially with the other pilgrims. Although the narrator is unnamed as a participant within the tales themselves, in the Introduction to the Man of Law's Tale, Chaucer is mentioned patronizingly as the teller of lovers' tales "Mo than Ouyde made of mencioun / In his epystels" (xxi^{v}).[13] Inside manuscript and early printed collections of *The Canterbury Tales*, albeit in statements that frame segments of the tales themselves, Chaucer is also identified repeatedly by name as the recounter both of two tales and of the pilgrimage as a whole. In more inclusive collections of his poetry, such as the Renaissance editions of his corpus, he is also identified as "Geffray" within *The House of Fame* (cccxvi^{v}) and named in captions or endnotes as the maker of various other poems.

In comparison, Spenser's name never appears explicitly *within* his poetry, or at least within his English poetry.[14] His Faerie narrator is also a less mimetically embodied figure than Chaucer's Canterbury pilgrim, but like several of Spenser's other speakers, he has nonetheless personalized markers within the fiction itself, for example, "*Mulla* mine" or "my mother Cambridge" (IV.xi.34, 41). At another, considerably more complicated level, Spenser's narrator becomes the socially contextualized speaker of the proems and the self-citational figure whose words recall not only earlier passages of *The Faerie Queene* but also Spenser's shorter poems, including the personally allusive *Amoretti* and *Epithalamion*, and they likewise image other contours of Spenser's own life, such as his friendship with Ralegh and his final withdrawal to Ireland; and, indeed, in Book VI, the words of the Faerie narrator pass into those of Colin himself.

While the primary narrators of both Chaucer and Spenser acknowledge responsibility for the texts in which they appear, Chaucer's anxious narrator, who disclaims artistic ability, would limit his role to reporting, while Spenser's narrator often identifies himself as the singer of his poem and thereby claims an identity more specifically poetic. Overtly neither a pilgrim nor even a dreamer, Spenser's narrator is more openly the creator of his poem and more openly a fiction. All personalized references, of course, can be regarded as conventions and potentially as material to be mocked, but there is still an appreciable difference, even within deconstructive norms, between a personally marked text and one lacking such gestures. Form, after all, has meaning. It could be here, in fact, that an internal contradiction arises in any textual theory that indiscriminately levels as convention conspicuous personal signatures in the text. In practice this is merely to discount them in the interest of a meta-narrative characterized by its own self-identity. Does the absorption of text into metanarrative, and of personalized reference into convention, leave not a trace behind?

Describing intertextual dialogics, Don H. Bialostosky remarks that the worst misconception of formalism "is to imagine that what does not [directly or explicitly] appear in the text does not impinge upon it."[15] While Bialostosky is unlikely to have had the writer in mind, there is no logical reason to exclude him alone, along with his culture, from this statement. Nonexclusion is not the same as attributing ultimate control—originary, causal, intentional, or determinative—to the writer, and inclusion of him remains a highly problematical, densely mediated interpretive act, not a literal one. My point is that inclusion remains an interpretive option and one textually grounded—even insistent. The hard question is how to get at it.[16]

There is parody aplenty in *The Faerie Queene*, but reading the Spenserian narrator or, rather, narrators *only* as figures of parody seems to me at odds with the variousness of the poetry itself—perversely, if you will, too self-consistent. Such reading produces a poem that lacks agency and commitment and, more exactly, the urgency and emotional investment of real exploration, including self-questioning. There is too much internal distance in it, if this is a distance always maintained. In Spenser's writing, there is instead an irreducible doubleness—not in the strictly numerical sense, but in the sense of irony, ambiguity, variety, and elusiveness—that nevertheless implicates the poet in suggestive and persistent ways, although it can never be simply equated with him. As already indicated, Chaucer's writing offers a likely precedent for this doubleness (indeed, sometimes this tripleness and quadrupleness), the conceptual roots of which emerge in the General Prologue.

Within this Prologue, the decentering of self-representation is concentrated in techniques of *impersonation*, by which term I intend a modern dead metaphor that is enlivened—literalized, or more accurately, actively or performatively figuralized—in Chaucer's and Spenser's texts, where one character can literally become or blend into another. A second relevant dead metaphor that I would reactivate involves the term *investment*. In Chaucer criticism it has been common to debate, then deny, Chaucer's "investment" in a particular character or tale such as Melibee's, but if *investment* is understood etymologically as a covering or as clothing, as a mask and very possibly an emotionally charged or "invested" (that is, cathected) one, it offers, along with *impersonation*, a specific and suggestive term for discussing Chaucerian and Spenserian storytellers. These storytellers, who dominate *The Canterbury Tales* and appear with a frequency we tend to overlook in *The Faerie Queene*, are at once masks and the ascribed voices that animate them. A mask suggests the same mediation that representation does, but a mask typically has holes and therefore implies something or someone behind it, whether a vacancy, a historical person, or a doubled, deliberately elusive, and fleeting identity, perhaps one that is not unlike the fleeting figure of Arthur's dream or, indeed, not unlike the poet's.[17] A mask could also be a way of representing an identity that is schizophrenic in the currently loosened, unclinical sense—fragmented or momentary, glimpsed, cumulative, multiple, indefinite, and above all experimental, even searching.

In *The Faerie Queene*, *mask* is itself a privileged term, occurring in the first line of Book I—"Lo I the man, whose Muse whilome did maske"—and later recurring with ironic thematic insistence in the House of Busirane and the fourth and fifth books.[18] In all these instances, the word *mask* is associated with cultural forms—conventional, social, poetic, mythic, personal, and subjective. These are seen to be falsifying but necessary, provisional but also expressive and powerful.[19] Impersonation is likewise an idea—in fact, a conceptual pun—that is introduced early, specifically, and ironically in *The Faerie Queene*. When Archimago, that purveyor of images, separates Redcrosse from Una and masks himself in the sign of Holiness, the armor with the bloody cross, he is said "the person to put on / Of that good knight," namely Redcrosse; thus he literally and duplicitously *impersonates* him, *enacting* the combination of Latin *in* and *persona*, "into the person [of]," an act that Archimago has already anticipated in poisoning the imagination of the Redcrosse Knight. When, after pointedly recalling the first stanza describing Redcrosse, the Spenserian narrator remarks—it cannot be innocently—of Archimago's guise, "*Saint George* himself ye would haue deemed him to be," the whole issue of the reliability or deception of representation is put on the table, and since Archimago is a figure of the poet, the whole issue of self-representation appears here as well (I.ii.11). For Spenser, even more explicitly than for Chaucer, the idea of impersonation is thematized, problematical, and self-reflexive from the start.[20] Moreover, this self-reflection implicates the narrative and the self, or the subjectivity, who in this case, whatever else he is, is the absent-but-not-absent poet.

In Chaucer's General Prologue (and in the subsequent tales), there are certain pressure points where the difference between character and characterizer blurs conspicuously, displaying an instability of intention, origin, and identity that is explicitly thematized in the narrator's subsequent apology, which I cited earlier: "Who shal tellen a tale after a manne / He mote reherce as nye as euere he canne / Euerych word." This blending, obvious just often enough to become openly an issue, affords a paradigm of relationship between character and characterizer, mask and masker, voice and projector. This model seems to me to offer the most authentic and suggestive indication we have of the self-reflexive relationship between the narrator of the poem itself and its poet. Throughout the medieval and Renaissance periods, when human beings were thought to share a common essence and the body was supposed to be permeable, its borders open and porous rather than hard-edged, there is considerable historical warrant for such a relationship.[21]

Probably the best known Chaucerian example of paradigmatic blending occurs in the portrait of the Monk. Characterizing the Monk's disregard of monastic rules with increasing engagement and tonal ambiguity (a frequent and psychologically suggestive combination in Chaucerian texts), the narrator remarks of the Monk's dismissal of cloistered confinement,

> And I say his opynyon was good[:]
> Wherto shuld he study, and make him selfe wood
> Upon a boke alway in cloystre to powre
> Or swynke with his handes, or labowre
> As Austyn byd[?] Howe shul the worlde be serued[?][22]
> Let Austyn haue his swinke to hym reserued[!]
> Therefore he was a pryckesour a right. (B.iii^r)

Whether this passage is mocking or approving, and whether its penultimate line—"Let Austyn haue his swynke to hym reserued"—expresses disapproving mimicry, ambivalent ventriloquism, or the very words of the Monk is left utterly and deftly unclear.[23] The Monk's attitude speaks through the narrator, and momentarily the narrator's voice enters the role of the Monk, even while the lines framing the passage ensure that the difference between Monk and narrator remain audible and visible. The irreducible doubleness of the passage implies criticism of the Monk but also denies it. What we have here is a version of the blending of one figure with another that Spenser made virtually a hallmark of *The Faerie Queene*, and what is significant in this instance is that the blending involves a relatively mimetic figure of the poet.

The same phenomenon occurs to varying degrees throughout the General Prologue, and in the interest of variety, I shall address two other instances of it. The distinction of the first is the narrator's engagement with a good character, the Parson.[24] Reflecting on the relation of the Parson's words to his deeds, the narrator remarks that the Parson explained a relevant biblical passage with a homely proverb:

> And this fygure he radde eke therto[,]
> That if golde ruste, what shulde yron do[?]
> For if a preest be foule, on whom we trust[,]
> No wonder is a leude man to rust[;]

And shame it is, if a preest take kepe[,]
To se a shytten shepherde, and a clene shepe. (Biv^{v})

Again, in the latter half of this passage, the difference between the attitude and even the words of the narrator and those of the pilgrim he describes becomes indistinct, and this momentary indistinction suggests a self-reflexive model for the relationship of the decentered poet himself to his narrator. If read in one direction, namely from Parson to narrator to poet, the model implies that any person behind the mask will be only a recessive figural construct; read in the other, from poet to narrator to Parson, it indicates not only expression—literally, a pressing out, a form, a representation in image and word—but also some degree of allegorical projection, however partial, brief, and soon deflected.[25] This latter reading, which starts with an undifferentiated figure of the poet, involves an act of faith in the fact that there actually *was* historically not an autonomous self but a poet, a documented and textualized assumption that I do not hesitate to embrace.

My final example of Chaucerian blending occurs in the portrait of the Summoner. Here the narrator reports how the Summoner corrupts justice by reducing it to bribery: he teaches "a good felawe . . . to haue none awe . . . of the archedekyns curse,"

But if mans soule were in his purse[,]
For in his purse he shulde ypunysshed be[.]
Purse is the archedekens hel, sayde he. (Bv^{v})

The more I look at this passage, the more the two explanatory lines that precede the last, which is a direct quotation of the Summoner's words, sound like the narrator's glossing, and the lines that immediately follow the passage muddy the attribution of attitudes still further. In them, the narrator continues,

But wel I wote he lyed right in dede[;]
Of cursyng ought eche synful man drede
For cursyng wol slee, riȝt as assoyling saueth[—]
And also ware him of a Significauit. (Bv^{v})

Meeting the first three of these lines, which initially seem pious, fearful, and also indignant, a reader is likely to cancel any previous doubt about the identity of the cynical speaker in the lines immediately preceding. "Aha," one concludes, "it was all the Summoner." But then comes the line with a wallop, "And also ware him of a Significauit." The likely speaker of this warning is by all odds the narrator, since the line continues his explanation, even while radically altering its basis. A *significavit* is the sort of writ likely to entail harsh physical punishment, and the one-liner mentioning it casts doubt on the sincerity of the three lines before it, making their conventional piety sound like the pious lip service that masks a worldly pragmatism wary of fleshly punishment. Their imputed insincerity in turn reaffirms that the cynical assessment of the archdeacon's greed with which all this ambiguity started might as readily belong to the narrator as to the Summoner. Once again, two figures, the narrator and his character—in the dramatic, personal, and graphic senses of this word—have blended. More precisely, their attitudes, or voices, have momentarily become indistinguishable or, from another viewpoint, they have doubled and become duplicitous. If this duplicity is not Chaucer's as such, being distanced from him through his narrative speaker, it is a characteristic trademark of his writing, or poetic identity, and in this way a trace of the poet himself.

Spenser seems to me an incredibly astute student of Chaucer's work, and variously throughout *The Faerie Queene* he—or rather, his narrative voice or attitude—slips ambiguously, duplicitously into a mask or into the techniques of impersonation.[26] This slippage is more indirect and implicit and, like the rest of Spenser's poem, less realistically mimetic than Chaucer's. Recently it caught my attention while I was working on other Spenserian essays, to which it bore an incidental relation. As a critical shorthand, I want to describe the relevant passages in these essays, an exercise that will appropriately be a Spenserian process of self-citation. One of the passages occurs in an essay on the Giant with the scales in the fifth book of *The Faerie Queene*, who debates with Artegall the justice of the old world order.[27] The leveling Giant's materialistic argument is wholly based on quantity, appearance, and sight: "*Seest* not, how badly all things present bee," he demands and then continues, "The *sea* it selfe doest thou not plainely *see* / Encroch vppon the land there vnder thee?" (V.ii.37: my emphasis). In these lines, the insistent punning (see/sea), which is only nominally and inadvertently the Giant's, is unusually obvious, and it pointedly anticipates the leveling of the Giant himself, who is literally "thrust downe into the deepest maine," and drowned "in the sea" with a narrative irony so pronounced as to be vindictive (V.ii.38, 49). Like Talus's shouldering the Giant from the cliff to the rocks below, this irony participates in violent suppression, as the narrator's subsequent comparison of the Giant to a doomed ship—"misfortunes piteous pray," driven onto the rocks by a "cruell tempest"—appears to acknowledge (V.ii.50).

But who is this narrator and what does he have to do with the poet—that is, with an identifiable voice of the text, or with the more specific voice of the fifth proem, which appears to agree with the Giant? And what is his relation to Artegall, the Giant's virtuous opponent, whose fortunes to this point have often been ironized or strongly ambivalent? Since I read the debate between Artegall and the Giant as a real one with two sides and not merely a showcase for Artegall's righteousness, these redoubled signs of ironic doubling indicate to me a divided narrator who is invested in both sides and as much engaged in self-debate as is Redcrosse in the encounter with Contemplation. Without turning *The Faerie Queene* into a panorama of direct, neurotic authorial projections or regarding it as an unmediated transcription of Elizabethan culture, we can see in its heightened moments of narrative dédoublement a process of self-definition and, again, some trace of the poet's identity.

The second instance of slippage I have recently encountered occurs in Book IV of *The Faerie Queene*, when Scudamour engages Amoret's hand to lead her from the Temple of Venus.[28] Here it is not clear whether the simile "Like warie Hynd within the weedie soyle" refers to Amoret's hand or to Scudamour himself, in either case a problematical reading (IV.x.55). If Scudamour is the more likely referent, despite the fact that a hind is a female deer, the confusion (or conflation) of the roles of hunter and hunted in the simile suggests how much Scudamour, the Knight who compares himself to Orpheus leading Eurydice from hell, is threatened by this Venerean place, to which he has been drawn so unerringly and in poetry of such power. Love and hate are as hard to distinguish here as is the author of their confusion, whether Scudamour, who is the Chaucerian teller of this tale, or the narrator behind him. The appearance of a deer in the canceled ending of Book III, where it images Scudamour, and in the *Amoretti* as well, further enforces its connection with Spenser, the Orphic poet of the *Epithalamion*.[29] Once again, the trace of a poetic identity surfaces in a moment of impersonation, as the narrator's closing line in the Temple episode acknowledges: "So ended he his tale, where I this Canto end" (IV.x.58).[30] With this line, a specific figure of the figure behind the curtain comes openly into view, and it affirms an allegory of authorship in which the poet himself lies concealed but implicit.

Writing autobiographically, Roland Barthes once asked, "why should I not speak of 'myself' since this 'my' is no longer 'the self'?" Decentered, various, and ungrounded, Barthes' "subject apprehends himself *elsewhere*."[31] To apprehend the self is literally to grasp—to seize and arrest it. To the extent that apprehension occurs its alienated site will preeminently be language, and its means the methods of dédoublement, notably including mask and impersonation.

The Bower of Bliss, in which most readers find heightened poetic engagement, affords an especially concentrated example of doubling as Guyon and the Palmer approach Acrasia herself. Their approach is framed by insistent memories of Chaucer's narrative in *The Parliament of Fowls* and therefore of the identity of his poetic narrator, whose character in the *Parliament* resembles the one in the *Canterbury Tales.* Here, "all that pleasing is to liuing eare, / Was there consorted in one harmonee" (II.xii.70). "The ioyous birdes"

> Their notes vnto the voyce attempred sweete;
> Th'Angelicall soft trembling voyces made
> To th'instruments diuine respondence meet.

The sounds of waterfalls "vnto the wind did call: / The gentle warbling wind low answered to all" (xii.71).[32] There is no denying the appeal of the narrator's joyous voicing of this place. At this moment we are in a "Paradise" of "melodious sound" and without qualifying reminders of Rhodope, Thessalian Tempe, or "*Eden* selfe" (II.xii.52). Yet the narrator passes next to a critical description of Acrasia, "the faire Witch her selfe." This is his most distanced appraisal of her, and it involves an abrupt and self-reflexive doubling.

Usually unremarked is the fact that this description of Acrasia, which occupies stanzas 72–74 and affords the first immediate vision of her, is specifically the narrator's, since Guyon and the Palmer are not within sight until stanza 76. The narrator's description is analytical:

> And all that while, right ouer him she hong,
> With her false eyes fast fixed in his sight,
> As seeking medicine, whence she was stong,
> Or greedily depasturing delight:
> And oft inclining downe with kisses light,
> For feare of waking him, his lips bedewd,
> And through his humid eyes did sucke his spright,
> Quite molten into lust and pleasure lewd;
> Wherewith she sighed soft, as if his case she rewd. (II.xii.73)

This stanza acknowledges the narrative's implication in Acrasian pleasure more explicitly than the seductive stanzas that precede it and does so while holding Acrasia at bay. Acrasia's eyes, "fast fixed in his sight," ambiguously and bisexually suggest her sight beholding, his sight beheld, and his sight beholding. In accord with Renaissance medical practices, she seeks healing "whence she was stong," or else she feeds on delight.

Thus vulnerable and already wounded, or else consuming, she is variously recipient or seeker. She fears to wake him, yet gets her sustenance through his "humid eyes." The sleeping Verdant has some connection with the vision of Acrasia (in all senses of *vision*), and her fear of waking him implies that they exist for one another in a dream. Acrasia is the dreamer's as the dreamer is hers. No matter how morally the narrative here distances this vision of symbiosis, the poet figuratively—indeed allegorically—acknowledges his implication in its authorship, as, indeed, he must, "The whiles some one did chaunt this louely lay" (74). Tasso's lay it is, but not in English.

When Guyon and the Palmer finally catch up with the narrator, they have crept—the word is Spenser's—through groves and thickets "at last [to] display" Acrasia, Spenserian phrasing that surely sounds prurient enough to compromise their creeping: *display* means "exhibit," but for this etymologically informed poem, it means also "fold apart or asunder." Borne on the wings of my allegory of authorship, I am tempted to add that it means "de-implicated," or unfolded, in another sense as well. The reasserted presence of Guyon and the Palmer, with all the de-implicating moral control that it signifies, enables the narrator's second description of Acrasia; once again, the description is emotive, and it alludes to Chaucerian narrative:

> Vpon a bed of Roses she was layd,
> As faint through heat, or dight to pleasant sin,
> And was arayd, or rather disarayd,
> All in a vele of silke and siluer thin,
> That hid no whit her alabaster skin,
> But rather shewd more white, if more might bee:
> More subtle web *Arachne* can not spin,
> Nor the fine nets, which oft we wouen see
> Of scorched deaw, do not in th'aire more lightly flee. (II.xii.77)

More follows, but in a properly sequential reading of the poem, the narrator returns here to an erotic appeal in which the word (let alone the idea) *sin*, rhyming with "thin," "skin," and "spin," is barely distinguished. My conclusion from such striking evidence of multiple narrative voices in the Spenserian text would reject both the ideas that there is a single Spenserian voice and that there is none. What I want to say instead is that complexity, conflict, and a multidimensional awareness—an awareness subtly, complexly, and equivocally patterned—are characteristic of Spenser's identity as a poet, the details of whose figure—"*Mulla* mine" or "mother Cambridge"—elsewhere gesture pointedly enough toward his life to invite, but not to delimit or define, connections. Thus the poet I describe is a personal, not an impersonal, pronoun, and he is also a figure whose essential humanity may lie—may even lie punningly—precisely in his decenteredness. In Manfred Frank's *Neostructuralism*, it would lie in the determinacy needed even to determine that it is, indeed, indeterminate.[33] And yet it *would* lie there.

Notes

1. *The Faerie Queene*, IV.ii.34. All references to Spenser's poetry are to the *Variorum Spenser*, cited as *Var.* Subsequently, *The Faerie Queene* is cited as *FQ*.

2. This is the reading of Patterson in "'What Man Artow?'" e.g., 123. See also David, *Strumpet Muse*, chap. 15, esp. 215–21, on *sentence* and *solas* in *Melibee* and *Sir Thopas*.

3. See my discussions of *Sir Thopas* and *Melibee* in "'A Gentle Knight,'" "The 'couert vele,'" 646–48, and "Prudence and Her Silence."

4. E.g., *Colin Clouts Come Home Again*, vv. 652–87; and *FQ* VI.ix.24–25, x.2–3.

5. Berger, "'Kidnapped Romance,'" "Narrative as Rhetoric." For discussions related to Berger's, albeit also distinguished from his, see Miller's argument for Spenserian "authorship under erasure," in "The Earl of Cork's Lute." Cheney's afterword in Anderson, Cheney and Richardson, eds., *Spenser's Life*, pertinently describes a "dialogic" Spenser.

6. All Chaucerian references are to *The Works, 1532*, ed. Thynne, here Bvi[r]. I have expanded the contractions in Thynne's text and changed the solidi to commas; in the interest of intelligibility, I have also added minimal modern punctuation, which is enclosed within brackets. Unless otherwise noted, reference to Chaucer's texts is to this edition. Although Hieatt (*Chaucer, Spenser, Milton*, 19–24) offers speculations regarding the specific edition of Chaucer that Spenser uses, his hard evidence—the word "checklatoun"—establishes only that this was one of the Thynne family of editions. I cite the facsimile of Thynne's 1532 edition for three reasons: its wide availability; the irrelevance to my argument of the texts added to later editions; the absence of substantial variants among Thynne editions that relate to my citations and indeed, in my experience, of substantial textual variants among these editions in general. Craig Berry's welcome discovery (n. 14 of his chapter in this volume) that Spenser might have known more than one edition of Chaucer—and an earlier edition than Thynne's at that—does not cancel Hieatt's evidence that Spenser knew one Thynne edition or more.

7. In the main, I am following—and indebted to—the reading of Leicester, *Disenchanted Self*, 383–417, here 397–98, 400–5. But see also Lawton, *Chaucer's Narrators*, 1–8, 102; and Donaldson's classic essay "Chaucer the Pilgrim."

8. Berger, *Revisionary Play*, 59–60, has a provocatively entertaining discussion of the irony in this passage. My *Growth of a Personal Voice*, 97–98 and 219–20n.3, is skeptical about Spenser's ironical treatment of Una in a way that I no longer embrace, although I continue to find this treatment problematical. On irony in the proem to Book V, see *Personal Voice*, 184–86.

9. While recent criticism has considerably qualified the Knight's ideality and the Pardoner's degeneracy, the general moral contrast between them remains obvious.

10. Barney's *Allegories of History*, 17–18, 20–21, is pertinent; but see also Fineman, "Structure of Allegorical Desire," esp. 31–36.

11. de Man, "Rhetoric of Temporality," 194–95. Cf. de Man on "Pascal's Allegory of Persuasion." On the debate about the dédoublement of de Man's own life and its bearing on authorship, see the prologue of Burke's *Death and the Return of the Author.*

12. Teskey, "Irony, Allegory, and Metaphysical Decay."

13. Responding to my essay, Alfred David asks whether this reference to Chaucer by the Man of Law makes "the narrator a different person" or whether it indicates his failure to recognize Chaucer as pilgrim. In any case, the ironic effect is to destabilize the subject, as David and I would agree. (David, *Strumpet Muse*, 231, also suggests a Chaucerian signature in the Second Nun's Prologue, when the narrator, presumably the second nun, prays Mary, "though that I, unworthy sone of Eve, / Be synful, yet accepte my bileve": cited from *Riverside Chaucer*, 263, vv. 62–63. Insofar as the Thynne editions of Chaucer that Spenser used change "sone" to "doughter," the question of whether this self-assertive filiation differs from the momentary blending of narrator with character that suggests self-projection, my present concern, is moot as regards Spenser: lxv^{V}. In Caxton's 1478 edition, which Spenser might have seen, the word *sone* remains, however, and could be read as an authorial signature, albeit a notably indirect one.)

14. I regard as an exception the occurrence of "Edmundus" in Spenser's Latin verse epistle "Ad Ornatissimum virum . . . G. H.," v. 233, where Spenser's first name is ventriloquized as issuing from Gabriel Harvey's mouth (*Var.* X, 11). Like Milton, Spenser appears to have felt Latin not only an intimate form but also a protecting (and mediating?) one. Insofar as John Donne and Ben Jonson are contemporaries of Spenser, in both cases writing during the 1590s, Spenser's evident avoidance of explicit nomination other than in Latin, for a dedication, or on a title page or such a letter as that to Ralegh (belatedly introducing *The Faerie Queene* at the end of Book III in 1590 and not at all in 1596), is all the more noticeable; but see Loewenstein, "Spenser's Retrography." Jonson, of course, employs his name explicitly in his poetry, and Donne plays openly on his.

15. Bialostosky's statement is taken from an unpublished paper cited in Graff's *Professing Literature*, 257, 303n.

16. Frye's *Elizabeth I*, 124–35, instances a relevant effort to identify Spenser and his narrator with Busirane's perversions. A number of Frye's fascinating read-

ings are questionable, however, and her assumptions about the relation of poet to poem need fuller theorization.

17. According to the *OED*, *mask* is usually thought to have been adopted from French *masque*, in turn an adaptation of the synonymous Spanish *máscara* and Italian *maschera*. But the *OED* also suggests a connection between *mask* and medieval Latin *mascus*, *masca* "mask" or "specter." Žižek describes a suggestively similar phenomenon in *The Sublime Object*, 193–94: "If, behind the phenomenal veil there is nothing, it is through the mediation of this 'nothing' that the subject constitutes himself in the very act of his misrecognition. The illusion that there is something hidden behind the curtain is . . . reflexive . . . [for] what is hidden behind the appearance is the possibility of this very illusion." Likewise suggestive in relation to my argument are Judith Butler's ideas about the performativity of identity: e.g., *Gender Trouble*, 128–49, and *Bodies That Matter*, 1–23.

18. Cf. the use of *mask* in *Amoretti* LIV:

> Of this worlds Theatre in which we stay,
> My loue lyke the Spectator ydly sits
> beholding me that all the pageants play,
> disguysing diuersly my troubled wits.
> Sometimes I ioy when glad occasion fits,
> and mask in myrth lyke to a Comedy. . . .

19. Discussing the social fashioning of identity in the Renaissance, Stephen Greenblatt observes that Thomas Hobbes derives the English word *person* from Latin *persona*, "'*disguise*, or *outward appearance* of a man, counterfeited on the stage; and sometimes more particularly . . . a Mask or Visard.'" Glancing at Shakespeare and Spenser, Greenblatt continues, "for Hobbes there is no person, no coherent, enduring identity beneath the mask. . . . Identity is only possible as a mask, something constructed and assumed" ("Psychoanalysis and Renaissance Culture," 221–23).

20. Curiously, the word *impersonation*, as distinct from the conception, does not appear until the early decades of the seventeenth century and does not occur in a specifically theatrical sense until the eighteenth: *OED*, s.v. *Impersonate/-ion*. The *OED* records occurrences in 1598 and 1602 of the verb *personate*, from Latin *persona* ("mask"), meaning "to act or play the part of (a character in a drama or the like)." Spenser employs this verb in the dedication to "Mother Hubberds Tale," where he refers to "the simplicitie and meannesse thus personated"—i.e., "thus represented."

21. See Paster, *The Body Embarrassed*, 1–15, here 9; and Bakhtin, *Rabelais and His World*, 26. Additional warrant for such blending might be found in the various philosophic ideas concerning a common human nature, which were often developed more confidently and consensually than were those concerning individuation.

22. In this line, after "byd" I have replaced Thynne's solidus with a question mark rather than a comma, and I have capitalized the *h* in "howe."

23. Leicester, *Disenchanted Self*, 387, makes the same point, one that is generally familiar.

24. On the bearing of the portrait of the Parson on the dramatic personae in the General Prologue, see Donaldson, "Adventures with the Adversative Conjunction," 355–56; and my relation of Donaldson's essay to *The Faerie Queene*: "What Comes After Chaucer's *But*," esp. 105, 118.

25. My definition of *expression* has been adapted from *OED*, s.v. *Express, v. Express* derives from Latin *exprimere*: "to press out," "to form (an image) by pressure," "to represent in sculpture or painting," "to represent or set forth in words or actions."

26. In this connection, cf. the envoy to *The Shepheardes Calender*, in which the poet dares not match his poem "with Tityrus hys style, / Nor with the Pilgrim that the Ploughman playde a whyle." The pilgrim playing plowman (or plowman playing pilgrim) alludes to a similar technique: see my *Growth of a Personal Voice*, 1–2.

27. The remainder of this paragraph draws on my discussion of the Giant in the final chapter of *Words that Matter.*

28. Discussion of the Temple draws on my "The 'couert vele,'" esp. 645, 656–57.

29. On Orpheus in *Epithalamion*, see Loewenstein, "Echo's Ring"; and on Spenser as Orphic poet more generally, see Cain, *Praise in "The Faerie Queene,"* 14–24, 169–73, and Cheney, *Spenser's Famous Flight*, chap. 1.

30. In the prologue to Chaucer's Miller's Tale, compare the slipping of the pilgrim's mask in the line "Turne ouer the lefe, and chose another tale" (xiii^{v}). See David, *Strumpet Muse*, chap. 8, esp. 120.

31. *Roland Barthes by Roland Barthes*, 168. The original French reads, "pourquoi ne parlerais-je pas de 'moi,' puisque 'moi' n'est plus 'soi'?" and "le suject se prend *ailleurs*": *Roland Barthes par roland barthes*, 171. "Apprehends" is a sensitive translation of "se prend" in this context. See also Paul Smith, *Discerning the Subject*, 6: "the singular is not necessarily to be conceived of as a unity: to think of it as such would be to posit it as purely the effect of the ideological processes in which it lives." Likewise, Burke, *Death and the Return of the Author*, 27: "Observing light passing through a prism . . . we do not deny its effect upon the light, still less call for the death of the prism. . . . One must, at base, be deeply *auterist* to call for the Death of the Author"; cf. 25, 154, 167. Cf. Norris, *Derrida*, 213; also Haraway, *Simians, Cyborgs, and Women*, 191: "The alternative to relativism is partial, locatable, critical knowledges. . . . Relativism is a way of being nowhere while claiming to be everywhere equally. . . . [It is the] twin of totalization . . . [since] both deny the stakes in location, embodiment, and partial perspective."

32. Cf. *FQ* II.xii.70–71, 77 with Chaucer's *Parliament*, cclxxx^{r-v}.

33. Frank, *What Is Neostructuralism?* lectures 25–27, esp. 408, 424, 432–33, 436–37; cf. xxxix, xxxiv–xxxv. Frank's theory of individuality as difference/*différance* in these lectures is also pertinent. Cf. the mathematician Rotman's *Signifying Nothing*, 105: "The very function which zero enjoys within mathematics as the mark of an origin requires there to be . . . a certain sort of subject present, a conscious intentional agency, whose 'presence' at the initiation of the process of the counting is precisely what zero signifies."

CHAPTER 6

"Sundrie Doubts"

Vulnerable Understanding and Dubious Origins in Spenser's Continuation of the Squire's Tale

CRAIG A. BERRY

My goal in this chapter is to explore the theme of doubt in the early cantos of Book IV of *The Faerie Queene* in a way that illuminates Spenser's struggle to overcome doubts about his place in an English poetic tradition and about the creation and reception of his poem. The fourth book launches the second installment of the poem after a six-year period in which the poet could formulate a poetic response to the reception of the first three books, and it seems clear from the discussion of "Stoicke censours" in the opening lines of Book IV that Spenser felt at least part of that reception to be a misunderstanding (IV.Proem.3).[1] It is no coincidence, I argue, that Spenser's most overt appeal to his greatest English predecessor comes precisely at this moment of doubt. Chaucer's presence—never explicitly acknowledged in the first three books of *The Faerie Queene*—surfaces here in a proposal to continue the fragmentary Squire's Tale through "infusion sweete" of Chaucer's "owne spirit" (IV.ii.34), but a detailed reading of this invocation shows that Spenser has at least as many doubts about his poetic parentage as he does about his contemporary audience.

Examining Spenser's intertextual strategies for coping with doubts about poetic origins as well as doubts about contemporary reception is more than a convenient juxtaposition, for both kinds of doubt inspire even as they challenge Spenser's highly allusive brand of moral allegory. "Spenser's writing . . . may be said to feed on certain species of doubt," writes Kenneth Gross; the successful production and reception of *The Faerie Queene* depend on an originating doubt but, as Gross explains, may ultimately be threatened by the doubts thus generated: "in every attempt to achieve something like a visionary identification with a sacred emblem, the fear of fixation or of subsequent misreading haunts the literary quest like a demon."[2] As we shall see, a poem that represents its author reading his sources in the same figures that represent its readers reading—or failing to read—the poem itself becomes an arena where the past-oriented concerns of intertextuality meet the present-oriented concerns of contemporary reception. My specific focus is with how—by his intertextual presence in the early cantos of Book IV—Chaucer can function simultaneously, in Gross's terms, as "sacred emblem" and as "demon," as an authoritative hedge against misreading and ill reception who also haunts his successor with doubts about the durability of written monuments, the limitations of an English poetic heritage, and the viability of poetic vocation.

The Squire's Tale shares with Book IV a preoccupation with doubtful interpretation, specifically doubts that arise in the presence of the unfamiliar or exotic. The Squire narrator harshly criticizes those characters who find difficulty interpreting the tale's marvels, but he also apologizes profusely to his audience about his own inability to describe the wonders at the court of the Tartar king Cambyuskan. The desire to engage the remote and alien seems to go hand in hand with a fear of being misunderstood. As John Fyler argues, "The Squire repeatedly leaves us at the line between sameness and otherness, innocence and experience, the familiar and the exotic."[3] That the tale oscillates between two imperatives—the enlightening confrontation with otherness and the anxious retreat to the familiar—makes it an especially appropriate staging ground for Spenser's encounter with his Chaucerian roots, for the people of England in Spenser's time had a deeply ambivalent attitude toward their own past. As Alice Miskimin notes, "the Middle Ages were paradoxically both despised by Elizabethans as the primitive darkness of superstition and ignorance from which they had emerged, and yet honored, as the origin of uniquely English institutions, the common law, the English language, and the monarchy itself."[4] The English past, like Cambyuskan's court, was both uncomfortably familiar and tantalizingly foreign, frighteningly different yet reassuringly recognizable.

Spenser found inspiration in the Squire's Tale for working out his own fear of being misunderstood, but such historical separations as fifteenth-century language changes and the Protestant Reformation made Chaucer in some respects a remote and dubious origin.[5] A brief comparison of Spenser's Chaucerian and Ariostan allusions near the end of this chapter shows that Chaucer was not Spenser's only difficult ancestor but that he figured as no other precursor could the particular risks of claiming an English poetic heritage. By writing rhymed verse in emulation of an English model, Spenser invited not only the objections of poetry's detractors but also the criticism of some of its most prominent Elizabethan apologists. Roger Ascham assumed that only Latin and Greek models were worthy of imitation and deplored the "barbarous and rude Ryming" of even the greatest English poets; Spenser's friend Gabriel Harvey, among others, argued that English verse should use the quantitative meters of the classical languages; George Puttenham frequently criticized the rudeness of Chaucer's language or disparaged the form of his verse even while praising him; and Sir Philip Sidney, as we shall see in more detail later, also found fault with England's medieval poetic heritage.[6] In such a context Spenser could hardly think of Chaucer as his father or master in the relatively direct manner of Chaucer's fifteenth-century imitators, and in fact he replaces filiation as begetting with filiation as spiritual infusion—a more flexible, and thus safer, imitative strategy for a poet who wants to be identified with a famous predecessor for support in facing a potentially doubting audience—but at the same time finds it necessary to distance himself from some of that predecessor's dubious associations.

The title page of Book IV informs its readers that the book will be devoted to the virtue of friendship, and by frequently characterizing the obstacles to friendship as doubts, Spenser links the pursuit of virtue with the pursuit of understanding. Such is the case in the first episode in Book IV, where the doubts of Spenser's characters figure the doubts of his readers. Britomart has just rescued Amoret from the psychological terrors of love in the House of Busyrane, but Amoret fears that her rescuer, whose armor leads her to the interpretation that Britomart is a man, may become her oppressor. Amoret's doubts about Britomart are based on a misreading of the latter's chivalric trappings, and her fears are compounded when they reach the gate of a castle where only knights in possession of ladies may enter, and a lone knight claims his right to her by proof of arms. Britomart defeats the knight, but more than that, by reading virtuously in doubtful circumstances she transforms the entire situation into a scene of concord and friendship.

After Britomart defeats the challenger, we are told,

> She that no lesse was courteous then stout,
> Cast how to salue, that both the custome showne
> Were kept, and yet that Knight not locked out,
> That seem'd full hard t'accord two things so far in dout. (IV.i.11)

By the rules of the castle, the defeated knight is to be "locked out," but Britomart seeks an interpretation of "the custome" which also satisfies the demands of the virtue of friendship by allowing him entrance. Her imaginative solution is simply to unlace her helmet and reveal herself to be a woman. She has won passage for Amoret in her role as a knight, but she also gains entry to the castle for the defeated knight by offering to be his lady, and thus subverts the capricious social order by an act of personal charity. Britomart has faced a seemingly overwhelming set of mutually exclusive constraints, and the force separating the poles of the dilemma is described as "dout," but she resolves the doubt and brings concord to the situation through her imaginative reading of courtly mores.

The next stanza, however, betrays an underlying sense that not all the doubts are accorded; when Britomart removes her helmet and displays her "golden lockes" (IV.i.13), the reactions of those present reveal a troubling sense of hermeneutic uncertainty:

> Such when those Knights and Ladies all about
> Beheld her, all were with amazement smit,
> And euery one gan grow in secret dout
> Of this and that, according to each wit:
> Some thought that some enchantment faygned it;
> Some, that *Bellona* in that warlike wise
> To them appear'd, with shield and armour fit;
> Some, that it was a maske of strange disguise:
> So diuersely each one did sundrie doubts deuise. (IV.i.14)

Britomart's martial feat causes no raised eyebrows when everyone believes her to be a man, but in showing her true identity she suddenly becomes an interpretation problem. The "sundrie doubts" are all attempts to limit Britomart to something within the experience and understanding of those making an interpretation, and by emphasizing that doubt is a solitary event ("euery one gan grow in secret dout"), Spenser identifies it as the opposite of the trust necessary for community and friendship.

To borrow the terminology of reception theory, for these onlookers the hermeneutic circle has ground to a halt; there is no back and forth movement between part and whole that might allow them to integrate the presence of a virtuous and powerful female warrior into their closed courtly system, and they are unable to broaden their horizon of expectation or engage in a dialogic process of adjustment between their preconceptions and the empirical other before them.[7] Gerald Bruns writes, "Allegory is, crudely, the squaring of an alien conceptual scheme with one's own on the charitable assumption that there is a sense (which it is the task of interpretation to determine) in which they are coherent with one another."[8] The assumptions of Britomart's interpreters are anything but charitable, and for Spenser their worst sin seems to be that they—and the sort of readers they represent—are unable or unwilling to allow the alien texture of his allegory to cure their moral tunnel vision.

Significantly, the onlookers confounded by Britomart's appearance are "Knights and Ladies," and thus, unlike the "raskall many"[9] whom Spenser denounces throughout the poem, should show an innate sensitivity to the allegorical representation of virtue. In the explanatory letter to Raleigh, Spenser states, "The generall end therefore of all the booke is to fashion a gentleman or noble person in vertuous and gentle discipline,"[10] and the failure of these knights and ladies to make sound interpretations figures the risk that the gentleman or noble person whom the poet hopes to fashion may be less perceptive and more hostile than he or she should be. How could Spenser be sure that his readers would be able to follow such twistings and turnings of an allegory in which—as the letter to Raleigh explains—the same figure may not only represent glory in the abstract and the Queen in particular but also may give place to other figures with overlapping sets of referents? Indeed, Spenser prefaces his explanations with an acknowledgment of the difficulty, "knowing how doubtfully all Allegories may be construed," and by the time he published Book IV in the 1596 edition of the poem, he may well have had further concerns about the "gealous opinions and misconstructions" which the letter had sought to preempt.

The competing interpretations of Britomart are absent in Spenser's Ariostan source, where Bradamante doffs her helmet to reveal that she is unambiguously a young woman (*Orlando Furioso* XXXII.79). Spenser renders the same Ariostan subtext more faithfully in Book III (III.ix.21), but somehow doubt has crept in during the move from Book III to Book IV. It is rare to see a poet quoting himself and a predecessor simultaneously, and Britomart's predicament as a misunderstood allegorical figure suggests that we are indeed getting a glimpse at Spenser reading Spenser; her situation figures the anxiety of an author whose poetic method is a particularly complex form of allegory.

There is more to the literary history of the passage at which we have been looking than Spenser reading himself reading Ariosto; Chaucer's incomplete Squire's Tale, which Spenser continues a canto after Britomart's encounter with the inept readers, also contains a parable about readerly doubt. The Squire's Tale begins with a foreign knight arriving at the birthday feast of a king to present gifts, namely a mirror, a ring, a sword, and a "steede of bras" (V.81); and since this is a romance, all the gifts have magical properties.[11] The steed of brass is a Pegasus-like flying horse that—like the fantastic narrative in which it occurs—can take its rider/reader wherever he or she wants to go in the space of one day (V.115–21); "He that it wroghte koude ful many a gyn," we are told (V.128); the maker of the horse, like the poetic *makere*, uses a number of ingenious contrivances in his craft. The horse, then, seems to say something about the relationship of the poem to its readers.[12] The diverse reactions to it of those present at the feast call to mind the interpretation problems which Britomart presented by the removal of her helmet:

> It was a fairye, as the peple semed.
> Diverse folk diversely they demed;
> As many heddes, as manye wittes ther been.
> They murmureden as dooth a swarm of been. (V.201–4)

In trying to account for the marvelous nature of the horse, the people of the court proceed to attempt explanations of it in terms of various literary precedents (notably Pegasus and the Trojan Horse), and the divergence of interpretation suggests a Babel-like frustration of understanding.

The narrator soon breaks in to shower withering criticism on the struggling interpreters, and—like the Spenserian narrator—he tells a story about interpretation which rhetorically deflects the responsibility for right reading onto his audience:

> Of sondry doutes thus they jangle and trete,
> As lewed peple demeth comunly
> Of thinges that been maad moore subtilly
> Than they kan in her lewednesse comprehende;
> They demen gladly to the badder ende. (V.220–24)

Like the failed interpretations of the helmetless Britomart, the "sondry doutes" of Cambyuskan's courtiers indicate a limited moral vision and an inability to engage the alterity of the marvel before them. Whereas the moral allegorist Spenser figures readerly limitation as the failure to comprehend a shape-shifting figure of chastity, Chaucer the *makere* depicts feeble reading as an inability to reverse engineer a subtle man-made engine, but both poets show us what good readers should be like by showing us what bad readers are like.

Spenser's hermeneutic lesson for his readers clearly owes much in both form and spirit to Chaucer. Not only are there similarities in the general atmosphere of contentious interpretation; both poets also characterize the diverging interpretations as doubts. "And euery one gan grow in secret dout / Of this and that, according to each wit," says Spenser; "As many heddes, as manye wittes ther been," says Chaucer. "So diuersely each one did sundrie doubts deuise," says Spenser; "Of sondry doutes thus they jangle and trete," says Chaucer.[13] The words *sondry* and *doute,* both quite common in Chaucer's vocabulary, occur together nowhere else in the Chaucerian canon, and although Spenser could have arrived at such a simple construction independently, his use of the expression in the context of readerly doubt must almost certainly be a verbal echo of the Squire's Tale.[14]

Both allegories of reading are preoccupied with doubt leading to multiple and conflicting interpretations, but Spenser is less willing than Chaucer is to leave doubting readers to fend for themselves. The young knight whom Britomart has defeated but to whom she has also graciously offered the hand of friendship is "to that goodly fellowship restor'd" (IV.i.15), and Amoret no longer fears to share a bed with her traveling companion because she now knows Britomart is a woman. Spenser seems to be saying that his poem should be judged by its fruits; doubts resulting from the twistings and turnings of the allegory should not be allowed to obscure the fact that it is a *moral* allegory capable of harmonizing and dispelling far graver doubts than those caused by the poem's inner workings. This is something of a smokescreen, of course, one which hides the fact that problems with reading the poem and problems with exercising the virtue of friendship are both threats to Spenser's success in fashioning gentlemen. By representing moral victory in spite of a conglomeration of misguided or inadequate readings, Spenser attempts to resolve doubts about the interpretation of his poem and its success in accomplishing the ambitious moral influence he intended for it.

Chaucer, by contrast, revels in the multiplication of doubt. Unlike the misguided young knight whom Britomart chastens and restores to his companions, the Squire narrator—just as he outlines Part 3 of his tale—is cut off in mid-sentence and never heard from again, effectively shutting him out of the Canterbury fellowship.[15] The tale's audience remains forever in doubt about the fates of Cambalo and Canacee, at least until Spenser takes up their story two centuries later. The foreign knight reveals the secret of the horse's operation to Cambyuskan, but the people who struggled to interpret it are left in the dark, and the tale ends before we see it in action. For Spenser, Chaucer's willingness to leave such breaches of understanding unresolved must have become increasingly attractive as he began to complicate his own happy resolutions. In the revised ending of

Book III published with the 1596 edition of *The Faerie Queene,* Amoret and Scudamour no longer embrace, and Book IV is often thought of as the place where the harmony and concord which are the whole point of the virtue of friendship never happen in a complete and satisfying way. The structure of the narrative itself was long ago noted for its disharmony, whereas recent critics are more apt to find a harmonious story line that may be read against the grain to discover a deeper deferral of closure.[16] In any case, as Sean Kane says of Book IV, "the reader is encouraged to imagine harmony . . . in terms of the force that disrupts it."[17]

I have already commented that doubt creeps in during the transition from Book III to Book IV, and taking this turn at the beginning of the second installment of *The Faerie Queene* may reflect the deferral of easy fulfillments in Spenser's career. Whatever the reasons for the increasing dissonance, it coincides with a new attitude toward precursor poets. Ariosto, whose extensive contributions to the first three books are nowhere acknowledged explicitly in the poem, is now referred to as "that famous Tuscane penne" (IV.iii.45), and Chaucer emerges not only as a significant subtext but as an overtly revered predecessor. We have seen that Spenser found a coping mechanism to emulate in the shifting of the burden of understanding in the Squire's Tale onto the reader, but unlike the Squire narrator, who scorns those who seek to understand the brass horse in terms of literary precedent, he tries to go his own source one better by acknowledging his indebtedness to other poets.

Thomas Greene has taught us to view the acknowledgment of historical difference from a precursor as "the admission of a risk, the risk of being smaller, of appearing blind, of betraying a degeneration, of falling into travesty or pollution."[18] Greene's discussion is about Renaissance imitations of ancient models, but the risks are equally great, if different, for a Renaissance poet following in the footsteps of a medieval one. It is less clear in this case what constitutes "the risk of being smaller," for attaining equality with a medieval model could be a mixed blessing in the sixteenth century.

As we have seen, several prominent Elizabethans harbored ambivalence toward their medieval poetic heritage, and Philip Sidney's comments on Chaucer in his *Apologie for Poetrie* identify with particular force the risks Spenser took by imitating Chaucer. "*Chaucer,*" says Sidney, "vndoubtedly, did excellently in hys *Troylus* and *Cresseid;* of whom, truly, I know not whether to meruaile more, either that he in that mistic time could see so clearely, or that wee in this cleare age walke so stumblingly after him. Yet had he great wants, fitte to be forgiuen in so reuerent antiquity." The way these sentences double back on themselves, negating whatever they assert, reveals the depth of Sidney's ambivalence and suggests that he had little or no interest in bridging the gap between his own age and Chaucer's "reuerent antiquity." A few lines further on, Spenser's own *Shepheardes Calender,* which had been dedicated to Sidney, receives the same mixture of praise and censure that Sidney had bestowed on Chaucer. Spenser's debut, says Sidney, "hath much Poetrie in his Eglogues: indeede worthy the reading, if I be not deceiued. That same framing of his stile to an old rustick language I dare not alowe, sith neyther *Theocritus* in Greek, *Virgill* in Latine, nor *Sanazar* in Italian did affect it." While Sidney is vague about both the faults and merits of Chaucer, he is quite explicit about the shortcomings of Spenser's first public performance, sternly criticizing the archaic language as a departure from classical and continental tradition even as he praises it as one of very few works in English having "poeticall sinnewes."[19]

For Sidney, who fails to recognize that engagement with one's origins holds promise as well as danger, the risk of evoking the English past is so great, the domestic literary heritage so embarrassingly meager, that he "dare not allow" the archaism which *The Shepheardes Calender* flaunts. The implication for any late sixteenth-century emulation of Chaucer is that Chaucer was not only—as Chaucer's fifteenth-century followers claimed—a great father who had left a formidable legacy to follow but also a dependent Anchises who had to be packed up with the household gods and carried into the future. To invoke Chaucer, then, is not simply to bring in, as I have suggested above, an expert on doubt but also to engage in an enterprise which itself has dubious prospects, for there is the double risk that Spenser may appear either smaller than his medieval predecessor or smaller than he would have had he stuck with classical models and their less ambiguous reputations.

Spenser probably smarted from Sidney's remarks, perhaps enough to avoid direct allusions to Chaucer for the first half of *The Faerie Queene,* but in the second half he embraces his revered, rustic precursor in a way that addresses Sidney's doubts—and his own—about the prospects of writing great poetry from within an English tradition. Spenser tells us about the origin of Cambel and Triamond, the heroes whose names appear on the title page of Book IV, in the homage he pays his own original:

> Whylome as antique stories tellen vs,
> Those two were foes the fellonest on ground,
> And battell made the dreddest daungerous,
> That euer shrilling trumpet did resound;
> Though now their acts be now where to be found,

As that renowmed Poet them compyled,
With warlike numbers and Heroicke sound,
Dan *Chaucer,* well of English vndefyled,
On Fames eternall beadroll worthie to be fyled. (IV.iii.32)

Spenser here depicts the Squire's Tale as an epic rather than a romance by implying that the poet's purpose is to record the deeds of heroes in the manner of a herald and thereby to earn a place on "Fames eternall beadroll." Few would now recognize this as Chaucer's purpose in writing the Squire's Tale, but by offering such a representation Spenser casts himself as the heir to an English epic tradition and thus one embarked on a serious and respectable enterprise. The first line of the stanza closely imitates the first line of the Knight's Tale, and by calling his predecessor "Dan *Chaucer*" Spenser posthumously promotes him to knighthood.[20] These details remind us that the knightly estate provides both the proper subject and the intended audience of epic and suggest that the poet who recounts epic deeds shares in the glory of the champions who perform them.

Spenser no sooner establishes the worthiness of his predecessor than he proceeds to address the risks of following a remote model:

But wicked Time that all good thoughts doth waste,
And workes of noblest wits to nought out weare,
That famous moniment hath quite defaste,
And robd the world of threasure endlesse deare,
The which mote haue enriched all vs heare.
O cursed Eld the cankerworme of writs,
How may these rimes, so rude as doth appeare,
Hope to endure, sith workes of heauenly wits
Are quite deuourd, and brought to nought by little bits?

Then pardon, O most sacred happie spirit,
That I thy labours lost may thus reuiue,
And steale from thee the meede of thy due merit,
That none durst euer whilest thou wast aliue,
And being dead in vaine yet many striue:
Ne dare I like, but through infusion sweete
Of thine owne spirit, which doth in me surviue,
I follow here the footing of thy feete,
That with thy meaning so I may the rather meete. (IV.ii.33–34)

Spenser presents his doubts about literary inheritance in terms of loss and mutability, and Ellen Martin makes a strong case that the principle motivating the poet here is "the transmutation of loss into invention."[21]

Spenser elaborately downplays his own inventive power, however, claiming only to "reuiue" the "labours lost" of his worthy predecessor, and in doing so he conjures up a rather traditional, self-effacing notion of poet and source: his own poem is "rude," whereas Chaucer's is "threasure endlesse deare." Moreover, by asking Chaucer's pardon for stealing "the meede of thy due merit," Spenser not only portrays himself as taking the reward due someone else; he also makes his own work out to be several times removed from the authentic original. "Meede" is an alternate spelling of "mead," the fermented drink made from honey, pertinent here because a bee making honey is an ancient figure of poetic imitation.[22] The figure of mellification, while highlighting the industry of the imitator and the fact that his work concentrates in one place the nectar gathered from many flowers, also emphasizes the derivative nature of that work. Moreover, mead is honey which has been diluted and—like Chaucer's "famous moniment"—altered by the passage of time; Chaucer's "merit" can only be obtained in a watered down and fermented version, and even that must be stolen. It can merely be hoped that such an "infusion sweete" will inspire an imitation worthy of its original.

Although he pushes the rhetoric of humility to an extreme, Spenser's attitude to his source at first appears to be a straightforward "admission of a risk" in Thomas Greene's terms, but we have seen that the risk of imitating Chaucer was double-edged in the sixteenth century. It is unlikely that Spenser simply disagreed with Sidney about Chaucer's shortcomings; a poet such as Spenser—with an unusually fine ear but a sixteenth-century understanding of Middle English pronunciation—could not help but feel a roughness in Chaucer's versification. As Theresa Krier has pointed out, "These stanzas articulate an unstable suspension of despair and hope, a sense of distance from Chaucer as well as one of intimacy with him," and this double feeling is evident even in Spenser's metrical revision of Chaucer's verse.[23] The opening line of Spenser's Chaucerian invocation, "Whylome as antique stories tellen vs," is, as I have noted, the first line of the Knight's Tale, but in Spenser's version "olde," having lost a syllable during the fifteenth century, is replaced by "antique" to make the meter work; for Spenser the well of English may be undefiled, but it needs filtering before being served to a sixteenth-century audience.[24] That Spenser makes reference to Chaucer's "warlike numbers and Heroicke sound" does not necessarily mean that he considered his predecessor, as one critic argues, a "martial poet," but rather that Chaucer's meter sounded strong and energetic but also harsh and undisciplined.[25] Like the overeager martial tendencies that must be brought into concord in Book IV, Chaucer's rough verse must be tamed and put to work in the service of the virtue of friendship.

Spenser's accommodation of Chaucer's metrical irregularity continues with a wordplay in the lines "I follow here the footing of thy feete, / That with thy meaning so I may the rather meete." Among the many possible constructions of this sentence, it may be rendered as "I imitate the feet of your verse in order to encounter your meaning more quickly"; Spenser tropes metrical imitation as a means of hermeneutic assistance, but since he has just performed foot surgery on his predecessor's verse, we would do well to ask in what way he follows in Chaucer's (limping) footsteps.[26] The entire stanza is in the second person, so it makes sense to read "the" in the last line as "thee": "That with thy meaning so I may *thee* rather meete." Appropriately, reading "the" as "thee" shifts the stress from the first syllable of "rather" to "thee," thus throwing off the rhythm of Spenser's alexandrine and making a literal truth out of following Chaucer's footing.[27] If Spenser's verse echoes the metrical roughness of Chaucer's, the follower erases the distance between himself and his mentor poet and meets him face to face, but if the meter works properly, the later poet must depend on his predecessor's spirit to overcome the debilitating effects of time and recover his meaning.

Is it Chaucer's presence, then, that is required to revive the meaning of Chaucer's verse, or does following the meter of Chaucer's verse give rise to a meeting with the poet himself along with or by means of his meaning? Jonathan Goldberg finds only negative potential here, equating Chaucer's footsteps with "a Derridean 'trace,'" and asserting that for the Spenserian narrator to follow them he "must abandon his voice entirely to Chaucer's, effecting a loss of voice so complete as to permit Chaucer to write through him, making his text a rewriting in another's voice," a rewriting which requires him to "pursue his own obliteration."[28] Judith Anderson captures the spirit of the passage better when she suggests that "pointing toward and participating in, rather than fully possessing or appropriating, are here the ideas that sustain and empower."[29] However, there are risks as well as benefits in figuring imitation as mutual participation, and in the very lines where Spenser claims to be following Chaucer's lead, he subtly resists the dangers of following too closely. Making the final alexandrine work two ways seems to be Spenser's method for coping with the paradoxical remoteness and closeness of Chaucer and his own uncertain provenance as a poet who writes in English; he can embrace his precursor with all of his roughness and hold the roughness at arm's length while enjoying a spiritual oneness with him.

Spenser's imitative purpose, then, is to "meete" both Chaucer's meaning and Chaucer himself in a way that accommodates the risks of such meeting, but not only does the object of the verb have multiple valences; the verb *meete* itself means far more than just "encounter," and the cornucopia of meanings tells us more about Spenser's attitude toward his intertextual endeavor. "To meet (with)" can mean "to be even with; to requite or 'pay out,'" and "meet" can also be rendered "to complete the full 'measure' or amount of."[30] Earlier in the stanza, Spenser has asked Chaucer's pardon for stealing his reward, but here he offers his own act of imitation as a requital that places him on par with his precursor and completes the unfulfilled potential of Chaucer's ambitious but fragmentary tale. Spenser joins the Canterbury fellowship, as it were, "quiting" the Squire's Tale with a tale of his own that responds to and dilates on the meaning of its predecessor.[31] But the requitals in the *Canterbury Tales* more often than not challenge or undermine the tales which they purportedly complement, so adopting this paradigm allows Spenser simultaneously to criticize and to render homage. Reviving the Squire's Tale is thus a balancing act between evoking a tradition to suggest an authoritative continuity of poetic endeavor and staking out new territory which escapes the limits of the tradition.

Spenser's continuation of the Squire's Tale is based on rather sparse hints in the tale itself, hints which leave a high degree of doubt about what a suitable conclusion to the fragmentary narrative might contain. Shortly before his tale abruptly ends, the Squire says, "And after wol I speke of Cambalo, / That faught in lystes with the bretheren two / For Canacee er that he myghte hire wynne" (V.667–69). Like Britomart outside the castle, Spenser has a rather odd and potentially threatening situation to resolve in continuing the tale. Jousting for the love of a lady is a common enough romance occurrence, but in what sense can Cambalo fight for and "wynne" his sister Canacee? Spenser chooses not to deal with incest directly here, but he does create a situation in which the love between brother and sister is in tension with Canacee's status as a romantic object.[32] In Spenser's version of the story, the princess Canacee has refused all of her many suitors, who vent their frustrations by fighting one another. Her brother Cambel, distressed by the strife in the kingdom, proposes to settle the situation by fighting the three doughtiest suitors himself and granting his sister's hand to the winner.

Priamond, Diamond, and Triamond, the three sons of Agape, are deemed to be the worthiest aspirants to Canacee's hand, and Cambel battles the three of them in turn. Before discussing the battle itself, it is important to note the origin of the three brothers, a dubious origin which figures Spenser's ambivalent relationship with his own poetic roots. "Their mother was a Fay," we are told, who "lov'd in forests wyld to space" (IV.ii.44). One day her solitude is interrupted by "a noble youthly knight," who "vnawares vpon her laying hold, / That stroue in vaine him long to haue withstood, / Oppressed her, and there (as it is told) / Got these three louely babes, that prov'd three champions bold" (IV.ii.45). The noble youthly knight who had "oppressed" Agape is not named, perhaps because no one would want to remember a father who was a rapist. Thus the three brothers have a dubious origin in two very traditional senses: first, the identity of their father is unknown, and second, the manner of their begetting is shameful. Their mother's response to her situation, however, suggests that liabilities arising from uncertain origins can be accommodated and to some extent overcome.

Agape's name means "love," especially charitable or self-giving love, and in Spenserian allegory such a name implies that while love may be powerless in the face of brute force, it has a moral force of its own with the ability to reshape that which has been inflicted on it. Agape not only lovingly nurtures her sons in spite of their violent origin, she also attempts to protect them from danger when they grow up to show "signes of their fathers blood," which is to say signs of chivalric zeal; like their father, who was "Seeking aduentures" when he encountered Agape (IV.ii.45), "They loued armes, and knighthood did ensew, / Seeking aduentures, where they anie knew" (IV.ii.46). The boys are "louely babes," and thus exhibit their mother's characteristic quality, but they are also imitations of their father, and while his image is reflected in their faces, it is also reflected in the martial proclivities which threaten to cut short their lives. In an attempt to prevent their early deaths, Agape visits the Fates, who refuse her request that her sons' lives be lengthened. She does, however, negotiate a compromise: when each son dies, "his life may passe into the next" through the process of spiritual traduction (IV.ii.52).

At the beginning of canto iii Spenser chastises such foolhardy grasping at life, but his own invocation of Chaucer's spirit suggests that he too found the deferral of extinction by spiritual infusion an attractive model. Like Chaucer's "warlike numbers and Heroicke sound," the sire of Priamond, Diamond, and Triamond provides a crude but invigorating force, which cannot be directly resisted but can be lovingly augmented and sustained by means of spiritual infusion. For Spenser no less than for the sons of Agape, filiation as spiritual infusion offers a model of inheritance more supple and more susceptible to fashioning than is filiation as begetting, for imitating the father too closely can be dangerous and limiting. Ignoring one's origins, on the other hand, is simply impossible, both for the chivalric hero, whose identity is inseparable from his heritage, and for the poet, who can only write from within a tradition.

In the battle for Canacee's hand, Cambel kills Priamond and Diamond (presumably the anonymous "bretheren two" from the Squire's Tale), and the spirit of each brother passes to the next by virtue of the deal Agape has struck with the Fates. Triamond proves tougher to kill than his brothers, aided as he is by their spirits as well as his own, but Cambel, aided by his sister's magic ring, keeps up with him. Only the appearance of Triamond's sister Cambina, an allegorical figure who, as Thomas Roche says, is "meant to represent Concord or Peace," can reconcile the warriors by means of her cup of Nepenthe.[33] Cambina does bring concord to the scene she enters, but her name means "change," and the nectar she brings certainly effects a radical change in those who drink it: after drinking "an harty draught" from Cambina's cup (IV.iii.48), Cambel and Triamond immediately forget their quarrel and become lifelong friends. Cambina and her cup are like the flying horse in the Squire's Tale, the power of which lies in its ability to translate those acquainted with its secrets to circumstances radically removed from their own.

Spenser further links the contents of Cambina's cup with the fashioning role of poetry by asserting the superiority of Nepenthe over another transforming drink:

> Much more of price and of more gratious powre
> Is this, then that same water of Ardenne,
> The which *Rinaldo* drunck in happie howre,
> Described by that famous Tuscane penne:
> For that had might to change the hearts of men
> Fro love to hate, a change of euill choise:
> But this doth hatred make in loue to brenne,
> And heauy heart with comfort doth reioyce.
> Who would not to this vertue rather yeeld his voice? (IV.iii.45)

In the fifth line of the stanza, "that" of course nominally refers to the "water of Ardenne" in line 2, but it might also refer to the "Tuscane penne" in line 4 and still do justice to the syntax; it is Ariosto's pen that effects "a change of euill choise," a reading confirmed by the traditional association of poets' pens and springs. Spenser's account of his Italian source is not quite complete, for in the *Orlando Furioso* there are two springs, one of which ignites love and another that extinguishes it, but this simply confirms that springs per se are not what interest Spenser here.[34] What does interest him is making a point about his famous Italian predecessor and the language, "Tuscane," in which he writes; unlike Chaucer, the "well of English vndefyled" (IV.ii.32), or the "pure well head of Poesie" (VII.vii.9), the river of Italian romantic epic is an impure source.

Spenser was not the first Elizabethan to find the Englishing of Italian sources problematic; Roger Ascham, for example, deplored the translation of Italian romances into English because of their decadent influence, and even Sir John Harington, that most enthusiastic Elizabethan champion of Ariosto, felt it necessary in his translation and commentary to engage in a moralizing revision of the exuberant Italian epic.[35] In any case, we once again find Spenser with a double-edged relationship to a source, emulating him with great fervor but then distancing himself from his predecessor's unwelcome associations. Ariosto's cynicism and lack of a zealous moral program are usually considered to have been strikes against him for Spenser, and at least part of the impetus behind this subtle slight must be Spenser's concern, as he expresses in the proem to Book IV, that by "magnifying louers deare debate" he will be viewed as a frivolous poet himself.[36] Ariosto's reputation as a superficial poet has only been conclusively shown wanting quite recently, whereas Chaucer's reputation always presented both serious and scurrilous possibilities, as in Puttenham's contrast between the "very graue and stately" meter of *Troilus and Criseyde* and the "riding ryme" of the *Canterbury Tales*.[37] In light of the elegiac tone in his invocation of Chaucer's spirit and his disparagement of Ariosto's love-quenching spring, it seems that Spenser, having borrowed avidly and often from the reputedly frivolous Ariosto in the first three books, now turns to the serious resonances of Chaucer's reputation to correct his image.[38]

Comparing Spenser's allusion to Ariosto with his invocation of Chaucer allows us to revise Patrick Cheney's explanation for Spenser's recourse to the Squire's Tale in Book IV. "Spenser is attracted to Chaucer's unfinished tale," Cheney argues, "primarily because he finds in it a conventional *mythos* featuring three modes of action central to the genre of romance: love, magic, and chivalric heroism."[39] The Squire's Tale, as Cheney notes, serves up a fuller menu of romance elements than do most of Chaucer's other works, but Spenser's invocation of Chaucer's spirit makes no appeal at all to the tale's romance elements and a very direct appeal to Chaucer's reputation as a serious poet. Two questions intersect: if his intention was to evoke Chaucer as a correction for frivolity, why did he choose to imitate the fantastic Squire's Tale rather than a more serious chivalric narrative like the Knight's Tale, and on the other hand, if his primary interest was in the tale's romance marvels, why did he bother with Chaucer at all when Ariosto offered a more reliable, if less pure, source?[40]

Spenser, like Chaucer, strove to set precedents in English poetry, but he was not content, as Chaucer was, to toy with the romance of marvels genre and then abandon it. *The Faerie Queene* seeks to integrate romance more fully into epic than even Boiardo and Ariosto had done in their genre-defining romantic epics, and Spenser's ambitious mingling of genres makes the Squire's Tale, which Jennifer Goodman has identified as a "composite romance," a natural source of inspiration.[41] But while the tale does provide an example of generic mixing, its self-consciousness about literary inheritance and audience reception speaks even more directly to Spenser's concerns. The Squire, unlike any other Canterbury pilgrim, must tell a tale that pleases both his father the Knight and the rest of the company, and the very presence of father-and-son tale-tellers evokes, as Seth Lerer points out, the genealogical nature of literary tradition.[42] But the Squire's relationship with his father also gives him an air of authority despite his fantastic and rhetorically excessive tale, and we have seen that in claiming to be Chaucer's follower, Spenser too engages the benefits as well as the risks of literary inheritance.

For Spenser, then, evoking the serious resonances of Chaucer's reputation even as he pushed ahead with a continuation of a fantastic Chaucerian romance was a way to embrace the contradictions of his own career, and the Squire's Tale serves the purpose because it sets up the problem most clearly. Spenser not only broke ground in making a serious career out of poetry; he also attempted to write serious poetry about love, and—like the Squire narrator, who in reporting the speech of the foreign knight at Cambyuskan's court says, "I kan nat sowne his stile" (V.105)—Spenser claims inability to match the style of his model and expresses nostalgia for the lost greatness of the past but meanwhile asserts the superiority of his own poem over the works of his predecessors.

Cambina's appearance with her cup of Nepenthe ends the strife of Cambel and Triamond as well as the continuation of the Squire's unfinished story, and thus implicitly claims not only that the Spenserian drink is more salutary than its Ariostan predecessor but also that the poem has the ability to heal its own conflicts. Such "sundrie doubts" as the warring friends, the roughness of Chaucer's verse, the restrictive dangers of literary filiation, and the risks of integrating romance into a serious epic for an English audience are all accorded by the poem's representation of its own operation. Of course, no such program could fully succeed, and if the meaning of Cambina's name alerts us to the power of the poem to bring about change, it also reminds us that the poem is susceptible to changes, historical ones. Both kinds of change carry potential problems for the understanding of poetry. A speaking picture may be the most enlightening form of instruction, but it is also vulnerable to literal-minded misreading, and no matter how well understood a poet is in his own time, he must face the prospect that his work may be "brought to nought by little bits." At the end of his career, Spenser would openly acknowledge that "all that moueth, doth in *Change* delight" (*FQ* VII.viii.2) and seek to project his poetic vision beyond its historical limits. In Book IV, however, we see him coping with doubts about his authors and his readers by becoming the wielder of change, mirroring the fashioning of his readers in the reshaping of his sources.

Notes

1. *Spenser: Poetical Works*, ed. Smith and de Selincourt. All subsequent references to Spenser's poetry and letters are from this edition and appear in the text.

2. Gross, *Spenserian Poetics*, 17.

3. Fyler, "Domesticating the Exotic," 10. On otherness in the Squire's Tale see also Lynch, "East Meets West."

4. Miskimin, *Renaissance Chaucer*, 295. Greene, *Light in Troy*, also discusses the "Renaissance resistance toward its medieval roots," noting that Renaissance humanists often attempted "to exchange one recent past for another, distant one" (34–35).

5. As Miskimin notes, "Roger Ascham, John Fox, and many ardent sixteenth-century reformers read Chaucer's anticlerical satire as prophetic of the dawn to come" (*Renaissance Chaucer*, 97). That Renaissance Englishmen sometimes made Chaucer into a proto-Protestant merely confirms how conscious they were that a great divide separated them from their own past.

6. Roger Ascham, *The Scholemaster*, 289. See the Spenser-Harvey correspondence in *Poetical Works*, 609–43, especially 623–24, 635–36. On 623 Harvey cites Ascham, who had also criticized vernacular verse that did not observe quantity (Ascham, *The Scholemaster*, 291–92). George Puttenham, *Arte of English Poesie*, in Smith, *Elizabethan Critical Essays*, 2:117–24, also offered, with reservations, an argument for imitating classical meter in English; for disparagement of Chaucer's versification by Puttenham, see 2:64, 79, 93, 150.

7. For a lucid history of the hermeneutic model of horizons by one of its leading proponents, see Jauss, *Question and Answer*, 197–231.

8. Bruns, *Hermeneutics Ancient and Modern*, 85.

9. This phrase occurs at I.xii.9, V.xi.59, and V.xi.65. Similar expressions may be found at I.vii.35, II.ix.15, II.xi.19, III.xi.46, V.ii.52, V.ii.54, and V.vi.29.

10. *Poetical Works*, 407.

11. The Squire's Tale from *Riverside Chaucer.* All subsequent references are to this edition and appear in the text. Where early printed editions differ from the *Riverside* in ways that affect my reading of Spenser, I discuss the textual situation in the notes.

12. For a stimulating discussion of how the tale figures its own writing and reading, see the section entitled "The Hermeneutical Squire" in Frese, *"Ars Legendi,"* 169–77. See also Osborn, "The Squire's 'Steed of Brass' as Astrolabe." Both Frese and Osborn suggest the possibilities of the horse/astrolabe as a numerological map for reading *The Canterbury Tales.*

13. Related expressions occur at several other places in *The Canterbury Tales*: "Diverse folk diversely they seyde," (I.3857), which records the responses of the pilgrims to the Miller's Tale; "Diverse men diverse thynges seyden," (II.211); "Diverse men diversely hym tolde" (IV.1469).

14. The phrase in fact occurs nowhere else in the corpus of Middle English texts archived in the University of Virginia Electronic Text Center, Internet. *The Works, 1532*, ed. Thynne, prints "sondry thoughtes" rather than "sondry doutes," a reading left uncorrected in the expanded reprints of 1542, 1550, and 1561. However, "sondry doutes" appears in such editions of the *Canterbury Tales* as those of William Caxton (Westminster, 1484?), *STC* 5083, and Richard Pynson (London, 1526), *STC* 5086, which may also have been available to Spenser. Both Hengwrt and Ellesmere reade "doutes," and Thynne's printing probably began as a scribal mistaking of the initial "d" of "doutes" as an eth. In any case, the appearance of "thoughtes" in Thynne's editions may call for revision of Hieatt's argument concluding "it seems probable that Spenser at all times used only the editions between 1532 and 1561," *Chaucer, Spenser, Milton*, 23. See also Hieatt's essay in the present volume, n. 5, and Anderson's essay, n. 6.

15. My view on the abrupt ending of the tale depends on an overall reading in which I see the intentional "multiplication of doubt" as integral to its meaning, but whether or not Chaucer meant to finish the tale has been an issue hotly debated among Chaucerians. See Peterson, "Finished Fragment"; Duncan, "'Straw for Your Gentilesse'"; Clark's reply to Duncan, "Does the Franklin Interrupt the Squire?" and Seaman, "'Wordes of the Frankeleyn'." In sixteenth-century editions of Chaucer's works, the Merchant, rather than the Franklin, follows the Squire, but the puzzling commentary on the Squire's performance is the same regardless of speaker assignment.

16. Kate Warren called the book "a riot of formlessness." Cited in the *Variorum Spenser* 4:182. See Heberle, "Limitations of Friendship," who says that the virtue of friendship "may be fully realized only in stories" (108).

17. Kane, *Spenser's Moral Allegory*, 109.

18. Greene, *The Vulnerable Text*, 14.

19. Sir Philip Sidney, *Apologie for Poetrie*, in Smith, *Elizabethan Critical Essays*, 1:196.

20. Higgins, "Spenser Reading Chaucer," notes that "Spenser's use of this title (the equivalent of 'Sir') with a surname is a prominent anomaly; the orthodox form would be, in this case, '*Dan Geffrey*'" (19), and cites Pyles, "Dan Chaucer." Higgins goes on to argue that "what Spenser did . . . was to invent a 'lost' martial Chaucer to admire, a pose which allowed him filiation and independence at once" (20). I largely agree with this statement but would replace "martial" with "epic," for the point is not that Spenser represents Chaucer as a poet whose subject matter is warfare but that he greatly elevates his own and Chaucer's poetic importance with a fictionalized account of an epic tradition.

21. Martin, "Spenser, Chaucer," 107.

22. See Greene, *Light in Troy*, 62, 68–69, 73, 307n.33 for a history of the trope as begun by Lucretius and developed by Cicero and Seneca the Elder.

23. Krier, "Orality and Chaucerian Textuality."

24. Higgins sees the alteration "as a necessity imposed . . . by a change in pronunciation, and not as an effort to improve Chaucer's line" (22), but that metrical emendation is necessary at all supports Higgins's larger point that "Spenser's admiration for his literary father is complex and often equivocal" ("Spenser Reading Chaucer," 17).

25. Higgins, "Spenser Reading Chaucer," 19–20. See my note 20.

26. The ambivalence here may be usefully contrasted with Spenser's more straightforward use of this figure in the epilogue to *The Shepheardes Calender* (11). There Spenser tells his poem to follow the steps of Chaucer at a respectful distance, in a passage closely imitating Statius's deferral to Virgil in the closing lines of the *Thebaid* (12.816–17). Near the end of *Troilus and Criseyde* (1791), Chaucer had similarly followed Statius in instructing his poem to "kis the steppes" of the great poets of the past.

27. See chapter 9 of Hollander, *Melodious Guile*, for an account of how no less a versifier than Milton trips over this same imitative crux in Spenser. I am following Hollander's footing by seeing "a curious metrical limp" as an important point of insight into a particular poet's practice of *imitatio* (168).

28. Goldberg, *Endlesse Worke*, 31–33.

29. Anderson, "'Myn auctour,'" 30.

30. "Meet" 11i, *OED*; "mete" 1c, *OED*.

31. Later, after jointly winning the prize in the second day of Satyrane's tournament, Cambel and Triamond attempt to yield the prize to one another, "Each labouring t'aduance the others gest, / And make his praise before his owne preferd" (IV.iv.36). As noted by Goldberg (*Endlesse Worke*, 28), the word *gest* not only refers to the shared exploits of Cambel and Triamond but also suggests the shared storytelling of Chaucer and Spenser.

32. For a perceptive account of the literary history of Canacee, including John Gower's direct treatment of the incest theme and the insistence by Chaucer's own

Man of Law that Chaucer "'no word ne writeth he / Of thilke wikke ensample of Canacee, / That loved hir owene brother synfully'" (II.77–79), see Sanders, "Ruddymane and Canace, Lost and Found."

33. Roche, *Kindly Flame*, 23.

34. Ariosto borrows his account of the love-quenching spring from his precursor Boiardo, *Orlando Innamorato* IV.iii.32ff., where it appears as an elaborate fountain constructed by Merlin's magic. Ariosto describes both springs at *Orlando Furioso* I.78 and the love-extinguishing one at XXXXII.60ff.; Spenser may only be remembering the second passage.

35. Ascham, *The Scholemaster*, 230–31. Javitch, *Proclaiming a Classic*, writes, "having proclaimed that the *Furioso* was as morally edifying as the *Aeneid*, [Harington] had to make sure that nothing in the Italian fiction jeopardized its supposed educative function" (157). On Harington's moralizing revisions of Ariosto's fabulous episodes see Lee, "The English Ariosto."

36. See Helgerson, *Self-Crowned Laureates*, 55–67, for an account of how Spenser broke new ground in making love poetry a serious enterprise.

37. Ascoli, *Ariosto's Bitter Harmony*, while noting that the *Orlando Furioso*'s "strongest impulse is toward evasion from historical claims of church and state" (6), masterfully demonstrates how seriously engaged Ariosto was with various cultural and intellectual crises of his time. Whether or not Spenser perceived this engagement, the evasive—even escapist—surface of Ariosto's poem would have made Spenser's imitation of it a potentially risky endeavor. Puttenham's comment comes from the *Arte of English Poesie*, in Smith, *Elizabethan Critical Essays*, 2:64. Yeager, "Literary Theory at the Close of the Middle Ages," offers a finely nuanced argument about the varying degrees of Chaucer's seriousness implied by the selections of his works available in early printed editions.

38. For a different view on the reputations of the two poets, see Harington's preface to his translation of *Orlando Furioso*, where he defends Ariosto against the charge of lasciviousness by arguing, "I can smile at the finesse of some that will condemne [Ariosto], and yet not onely allow but admire our *Chawcer*, who both in words & sence incurreth far more the reprehension of flat scurrilitie" (Smith, *Elizabethan Critical Essays*, 2:215). This argument assumes Ariosto has a lascivious reputation and Chaucer a serious one (despite his scurrility) even as it suggests the range of Elizabethan opinion on the moral qualities of the two poets.

39. Cheney, "Spenser's Completion," 137.

40. Spenser does, however, make significant use of the Knight's Tale in Book IV even though it is the Squire's Tale that he explicitly claims to follow. As Hieatt has demonstrated, in matters of plot and theme Spenser borrows as much or more from the former as from the latter (*Chaucer, Spenser, Milton*, 77–78). My purpose here is not to deny the relevance of other Chaucerian texts but to show that Spenser's direct invocation of the Squire's Tale is more than a red herring, and in fact reveals what Spenser learned from Chaucer about a poet's relationship to his readers.

Lawton, *Chaucer's Narrators*, notes many parallels between the Squire's Tale and the *Orlando Furioso*, and even goes as far as to say that for Spenser, Chaucer "was the English Ariosto" (120). By emphasizing the tonal similarities between Chaucerian and Ariostan romance, Lawton, who takes Spenser's reference to Ariosto as a "passing tribute" (119), misses the radical difference in tone between Spenser's allusions to his English and to his Italian precursors.

41. Goodman, "Chaucer's Squire's Tale."

42. Lerer, *Chaucer and His Readers*, 58.

CHAPTER 7

Idolatrous Idylls

Protestant Iconoclasm, Spenser's *Daphnaïda,* and Chaucer's *Book of the Duchess*

GLENN STEINBERG

Edmund Spenser's *Daphnaïda* has been the object of considerable censure among critics. By far the most common response to the poem has been distaste. Francis Palgrave characterized the elegy as lacking "two elements which poetry can hardly dispense with, contrast and sincerity. And the sense of this latter deficiency is intensified by the pastoral form here used without any specific appropriateness, and prolonged through more than eighty stanzas."[1]

W. L. Renwick attributes what he takes to be the poem's failure to its "unsuitable model" and to the "*contaminatio* of pastoral allegory and medieval symbolism—of Virgil and Chaucer," a combination that yields "not a very happy result."[2] William Nelson judges Spenser's elegy "not the happiest of his experiments," while other commentators, including C. S. Lewis and Normand Berlin, are harsher, dismissing the poem as "radically vulgar" and "morbidly depressing."[3]

More recently, kinder critics have tried to redeem *Daphnaïda* by censuring its central character rather than the poem as a whole. Thus Duncan Harris and Nancy Steffen argue that Spenser intentionally portrays Alcyon as "repellent" and "solipsistic" in order to imply criticism of "the excesses of Alcyon's grief." William Oram characterizes Alcyon as "an impatient and excessive mourner," whose conduct amounts to "a warning against grieving too much." A. Leigh DeNeef views Alcyon as a "false poet," one who is "unable or unwilling, in Sidneyan terms, to translate fictional action into ethical action," failing to learn the ethical lessons implicit in his own fable of the white lion.[4] Such defenders of Spenser's poem still find most of it dreary and excessive, and they generally agree that the poem "will never be an inviting one."[5] The argument that Spenser intended the distaste that readers feel for Alcyon perhaps reflects our own embarrassment at bodily expressions of grief; in any case it takes the poem as an exhortation against the evils of Alcyon's self-absorption. According to this reading, the poem is a didactic meditation on the theme of moderation and calls upon Alcyon's historical original, Arthur Gorges, to temper his "outragious passion" at the death of his wife, Douglas Howard, the Daphne of the poem (*Daph* 555).[6]

But *Daphnaïda* becomes a more inviting and a more interesting text when we see it not as a failed experiment or a moralizing meditation but as a refiguration and response to Chaucer's *Book of the Duchess,* by a poet who brings to the formal and affective norms of elegy certain Protestant motifs and points of theology. By juxtaposing the two works, we may see, for instance, differences between the artistic decorum of the late Middle Ages and the passionate Protestant iconoclasm of Elizabethan England. While Dennis Kay, among others, argues that Spenser's poem enacts a relatively optimistic humanist view of the possibilities of human invention, I see the poem rather as reflecting a Reformation emphasis on the limits of the infected will and a distrust of art.[7] John King argues that "Spenser's poetry is inherently iconoclastic in its attack of the abuse or misapplication of art. . . . [He] shares the early Protestant assumption that iconoclasm involves a complex dialectic in which attacks on 'false' images are connected to a countervailing effort to construct acceptable forms of 'true' literary and visual art."[8] I see Spenser's *Daphnaïda* in precisely these terms—as an attack on a false image of grief connected to an effort to construct an acceptable form of true elegiac poetry. In this respect, the banishment of the Muses from Spenser's poem seems to me entirely and essentially iconoclastic. Thus it will not do to assume that Spenser's poem is an unsuccessful copy of Chaucer's, an abortive attempt to accomplish the same ends in the same ways, as if Spenser's poetic intent should coincide with Chaucer's in spite of the centuries that separated them. *Daphnaïda* movingly represents, in its implicit picture of Chaucer's work and in its imitative practice, a capacious vision of art which is no longer available to the Protestant poet two centuries later.[9]

The characters of the *Daphnaïda* live in an impoverished, fallen world, one that has lost innocence, beauty, and a lusty vitality associated with Chaucer. In this respect, Spenser's poem contrasts sharply with *The Book of the Duchess,* which celebrates the innocence and tragic beauty of loss. In *Daphnaïda,* loss is not innocent or beautiful but devastating and destabilizing, an effect of sin in the world. The Chaucerian literary past is attractive but also representative of an idyllic/idolatrous poetic. Chaucer's elegy arises out of an idiom of courtly decorum, out of an assumption of respect for privilege and an abiding faith in art as an ennobling and enabling medium. Spenser's poem, on the other hand, aims to destroy the artistic idols of literary grace and beauty in favor of an iconoclastic Christian truth and suffering, with tones of dark, impassioned complaint and apocalyptic prophecy. In this context, Spenser repudiates the Muses as idolatrous symbols of art and beauty:

> Ne let the sacred Sisters here be hight,
> Though they of sorrowe heavilie can sing;
> For even their heavie song would breede delight:
> But here no tunes, save sobs and grones shall ring. (*Daph* 11–14)

Given my insistence on Spenser's inversions of Chaucer's assumptions about art and faith, it is worth detailing the differences within the similarities of the two poems. Both Chaucer and Spenser describe themselves as restless and sad in the openings. Both speakers meet a mourning figure in black and try to discover the cause of sorrow in the mourner. Both mourners recite a formal complaint, tell a riddle as explanation for their grief, and complain against Fortune, who has robbed each of his wife.[10] These rough plot lines and character types are enough to suggest that Spenser's elegy quite consciously invites comparison with Chaucer's. So it is significant that Spenser's sketch of Alcyon—wandering, wild, "forlorne" (*Daph* 45)—casts a light on Chaucer's mourning Knight that makes the latter seem strong, stable, radiant with youthful beauty even in his grief. Alcyon first appears with "carelesse locks, uncombed and unshorne / . . . and beard all over growne" (*Daph* 43–44), carrying a "*Jaakob* staffe in hand . . . / Like to some Pilgrim, come from farre away" (*Daph* 41–42). Chaucer's Knight has "[u]pon hys berd but lytel her" (*BD* 456); he is "Of good mochel, and ryght yong therto" (*BD* 454). Chaucer's Knight carries no aura of wandering but is seated firmly against "an ook, an huge tree" (*BD* 447), surrounded by the vernal energies and extravagance of the Edenic "floury grene" (*BD* 398),

> As thogh the erthe envye wolde
> To be gayer than the heven,
> To have moo floures, swiche seven,
> As in the welken sterres be. (*BD* 406–9)

This is a world that "had forgete the povertee / That wynter, thorgh hys colde morwes, / Had mad hyt suffre" (*BD* 410–12). The boundless innocence of this world is affirmed in the grieving but fundamentally untainted

Knight; despite his loss, he is an ideal youth, noble in his naïve simplicity and promising in his beardless potential.

The unkempt beard of Alcyon, in this light, characterizes him as altogether wilder and more extreme than Chaucer's Man in Black, and Alcyon's behavior matches his coarse mien. Chaucer's mourner had failed to notice the Dreamer's greeting because he is absorbed in the deeply probing intellectual questions that accompany his grief; he "argued with his owne thoght, / And in hys wyt disputed faste / Why and how hys lyf myght laste" (*BD* 504–6), but Alcyon, restless and fierce, "lookt a side as in disdainefull wise, / Yet stayed not: till I againe did call" (*Daph* 59–60). His setting is wintry, "open fields, whose flowring pride opprest / With early frosts, had lost their beautie faire" (*Daph* 27–28); his world measures its fall not only from Eden but also from a loosely Chaucerian literary past, its vigor and luxuriance simultaneously lamented and suspected. Thus Alcyon was once one who "wont full merrilie to pipe and daunce / And fill with pleasance every wood and plaine" (*Daph* 55–56). In contrast to Chaucer, Spenser chooses not to idealize Alcyon's youth or his world, refusing outright to make Alcyon an innocent knight of "good mochel" or to place Alcyon in the idyllic setting typical of dream poems. Instead he inhabits a world of decay.

It is possible to argue that Spenser's decision not to idealize Alcyon's grief results from an implicit criticism of Alcyon's alleged excess and solipsism, from Alcyon's obsession with his own grief and the resulting reduplication of the consequences of the Fall in him and the world around him.[11] But Alcyon's "excessive" grief might also reflect a fundamental change in the conceptualization of suffering and death between Chaucer's time and Spenser's. Chaucer's sense of loss is sympathetic and awed. It does not minimize pain or belittle suffering, but it attempts to deepen and ennoble grief through art. As the encounter with the Black Knight progresses, the Knight's expressions of grief become increasingly personal as well as more noble and moving. He begins with a conventional complaint against death (*BD* 475–86), a complaint so conventional that the Dreamer may or may not even recognize it as describing a real loss.[12] Chaucer's Man in Black moves next to allegory (*BD* 617–86), the traditional language of courtly love (*BD* 759–1125), and personal history (*BD* 1145–1297), drawing closer and closer to an open, personal statement of grief, even as he brings himself, the Dreamer, and the reader to a greater understanding of his relationship with "goode faire White" (*BD* 948). The Knight is right to say, "thow nost what thow menest; / I have lost more than thou wenest" (*BD* 1137–38). Neither the Dreamer nor the reader nor even the Knight himself can fully understand or appreciate the revelation that "[s]he ys ded" (*BD* 1309) until they have been led from initial considerations of form and convention to a later, enlarged understanding of the mourner's loss—an understanding made possible only by a passage through time and the processes of reading. And this reading involves the reader in necessary discriminations among literary forms, discourses, and their implicit ethics.

The education proffered by Chaucer's poem leads the Dreamer and the reader to true, reliable knowledge of the meaning and depth of the Knight's sorrow and makes possible affective acknowledgments not available to the Dreamer initially. Early on he frankly admits, "I have felynge in nothyng" (*BD* 11), experiencing only a sentimental "pittee" for Alcyone, a "pittee" that lasts but a "morwe" (*BD* 97, 99). But much later he can stand in speechless sympathy: "Is that youre los? Be God, hyt ys routhe!" (*BD* 1310). Only after the "hert-huntyng," which Sandra Pierson Prior identifies as a hunt for the hurting heart, can the Dreamer and the reader awaken to full acknowledgment of the Knight's grief.[13] In this way, Chaucer displays a deep-rooted belief in the nobility of suffering and in the power of sympathy to encompass and circumscribe pain.

Spenser's understanding of grief and loss is qualitatively different from that of Chaucer in *The Book of the Duchess*. Spenser's representation of loss in his elegy precludes the closure of Chaucer's poem, just as it precludes the idealized and ennobling innocence of Chaucer's dreamlike Knight. Not surprisingly, it also precludes much of Chaucer's slow "hert-huntyng," eliminating all of Chaucer's prefatory material, including nearly all the dream frame and the initial, symbolic episodes of the dream itself. In *Daphnaïda,* Spenser is a poet of more immediate and more piercing loss, and his poem contrasts with the innocence and grace of his predecessor's richly adorned—and artistically contained—"hert-huntyng." Alcyon's "uncombed and unshorne" appearance is therefore less the result of blameworthy and excessive grief than it is the result of living in a world in which pain is immediate and overpowering—not a potential object of artistic beauty and grace. The stained-glass windows and paintings of "the story of Troye" and "al the Romaunce of the Rose," which Chaucer sees at the very beginning of his dream—artwork portraying love and loss so beautifully "[t]hat to beholde hyt was gret joye" (*BD* 325–26, 334)—are wholly inappropriate to Spenser's poem, while in Chaucer they are figures for the aesthetic artifact itself. The making of them formalizes, idealizes, and ennobles art's origins in pain, loss, mutability. This richness and grace are foreign to Spenser's perspective on loss in *Daphnaïda*.

It does not follow that Chaucer's work, embracing traditional aesthetic values and their role in suffering human lives, is necessarily superior to Spenser's work, embracing as it does contrasting values of passion, rawness, and iconoclasm. In contrast to Chaucer's idyllic dream world, made all the more beautiful by its transience and its momentary sadness, Spenser's poem effectively introduces his reader to a world and a kind of poetry marred and made ugly by loss and mutability:

> . . . all I see is vaine and transitorie,
> Ne will be helde in any stedfast plight,
> But in a moment loose their grace and glorie. (*Daph* 495–97)

Spenser sacrifices the facile beauty of art, now identified as idolatrous, for the vivid, iconoclastic truth of mutability and, in the process, creates a new beauty and a new aesthetic—a dark and disturbing vision potentially as compelling as Chaucer's lovely, graceful one.

This dark vision arises specifically from Spenser's sense of himself in this poem as an apocalyptic poet, embodying a prophetic, Calvinist theology that sees and mourns the cosmic struggle between good and evil in the world. In the poem's riddle and complaint, Alcyon speaks the language of apocalyptic prophecy and biblical lament, the language adopted in Protestant, Calvinist circles to mourn the imperfections of this fallen world. Alcyon becomes a Protestant everyman, a voice "breaking foorth" in the Babylonian exile of this life (*Daph* 196), a voice that speaks for all who have glimpsed the promised land but must anxiously await "the redemption of our bodie" before they can enter the kingdom of God in its fullness (Romans 8:23).

In characterizing the Black Knight's loss, Chaucer uses first and foremost the image of a game of chess played with "fals Fortune" (*BD* 618), an image that portrays death as a product of chance and the world's mutability. Spenser, by way of contrast, represents Alcyon's loss through "[t]he riddle of thy loved Lionesse" (*Daph* 177). The white lion was central in the Howard family's arms. But the Howard lioness of Douglas Howard is also intimately linked to a famous passage of messianic prophecy in Isaiah:

> The wolfe also shal dwell with the lambe, and the leoparde shal lye with the kid, and the calfe, and the lyon, and the fat beast together, and a litle childe shal lead them. And the kowe and the beare shal

> fede: their yong ones shal lie together: and the lyon shal eat strawe like the bullocke. (Isaiah 11:6–7)

While Alcyon's Lionesse lives, this earthly paradise of peace and prosperity is temporarily realized, for

> I her fram'd and wan so to my bent,
> That shee became so meeke and milde of cheare,
> As the least lamb in all my flock that went. (*Daph* 124–26)

Like the straw-eating lion in Isaiah's apocalyptic vision, Alcyon's Lionesse peacefully coexists with lambs, even guarding them most carefully (*Daph* 134–38). Alcyon is therefore greatly blessed in the possession of this Lionesse, blessed with the early, earthly fulfillment of Isaiah's prophecy. In his love for Daphne, he has glimpsed the kingdom to come.[14]

Because Alcyon's Lionesse is linked to Isaiah's prophecy in this way, her death becomes more than the simple loss of a beloved wife and companion. The fulfillment of Isaiah's prophecy of messianic peace and prosperity, temporarily glimpsed in the Lionesse, is unexpectedly disrupted and postponed. Alcyon is suddenly and painfully deprived of the joy of the world to come and returned to the imperfect world of the present, so that, like Paul, he must suffer until "the sonnes of God shalbe reueiled" and justice be finally restored on earth (Romans 8:19). As Paul writes:

> we knowe that euerie creature groneth with vs also, and trauaileth in paine together vnto this present. And not onely *the creature,* but we also which haue the first frutes of the Spirit, euen we do sigh in our selues, waiting for the adopcion, *euen* the redemption of our bodie. (Romans 8:22–23)

Because of his experience with the Lionesse, Alcyon too sighs within himself, waiting for the redemption of his life and body in this world, and that sighing breaks forth in his bitter complaint against the imperfections and injustices that postpone the promised paradise on earth.

Like the Psalmist mourning in exile, Alcyon experiences an undying grief over the postponed redemption, vowing that

> My bread shall be the anguish of my mynd,
> My drink the teares which fro mine eyes do raine,
> My bed the ground that hardest I may fynde[.] (*Daph* 375–77)

> My teares haue bene my meat daie and night, while they daiely say vnto me, Where is thy God? (Psalm 42:3)

Even Alcyon's beloved Daphne, whom some readers have seen as the model of Christian resignation and consolation in the poem,[15] bemoans the unredeemed suffering of this world in terms very like those of another psalm:

> Our daies are full of dolour and disease,
> Our life afflicted with incessant paine,
> That nought on earth may lessen or appease. (*Daph* 274–76)

> The time of our life *is* threscore yeres & ten, and if they be of strength, foure score yeres: yet their strength *is* but labour and sorowe. (Psalm 90:10)

Alcyon's grief is therefore hardly the excessive grief of one without reason or faith. Rather, it is the overpowering sorrow of a spiritual exile who has glimpsed paradise for a brief moment and longs for the permanent realization of that paradise on this earth. As Calvin writes, "seeing we are not yet indued with fulness, it is no marvel though we be moved with disquietness . . . for where there is a feeling of misery there is also mourning."[16] The Black Knight's loss of his "fers" at chess simply does not compare with this intense spiritual deprivation (*BD* 654).

Indeed, every death is a painful reminder of the postponement of spiritual "fulness." Death is not merely the result of the mutability of "fals Fortune," although it does arise from this "worlds ficklenesse" (*Daph* 150). Death is also the great adversary, the continuing sign of human sinfulness and imperfection, "the wages of sinne" (Romans 6:23), unconquered in us as yet by Christ despite our having received "the first frutes of the Spirit" (Romans 8:23). As Calvin notes, "the price of our redemption was so paid of Christ, that death, nevertheless, might hold us yet bound in his bonds; yea, we carry it within us."[17] Death's hold on us will continue until the end of time, because "[t]he last enemie that shalbe destroyed *is* death" (1 Corinthians 15:26). The Lionesse's death is therefore much more than the mere loss of a wife. Her death is a reminder of our state of deprivation and suffering as we await the final redemption to come—a reminder that justifies Alcyon's passionate grief.

In the face of that deprivation and suffering, good Christians should, according to Calvin, experience "a twofold affection . . . namely, that they, being pressed with the feeling of the present misery, mourn. Secondly, That, nevertheless, they do patiently expect a deliverance."[18] Alcyon in fact experiences this "twofold affection." He is clearly "pressed with the feeling of the present misery," so much so that he appears at times to abandon the patience and hope of Calvin's second "affection." He cries out, for example, against the gross injustice of the heavenlie powers,

> Which so unjustly doe their judgements share;
> Mongst earthly wights, as to afflict so sore
> The innocent, as those which do transgresse,
> And doe not spare the best or fairest, more
> Than worst or fowlest, but doe both oppresse. (*Daph* 198–203)

But this near blasphemous lament is not Alcyon's final word on the matter. In fact, it is quite literally his first word—at the very beginning of his complaint. In the course of that complaint, he comes to express in at least one sense how God's actions might be just, since

> The good and righteous he away doth take,
> To plague th'unrighteous which alive remaine:
> But the ungodly ones he doth forsake,
> By living long to multiplie their paine[.] (*Daph* 358–61)

In this way, the death of the innocent even becomes a form of mercy on God's part, a way of limiting their "paine" in contrast with that of the unrighteous.

Alcyon's anguished cry against the unjust "heavenlie powers" is therefore merely the initial, impassioned response of one who mourns, "being pressed with the feeling of the present misery." That passionate response is not at all condemned by Calvin, since mourning is an essential part of Christian salvation itself. God "doth not call his [people] unto the triumph before he have exercised them in the warfare of sufferance." As a result,

> it is expedient for us to labour in earth, to be oppressed, to mourn, to be afflicted, yea, to lie as it were half dead. . . . For they who covet a visible salvation, they put themselves by it, renouncing hope which is ordained of God to be keeper of it.

If salvation did not include suffering and grief, it would not try our faith and hope. It would not "exercise" our "sufferance." Salvation therefore comes precisely through the sobs and groans of prayer, "because God doth not . . . afflict his [people] with miseries, that they should inwardly devour up a hidden or secret sorrow; but that, by prayer, they should (exonerate and) ease themselves, and so exercise their faith."[19]

But that faith must result in Calvin's second "affection," by which the godly "patiently expect a deliverance." In Alcyon's case, he in fact explicitly experiences this "affection." Indeed, Alcyon confidently assumes that Daphne will deliver him because of her promise to him. He is sure that

> when I have with sorrow satisfyde
> Th'importune fates, which vengeance on me seeke,
> And th'heavens with long languor pacifyde,
> She for pure pitie of my sufferance meeke,
> Will send for me; for which I daylie long,
> And will till then my painfull penance eeke[.] (*Daph* 386–91)

He is sure that at Daphne's invitation he, too, will enjoy "deliverance" and "toward joyes" at "the bridale feast," a place where "no worlds sad care, nor wasting woe / May come their happie quiet to molest" (*Daph* 268, 279–80, 283–84). As a result, until her summons comes, he will willingly endure his suffering at being left behind with patient "sufferance":

> Sith then they so have ordred, I will pay
> Penance to her according their decree,
> And to her ghost doe service day by day. (*Daph* 369–71)

He will mourn, "being pressed with the feeling of the present misery," but he will willingly endure that misery as long as necessary—with patient expectation and unshakable faith.

Such Calvinist doctrines have ethical and epistemological consequences for Spenser's narrator and for the whole of the poem. As in Chaucer's poem, the reader of *Daphnaïda* learns much about the nature of mutability and suffering through the figure of the narrator. But unlike Chaucer's Dreamer, who is humble and uncertain, Spenser's narrator is at first confident and unabashed, absolutely certain of his grasp of Alcyon's situation. Also unlike Chaucer's Dreamer, Spenser's narrator sees his understanding and confidence diminish rather than increase as the poem progresses. His grasp of "this worlds vainnesse and lifes wretchednesse" (*Daph* 34) is unsettled rather than clarified in the course of the poem, making him a sadder and a wiser man by the poem's end. Alcyon's grief confronts him with the living, breathing reality of his own "troublous thought" and "meditation" on mutability (*Daph* 29, 33), confronting him also with the poverty of those musings before the immediate, overpowering presence of real pain. In the end, the narrator proves powerless before that pain—in stark contrast to Chaucer's Dreamer, who creates beauty out of the suffering in his dream, vowing upon waking "to put this sweven in ryme / As I kan best" (*BD* 1332–33). Unable to match this act of restorative, idolatrous creativity, Spenser's narrator becomes the means by which the reader learns the limits of consolation and art.

The initial confidence of Spenser's narrator leads him to brave Alcyon's "disdainefull" looks without fear. Unlike Chaucer's humbly polite Dreamer, Spenser's narrator actively and forcefully confronts Alcyon and his grief. Chaucer's Dreamer stands in humble silence before the Black Knight when that mournful figure fails to notice

> how y stood
> Before hym and did of myn hood,
> And had ygret hym as I best koude,
> Debonayrly, and nothyng lowde. (*BD* 515–18)

But when Alcyon is unresponsive to the gentle inquiry of Spenser's narrator he "againe did call," even though Alcyon clearly wishes to avoid him (*Daph* 57–63). His insistence that Alcyon speak to him, born of compassion and curiosity, will not be denied.[20]

This confidence on the part of the narrator is, however, vulnerable. It arises out of his overestimation of his own "miserie" (*Daph* 36). Before meeting Alcyon, he unabashedly characterizes himself as "of many most, / Most miserable man" (*Daph* 37–38). As a consequence, when he first encounters Alcyon, he confidently insists on his status as "fit mate thy wretched case to heare" (*Daph* 65). Unlike Chaucer's Dreamer, who stresses only his compassion and his desire "to make yow hool" (*BD* 554), Spenser's narrator emphasizes his own "like wofulnesse" and "like cause with thee to waile and weepe" (*Daph* 64, 66). Whereas Chaucer's Dreamer urges the Black Knight to tell his grief, simply because "[p]araunter hyt may ese youre herte" (*BD* 556), Spenser's narrator argues for revelation specifically because "[g]riefe findes some ease by him that like does beare" (*Daph* 67). He assumes that Alcyon's sorrow is no greater than his own, and he is therefore confident that he can provide "some ese" of pain through his commiseration.

When next he speaks, however, the narrator has heard Alcyon tell "[t]he riddle of thy loved Lionesse" (*Daph* 177), and his interpretive confidence is shaken. He is filled with "pittie" (*Daph* 170), and he admits that "painefull is thy plight, / That it in me breeds *almost equall paine*" (*Daph* 174–75; emphasis mine). He no longer presumes to call his own grief "like wofulnesse," and he is puzzled and unsettled by Alcyon's strange tale. As his understanding of the depth of Alcyon's suffering increases, his capacity to identify and sympathize with that suffering diminishes. Unlike Chaucer's Dreamer, he has already begun to realize that Alcyon has indeed "lost more than thow wenest" (*BD* 744), but he cannot fully comprehend or assimilate this greater loss.

Even after Alcyon reveals that "*Daphne* thou knewest . . . / She now is dead" (*Daph* 183–84), the narrator is at a loss to share in Alcyon's grief. Unlike Chaucer's Dreamer, who embraces the Black Knight's sorrow for his lady when he learns that "[s]he ys ded" (*BD* 1309), Spenser's narrator does not yield to pain, "[a]ll were my selfe through griefe in deadly drearing" (*Daph* 189). Instead, he tries in vain to console Alcyon and "mitigate / The stormie passion of his troubled brest" (*Daph* 191–92). Like Chaucer's Dreamer earlier in the encounter with the Black Knight, he cautions Alcyon—by "lightly him uprearing" when he swoons (*Daph* 187) and by advising him "with milde counsaile" (*Daph* 191)—to "[h]ave some pitee on your nature / That formed yow to creature" (*BD* 715–16), and Alcyon, becoming "more empassionate" (*Daph* 193), replies with his lengthy complaint, expanding upon the Knight's "I kan not soo" (*BD* 720). The narrator does not see that Alcyon's grief, like the "stubborne steed, that is with curb restrained" (*Daph* 194), cannot be controlled with mere words of comfort.

In Chaucer, the narrator's education in the true nature of sorrow develops via a progress through diverse literary discourses and generic affiliations, unsettling his initial lack of feeling. In Spenser, the narrator is more starkly dumbfounded before the relentless violence of "[t]he heaviest plaint that ever I heard sound" (*Daph* 541). He speaks no more of "almost equall paine." In the face of the depth and passion of Alcyon's complaint, he retreats from its incomprehensible suffering and vainly attempts "him to recomfort as I might" (*Daph* 546). But his pity is helpless and ineffectual, though "I sore griev'd to see his wretched case" (*Daph* 553). He is left powerless and lost, disoriented and frightened before a grief beyond his imagining or understanding. Unlike Chaucer's Dreamer, he neither fully grasps what has happened nor knows what to do. Whereas Chaucer's Dreamer eventually understands and embraces the Black Knight's loss, rendering that loss into a poetic meditation on poetry, Spenser's narrator fails either to touch or to capture Alcyon's wounded soul. Uncomprehending, he fails to restore order and is left, troubled and uncertain, amid chaos and fear.

Significantly, Chaucer's dream vision ends with a sense of stability and closure:

> this kyng
> Gan homwarde for to ryde
> Unto a place, was there besyde,
> Which was from us but a lyte—
> A long castel with walles white,
> Be Seynt Johan, on a ryche hil. (*BD* 1314–19)

But Spenser's poem ends without such closure. Instead, the narrator watches Alcyon depart and sadly acknowledges that "what of him became I cannot weene" (*Daph* 567). Alcyon's grief is so great and inscrutable that he disappears into a mist of mystery and silence. Order is disrupted, and Alcyon's violent, chaotic sorrow is still at large, threatening all other security with its incomprehensible violence, continuing on *out there* somewhere.

Through the narrator's unsettling experience of this pervasive sorrow, the reader, too, is unsettled. The reader, too, loses confidence and control before the unexpected intensity of Alcyon's grief. Alcyon is as much a threat to the reader's stability as he is to the narrator's, and like the narrator, we want to see Alcyon controlled and contained within "my Cabinet" (*Daph* 558). But Alcyon will not be contained. Instead, he emerges out of the shadows and returns to them at will, lurking just out of reach like the narrator's own

> troublous thought,
> Which dayly doth my weaker wit possesse,
> Ne lets it rest, untill it forth have brought
> Her long borne Infant, fruit of heavinesse[.] (*Daph* 29–32)

Alcyon fills our world, as he fills the narrator's "open fields" (*Daph* 27), with "death" and "hellish hags" (*Daph* 565–66). He becomes almost an allegorical figure for "lifes wretchednesse," a projection of our own—and the narrator's—fear.

Like Alcyon, moreover, Spenser is a man of passion, a man of faith, and a Calvinist who lurks just out of our reach in the poem. He was a man of apocalyptic longing for the kingdom to come, a man of sincere disquiet over the instability of this world, and a man of immediate, piercing loss and pain. His poem incarnates an apocalyptic, Calvinist system of images and paradigms much honored in Elizabeth's Protestant England, a system that includes zealous acts of iconoclasm. In the case of *Daphnaïda* that iconoclasm is, I think, a clear and powerful response to Chaucer. Spenser's poem does not lack sincerity, as Palgrave argues, nor is it a poor relation of Chaucer's poem, as Berlin supposes, nor yet is it a stern counsel against grieving too much, as Oram maintains. It is a "breaking foorth" that must break the idols of beauty in order to create a new, truer poetry.

Notes

1. Palgrave is quoted at length in the *Variorum Spenser*, 7:429.

2. Renwick, *Variorum* 7:432.

3. See Nelson, *Poetry of Edmund Spenser*, 69; Lewis, *English Literature in the Sixteenth Century*, 370; Berlin, "Chaucer's *Book of the Duchess*," 289. Martin understands these sorts of discomfort with *Daphnaïda* as "as a result of critical discomfort with the whole idea of elegy" ("Spenser, Chaucer," 83); "[t]aking a less dismissive attitude towards elegy's vagaries might help us to cease imposing our current definitions of health and sociability on imaginative work. . . . A rehabilitated appreciation of elegy reminds us of the poetic value of melancholia, withdrawal, intensity, and distraction" (108).

4. See Harris and Steffen, "Other Side of the Garden"; Oram, "*Daphnaïda*"; DeNeef, *Spenser and the Motives of Metaphor*, 41–50.

5. Oram, "*Daphnaïda*," 141.

6. Citations from *Daphnaïda* (*Daph*) and *The Faerie Queene* (*FQ*) are taken from the *Variorum*; I cite also from *Riverside Chaucer* (*The Book of the Duchess*, cited here as *BD*) and *The Geneva Bible*.

7. See Kay, *Melodious Tears*, 47–52. Kay argues that the poem's "consolatory structure" emerges from the elegy's "attempt to depict, to advocate, and teach the role artistic invention can play when human wit is challenged to make sense of premature and unexpected death" (48).

8. King, *Spenser's Poetry*, 65–67. There is a good deal of controversy on the nature and degree of Spenser's Protestantism and his commitment to Calvinism. Bieman sees a marked contrast between his poetic "stance as Christian-Neoplatonic *vates*" and the "harshly Calvinistic attitude to fallen creation" (*Plato Baptized*, 190). In *Edmund Spenser*, Hume emphasizes Spenser's ties to "militant Protestantism" (7–9). But Gross concludes that "Spenser . . . neither attempted nor could . . . master so extreme a rhetoric" as that advanced by the "tradition of Protestant iconoclasm" (*Spenserian Poetics*, 252).

9. For the view that Spenser failed to reproduce a Chaucerian poem, see Berlin, "Chaucer's *The Book of the Duchess*," 283.

10. This list is largely condensed from Nadal, "Spenser's *Daphnaïda*."

11. See, e.g., Oram, "*Daphnaïda*," 143–45. In this respect, one might compare Alcyon with Timias in *The Faerie Queene* IV or with Despair in Book I. Like Timias and Despair, Alcyon might seem to be making a hell out of this life by needlessly and wrongfully "[s]pending his daies in dolour and despaire" (*FQ* IV.vii.43). But unlike Timias, Alcyon neither becomes brutish and mute nor wrong-

fully retreats from life into "his cabin" (*FQ* IV.vii.38). Rather, he vows that his "wearie feete shall ever wandring be" and that he himself will serve as a living exemplum of this world's fickleness for all his fellow shepherds (*Daph* 457, 491–539). In much the same way, unlike Despair, Alcyon never once proposes suicide as a solution to grief, since "Daphne hence departing . . . bad me stay, till she for me did send" (*Daph* 454–55). Indeed, rather than enjoying the comfort of Despair's "[s]leepe after toyle, port after stormie seas, / Ease after warre, death after life" (*FQ* I.ix.40), Alcyon knows no sleep or rest until God, through Daphne, calls him from this life (*Daph* 456–76). As a result, Alcyon resembles Arthur at least as much as he resembles Timias and Despair, since Arthur also mourns his separation from his beloved and vows never to rest until reunited with her (e.g., *FQ* I.ix.15).

12. For debate on the Dreamer's responses through Chaucer's poem, see, e.g., Bronson, "*Book of the Duchess* Re-Opened"; French, "Man in Black's Lyric."

13. See Prior, "*Routhe* and *Hert-Huntyng*." Some critics interpret the Knight's sorrow as an error, to be corrected by the Dreamer, e.g., Shoaf, "'Mutatio Amoris.'" Fradenburg has argued that in essays on the *Book of the Duchess*, "all too frequently the dead, the woman, and the elegy itself are abandoned in favor of some form of transcendence," which Fradenburg sees as "elegiac misogyny"; see "'Voice Memorial,'" 185–86. But Chaucer's elegy overtly invites transcendence of death and mourning through *pitee* and *routhe,* in a way that makes it very unlike Spenser's poem. Although that overt invitation may be problematized, the gender implications of such transcendence are outside the scope of this chapter.

14. The contrast between Chaucer's secular image of a game of chess and Spenser's religious allusion to the lion of Isaiah draws attention to a significant difference between Chaucer's "idolatrous" poetic and Spenser's iconoclastic Protestant one. Chaucer's poem is decidedly pagan in flavor, largely without religious references or symbols. A few scholars have tried to see in its conclusion an allusion to the new Jerusalem—e.g., Huppé and Robertson, *Fruyt and Chaf*, 91–92. But by and large, critics agree that Chaucer's elegy ignores the Christian response to death in favor of a secular, poetic one. Spenser's conscious insertion of Christian imagery seems therefore to be a denial of the efficacy and relevance of Chaucer's secular poetic. By simultaneously alluding to Isaiah and the white lion of the Howard coat of arms, moreover, Spenser ingeniously combines apocalyptic and topical references in a single image. For other, less favorable views of Spenser's lion image, however, see Berlin, "Chaucer's *The Book of the Duchess*," 286; Harris and Steffen, "Other Side of the Garden," 30–31; Pigman, *English Renaissance Elegy*, 78.

15. Daphne's brief appearance in the poem has been cited by many critics as the only moment of Christian transcendence and consolation in the midst of Alcyon's gloom (see Harris and Steffen, "Other Side of the Garden," 30, 32–33; Oram, "*Daphnaïda*," 149–50; Pigman, *English Renaissance Elegy*, 78–80). My observations here, however, suggest that Daphne is no less gloomy than Alcyon.

16. Calvin, *Commentary*, 220.
17. Calvin, *Commentary*, 221.
18. Calvin, *Commentary*, 220.
19. Calvin, *Commentary*, 221–23.
20. Although many critics have commented upon Alcyon's rudeness in turning away from the narrator (e.g., Oram, "*Daphnaïda*," 143–45), few critics have commented upon the narrator's possible rudeness in foisting himself and his consolation upon Alcyon (cf. Oram, "*Daphnaïda*," 145–46). In the same way, few critics have noted the narrator's progressively diminished confidence in his "like wofulnesse," a development that I trace here (cf. Harris and Steffen, "Other Side of the Garden," 34–35).

PART III

Gender and the Translation of Genre

CHAPTER 8

Room of One's Own for Decisions

Chauncer and *The Faerie Queene*

A. KENT HIEATT

I follow two lines of argument in this chapter. Centrally, I attempt to clarify our fundamental exegetic confusion over the plotline of the central books of *The Faerie Queene* by tracing the agency of Spenser's most important debt to Chaucer, a conception of the relation between the sexes summarized in Spenser's three paraphrases of the same Chaucerian passage.[1] Marginally, I deduce that the tools of new historicism and social critique, useful as they are for much of the rest of *The Faerie Queene,* are powerless in dealing with what here is a case of disinterested vatic continuity, not of service to the political and religious centers of power in Spenser's England. Finally, quoting both the Chaucerian passage as Spenser probably found it and Spenser's paraphrases of it, I conclude the central argument by examining wider Chaucerian relationships, particularly with the Squire's Tale and the Knight's Tale.

Spenser said that in himself Chaucer's spirit was infused (a useful formula for defusing the anxiety of influence), even though for us what was born in Spenser was something very different from our Chaucer. Whichever way we look at it, the following reconsideration of Spenser's relationship to Chaucer incidentally promotes the conclusion that vatic continuity between canonical works had as much to do with the contents of *The Faerie Queene* as did the power structures and politics of Early Modern England, of which in another way Spenser was the creature. It's obvious that the invention of a literary past was in one way a political move glorifying England, but Spenser's use of that past was his own business. That use, in the Chaucerian respect to be outlined here, was seismic and doctrinal, not simply lexic and formal. It far surpassed the earlier parallel move in France to honor its own literary past so as to create a national literature, and there seems to be no useful parallel in the far more copious Italian evidence.

In its initial conception *The Faerie Queene* was another of the Early Modern heroic poems glorifying the aggrandizement, by supposedly righteous force, of the Christian, monarchical nation-state or Christendom conceived as a whole, and had nothing to do with Chaucer. As such it is surely intertextual with Italian Renaissance heroic poems, although the impress of fifteenth- and early sixteenth-century, partly native texts seems remarkable: we now begin to see that its curiously discontinuous narration, devoting nearly each book to one knight, is likely to look back to another late medieval English monument, the *Morte Darthur.*[2] Furthermore the specific mechanism of national aggrandizement, if Spenser indeed thought of it as the replacement of the Roman Church and Spanish power by a Protestant, English-led hegemony, descends from Arthur's conquest of Rome as presented in Malory and in Hardyng's *Chronicle.*[3] This, in turn, surely relates to Redcrosse's well-known postponement of his wedding with Una until he has dealt with the Paynim king who is afflicting the Faery Queen's realm.[4]

In terms of this religio-political conception, *The Faerie Queene* is scarcely canonical for us, or is so only secondarily: it allows us as readers to reinvent ourselves only in terms of a historical consciousness of what one pattern of belief in a Christian nation-state must have felt like. We can easily understand this conception in one new-historicist way, as narratively embodying what an English power-center wanted. It has nothing to do with Chaucer. The destiny of Gloriana and her court is a firm background ingredient in Books I (Holiness) and II (Temperance); it is in the foreground of V (Justice), and it is reacted against in VI (Courtesy), as it is in so much of Spenser's earlier work. It, and the foregrounded, individual subjects of each of these four books (also having little to do with Chaucer but often canonical in their own right) have historically preoccupied most exegetes and critics of *The Faerie Queene.*

On the other hand, the Mutability Cantos (VII) and Books III–IV, with their outlying symbolic locales in II and V, have little to do with the will-o'-the-wisp of Elizabethan imperium except in the transferred sense that two of the characters of III, IV, and V are distant progenitors of the Tudor line. Also, in III–IV the narrative organization in terms of one book to one knight breaks down, and the interlace pattern of narrative (shared by the French medieval prose romances and Ariosto, but moderated by Malory and, elsewhere, by Spenser) is more prevalent than anywhere else in the entire poem. Above all, however, III, IV, and VII provide the most interesting cases of Spenser's use of Chaucer in the whole oeuvre. They have nearly everything to do with a poet's honoring of a literary influence, little that can be explained in a new-historicist way. The decisive scene in Mutability is provided by the *Parlement of Foules* (or *Assemble of Foules*, as in Spenser's print of Chaucer).[5] The judgment of Chaucer's Nature in *The Parlement* concerns a far different subject from Spenser's, yet Chaucer's subject, in its concern to leave room for female choice, is at the center of Spenser's Books III and IV, which are an absorbed, almost completely nonpolitical narrative meditation, otherwise unexampled in a national epic, on what has to be added to the dark confusions of the sexual imperative to produce satisfactory, long-standing companionship.

Judith Anderson has recently emphasized the presence of Chaucer in Spenser, not simply in quotation or direct imitation, but suggestively, as Terence Cave and Thomas Greene have shown imitation to work elsewhere in the Renaissance.[6] I cannot always follow her in all these shades and half-lights, but I applaud one lesson with which she emerges: "the continuity—the impinging, implicating variety—of the forms of love" in Spenser.[7] Nevertheless, even in so dark and confused a subject as the erotic, certain distinctions can be made—enough to arrive at a general theory of what Spenser was at. It is with this conviction that I return to this matter. The problem calls for exegesis rather than for stepping back, as we often do today at a point like this, to say something about the nature of commentary and exegesis in general.

Two difficulties impede discussion here. One is that a bald specification of what Spenser took Chaucer to mean is something that we would rather hear from our psychotherapeutic experts than from a poet. Essentially what Spenser is articulating is a late courtly refinement of lovemaking that verges on a present-day social ideal of middle-class sexual relationships. Suummarily put, the bromide amounts to this: the steed of *natural* sexual passion has to be there, but it has to be bridled with the mutually considerate, socially acquired *art* of companionship without either deceitful, promiscuous tenders of affection or masterful sexual compulsion.

The embodiment of such a notion in narrative needs to be discussed in terms of concepts that critics are likely to share only in their extracritical lives in a larger community, and many academics are convinced that something more disturbing than this must resonate from the text to account for their high valuation of it. Disparate universes of critical discourse generate widely differing notions about all sorts of texts today, but the most enduring of new proposals about this part of Spenser's work depend on the claim for libidinal puns in it, going back as far as the revival of Spenser studies, circa 1960. My favorite is "perfect hole" as denoting vaginal sexual readiness, at the point where Amoret realizes that the wound given her by Busirane has been closed up with Britomart's help: "Tho when she felt her selfe to be vnbound, / And perfect hole, prostrate she fell into the ground" (III.xii.38).[8]

It's true that Spenser or his printer generally starts "whole[some]" with a "w," but consider Timias's and Calidore's growing "hole" of their wounds (III.v.43, VI.i.47) and a priest's supposedly "holesome" counsel (*Mother Hubbard's Tale,* 553). Or "How to save hole her hazarded estate" (VI.iii.12.7), "sweet spirit and holesom smell" (II.xii.51.9), "more sweet and holesome than the pleasaunt hill of Rhodope" (II.xii.52.1), "With holesome reede of sad sobriety" (VI.vi.5.7). A trouble with most such puns is syntactical inelegance: for the submerged meaning Spenser would have needed something like "*a* perfect hole," entailing (if that's the word) loss of the surface meaning (that is, "perfectly recovered") of this Early Modern English phrase. Given an adult sensibility and some learning, we easily grasp ribald Chaucerian or Shakespearean wordplay or Spenser's reference to a satyr's frequently ringing his matins' bell (III.x.48). But for a poet to need to hide the meaning "vulva" or "vagina" in "perfect hole" in a passage of exalted heroic verse, we have to posit a sexually repressive climate of the kind people tend to associate with Victorianism and Havelock Ellis.[9] The first generation of continental Freudians, in the early 1920s, were stimulated by finding sexual equivalents for everyday objects in one another's dreams, but only grievously uninstructed people suppose that our present revisionist psychoanalytic theory does not understand the process of intrapsychic symbol formation differently and more fluidly. In many social circles today the libidinal charge in saying a cigar connotes a penis is no greater than in saying it connotes a WWI submarine. We are less repressed.

Of course Spenser often puns productively, particularly in proper names, but to deal with the mindset according to which modern critics, freed from reactionary sexual evasions, are at last able to pull out such libidinal punning arcana deeply hidden in a text previously regarded with undue reverence, it's necessary to recognize how little late medieval or Renaissance figures were repressed or disposed to veil impenetrably anything erotic that they wanted to say. Rabelais obviously comes to mind, but his plain speaking is more scatological than erotic. The obvious candidate here is the German artist Hans Baldung Grien (ca. 1485–1545), one of the six most celebrated of the German Renaissance, who in his youth was left in charge of Dürer's workshop during Dürer's 1505–7 stay in Venice. He produced a range of remarkable work spanning all the usual Early Modern subjects. His predilection for sexual innuendo has been recognized ever since nineteenth-century study of him began: for example, Potiphar's wife exigently dragging at the cloak of a panicked Joseph to get him into her bed; a hauntingly beautiful, nude young witch arousing the rear end of a frantic, recumbent monster while she repressively micturates into his mouth; three naturalistically rendered woodcuts of the sexual exchanges of wild horses in the forest near Baldung's home in Strasbourg; a drawing of nude lovers side by side, passion spent, the male sleeping, the female indulging her private thoughts. One of his most beautiful paintings, the *Ottawa Eve,* rediscovered only in 1969, goes about as far as cloaked sexual allusion is likely to do in Early Modern times, which is not very far: in my experience no sexually initiated modern has inspected a reproduction of this painting closely without grins or giggles.[10] Adam steps forward from behind the fatal tree, which partly masks him, while the serpent encircles him and the tree in its coils. A compellingly nude, standing Eve, archly viewing Adam from the corner of her eye, gently pinches the serpent's tail, which emerges from the area of Adam's genitalia behind the tree. Adam simultaneously grasps an apple from the tree over his head with one hand and Eve's forearm with the other. Instantly, his ready collusion in the intent of Eve's aggressive female sexual gesture of pinching the male penis reduces him symbolically to the body of this death, so that he becomes as much an almost conventional figure of skeletal Death as of our progenitor, although considerably bloodier and terminally vital.

In practice, then, a lubricious reference only transparently concealed in an otherwise inexplicable action (Eve pinching the serpent's tail?), in an artist's oeuvre which has been recognized (unlike Spenser's) as daringly erotic ever since his work has been studied, differs qualitatively from Amoret's "hole" earlier theorized about. On the other hand, the dozen or so roughly contemporary Italian canvases of episodes from Tasso's *Gerusalemme Liberata* and Ariosto's *Orlando Furioso,* toward which the stanzaic narrative of *The Faerie Queene* aspired at the immediate level of narrative voice, are all decorous.[11]

Spenser could easily have made an aperçu in one of his dexterous nine-line stanzas of the Rube Goldberg sex of pressing a snake's tail to produce sexual aggression so as to precipitate instant transmutation of a man into a figure of death, or he could also as easily have rhymed Chaucer's episode of one hole extended from a window for a kiss and another extended to receive a burning-hot coulter. Instead he speaks of sex plainly (for example, the satyr, or Artegall-Osiris-crocodile impregnating Britomart-Isis in V.vii.16) but never in naturalistic detail.

Yet it is part of my argument that in a sense Amoret's sexual readiness is indeed being restored to her in this part of the narrative (although not by a pun on her vulva), which brings us to the second difficulty. Ridiculously, we aren't agreed to this day on the main *plotline* of III–IV—on who did what to whom. Far beyond usual critical disagreement about canonical texts, we have no agreed idea of how decisive parts of the narrative work, at the most primitive level of storytelling, in terms of characters' motives and aims.[12] We aren't agreed on why Amoret's husband Scudamour can't get into Busirane's house so as to rescue her in III.xii. We aren't agreed on why Busirane (whatever he represents) had succeeded in stealing Amoret away from Scudamour during the very celebration of their wedding in the retrospective account in IV.i. We aren't agreed, finally, on how to put all this together with Scudamour's even later account, in IV.x, of how he had initially won Amoret and of their subsequent troubles. Is he an overmasterful lover or an embodiment of the boldness that fortune is supposed to favor? Has Amoret contravened fortune by an unwomanly squeamishness about sex or is she properly defending an area of female decision? Or some third thing? And what did Spenser suppose he was doing when he inserted into this equation Busirane and an imperious love-god's pageant of illicit passion ending in shame and dishonor?

The practical effect of our perplexity about this narrative is that the principal episodes of III–IV, and some in V, which were generated as a powerful network interconnected with the story of Amoret and Scudamour, are reduced to little more than a congeries of events. The way out, I maintain here, lies in taking account of what is most crucially intertextual with Chaucer in the narrative of the middle books, a threefold paraphrase of Chaucer's Franklin's statement about sexual love in his prologue, in the print best known to Spenser (where the Franklin says nothing about *gentilesse* relative to his son, as I discuss later). Britomart's first words in her whole fictional existence in *The Faerie Queene* are: "Ne may loue be compeld by maisterie; / For soon as maisterie comes, sweet loue anone / Taketh his wings, and soone away is gone" (III.i.25). This is the narrative point at which she has first demonstrated her overwhelming martial prowess by quelling all six knights who allegorically signify the amorous resources of the masterful Malecasta. In a replay within the latter's castle, including allegorized qualities that return in Busirane's later Masque of Cupid, Britomart deals briskly with a Malecasta who, being as much a slave of Cupid as she is an embodiment of his mastery, seeks assuagement in Britomart's bed, deceived (as often happens) into thinking that such a manly knight must be a male.

Without setting out clearly a theory of who did what in *Faerie Queene* III–IV, it's hopeless to say what Chaucer (Spenser's Chaucer) has to do with it and how crucially important his part is. Correspondingly, the crucial importance of what is most evidently intertextual with Chaucer here—the threefold paraphrase of this passage from the Franklin's Tale (discussed with other Chaucerian matters at the end of this essay)—can most easily be explained on the theory that follows.

I am supposing that the story concerns three pairs of lovers—Florimell and Marinell, Amoret and Scudamour, Britomart and Artegall—whose interrelations speak differently to the question of *amor* and *amicitia*. The supremely desirable Florimell is in love with Marinell (III.v.8–10), associated by his name and actions with the cold sea. A churlish bachelor-caution supported by his mother (III.iv.26) impels him to reject Florimell frigidly, to give no sympathy, even, to her plight: he "nill marrie" ("doesn't want to get married"). We should be little concerned with this illustration of the exclusion of the possibility of any human response to another and would hurry on to the more specifically Chaucerian cases of the other two pairs of lovers, if it weren't for the second of three examples of Britomart's taking male-female relations into her own mighty hands. On the shore of the sea (III.iv), and moved by its turbulence in which she sees her own passion, Britomart falls into battle with Marinell. With a strength and a weapon that bespeak the power of femininity and the force of generous love, she wounds him, apparently mortally. His mother carries him off beneath the sea and finally restores him to physical health. Meanwhile Florimell, alone in the world and questing for him, is pursued by a succession of bestial louts and a monster (III.i.15–18, vii.1–26) and shortly ends up in Marinell's element, imprisoned by amorous Proteus (III.viii.26–43). Chastened, and overhearing her monologue of passionate sorrow, Marinell falls in love with her. The first, physical wound administered by womanhood is replaced by a second, psychic one: he sickens again until Florimell's release from Proteus and his marriage to her are finally achieved (IV.xi–xii, V.iii.1–3).

"That of *Amoret's* hart-binding chaine . . . / And this of *Florimels* vnworthie paine." Amoret's earlier career is much more fully recounted. Unlike her sister Belphoebe, whose biological destiny is virginity, she is raised from babyhood in the Garden of Adonis, under her patron Venus, in strictly natural surroundings that encourage her bodily perfection and readiness for the acts of generation (III.vi.28–52). She is discovered later, however, in full bloom on the Isle of Venus (IV.x), a landscape where nature has been trained up by art but never disappears into it, as though

William Kent had materialized a century and a half early to move its earth into vistas of hill and dale and to plant its flora most advantageously, as in an English country estate. Correspondingly its population is divided between lovers who do what comes naturally (as in the Garden of Adonis), and pairs of friends who have added to their natures the arts of understanding and companionship. Amoret herself sits surrounded by embodiments of those acquired virtues which Early Modern Europe thought would perfect a woman morally so as to impose durable marital unity on the sexual basis of mating. Her seat, however, is within the Isle's central temple, centrally dominated by a figure of Venus who embodies the ultimate supremacy of the generative passion—of sex—over all our acquired moral character.

On this scene enters her lover Scudamour, a very thrusting young knight, ignited with the fire of love. He has swallowed the macho hearsay that boldness is all a man needs with a woman. Because he thinks all comes by chance, he eschews the caution and reflection that Britomart later urges on him (chronologically later but narratively earlier: III.xi.23). His prowess enables him to overcome twenty other knights and all the allegorical embodiments of the delaying tactics which, in spite of contemporary narrative convention, were sometimes the proper test of the long-term possibilities of a suitor, to the point where he hales Amoret up by the hand out of the midst of her company of acquired virtues. She finds him compelling and is ready to love him (foreseen in III.vi.53), but (like Britomart in a similar situation) she wants room to make her own decision, which he steadfastly denies her. The virtue Womanhood accuses him of being "over-bold," but his display of his shield of Cupid with a dart, and the bold smile of Venus, give him what he needs to pull her out of the temple and the Isle. (I am not sure why Concord also smiles on him as he leaves, unless she is seeing the first step in a process which will finally produce an enduring union with Britomart's help.)

They are married (IV.i.1–4), but in the midst of the celebration (all being heedlessly inebriated) she is conveyed off by the enchanter Busirane to his house guarded by fire and smoke, in which he tortures her to make her love him (III.xii), working on her heart with a dart like Cupid's, through a cruel cut in her breast. In an outer room, Cupid with his own dart vaunts over the amorous gods and over a procession of figures representing the guilty, adulterous, loose amours that play so large a part in the abominable Castle of Malecasta and House of Malbecco elsewhere in the narrative.

Whether or not some loose ends about Busirane result from Spenser's other possible plans for him in a complete *Faerie Queene* or from some unknown historical episode, this Archimago-like enchanter embodies all those forces (surely not just love sonnets, as has been suggested) which are focused on inducing Amoret to desert monogamy for sexual adventure.[13] By wounding even Britomart superficially with his dart, he takes us back to her first encounter with promiscuity and Chaucerian *maistrye,* when she is almost identically wounded in Malecasta's castle (III.i.65). I deduce now that his presence is precipitated by Scudamour (not that he is himself Scudamour) and that Amoret (ultimately chaste) is susceptible to Busirane's practice on her, because an overbold, hasty Scudamour had initially practiced on her his own male mastery without the addition of companionable persuasion of her mind and will.[14] This association of Busirane with Scudamour, who did not know how to "use his bliss" (IV.x.8), seems demonstrated by the parallel between the five applications to Scudamour of the root *bold,* culminating (after the fourth one) in one "ouer bold" in the Isle of Venus and the multiple inscriptions "Be bold," culminating in "Be not too bold" in Busirane's House. Further, Britomart, chasing a bestial embodiment of male enforcement of women, had found only Scudamour when she arrived at the end of her chase, near Busirane's House. The association of the two seems patent, although it is a light touch. To put it another way, Amoret, like Britomart at one stage below, loves her suitor, now husband, but cannot yield herself unconditionally without having been given room to decide. Her reservations therefore leave her open to the compulsions of amorous deceits and illicit passion, although—unlike Malecasta, Hellenore, or Paridell, who succumb to them facilely—she continues to resist them; and she is finally saved by Britomart, who herself had indignantly rejected them in the Castle of Malecasta. She behaves much the same when later, in a reduplicative allegory (IV.vii.4–14), she "wanders" in a forest away from her protector and is carried off by Lust. Probably she ought not to have wandered, but when captured she finds an expedient to avoid surrendering: she is superficially subject to desire but fundamentally chaste. (Spenser often finds indulgent ways of stating the elective affinities of appealing female and male characters.) In an earlier case of her real indebtedness (IV.i.6), she recognizes that she owes love, service, and "her vtmost wealth," to Britomart, who has rescued her and seems to Amoret, up to this point, simply a male knight with amorous ideas. Yet still: "Die had she leuer with Enchanters knife / Then to be false in love, profest a virgine wife" (IV.i.6).

Lacking the arts of friendship, Scudamour in person, outside the castle, is clueless—his boldness inverted into despair—although he is pitiably eager to free his beloved (III.ii.7–24). Again, Britomart initiates the salvific action with her strength and weapon. This time in fiery, not watery, surroundings she pierces through the impediments with a rush, views the evidence, and frees Amoret, as the first step toward the reunion of a reformed Scudamour with his bride in a complete *Faerie Queene*.

Now for the third pair of lovers. The androgynously figured Britomart shows herself to be on a different plane from Amoret in two ways: in her dynastic aspect she shares with Artegall a syllable of Arthur's name, and she is elevated to a principle of chaste female power. But she is on precisely the same plane as Amoret in loving a man whom she rebuffs because of his exercise on her of male compulsion, expressed graphically in her third battle of the series I mentioned earlier, where she finally meets her match.[15] The difference here, which brings me to the end of my threefold pattern of lovers, consists in Artegall's artful reaction to the rebuff. Scudamour has been commendably bold but finally only callow in his reliance on male talk: "shaking off all doubt and shamefast feare, / Which Ladies loue I heard had neuer wonne / Mongst men of worth," he simply grabs Amoret (IV.x.53). Artegall, however, retreats from his exercise of force: "Yet durst he not make loue so suddenly, / Ne thinke th'affection of her hart to draw / From one to other so quite contrary" (IV.vi.33). When opportunity offers, he exercises "meeke seruice," "much suite," "faire entreatie," "sweet blandishment" (the tools of the bad guys but employed by a chaste lover): he gives her, that is, room to recognize her true mind (IV.vi.40–41). She accepts him fully, as Amoret (a graduate of the Garden of Adonis and the Isle of Venus) would have fully accepted Scudamour if, terminally, he had exercised friendly arts on her. The point is made again in the reduplicative allegory of Isis Temple in V.vii.13–16: crocodile-Artegall first tries to overcome Isis-Britomart by male force but is beaten back until, using blandishments, he impregnates her.

Now, what does Chaucer have to do with all this, or at least with Amoret's and Britomart's experiences? Most plainly, as already indicated, in Spenser's use of part of the following passage from the Franklin's Tale, in the text (so jarringly different from ours) that Spenser followed:

For one thing sirs, safely dare I seine
That frendes everich other must obein
If thei wol long holden companie
Loue wol not be constrained by maistrie
When maistry cometh, the God of loue anon
Beateth his winges, and farewell he is gon
Loue is a thing, as any spirite free

Women of kinde desiren liberte
And not to be constrained as a thrall
And so done men if I sothe saie shall
Loke who that moste pacient is in loue
He is at his auauntage all aboue
Pacience is an hie vertue certaine
For it venquisheth, as these clerkes saine
Thinges that rigour shall neuer attaine
For euery word, men may not chide or plaine
Lerneth to suffer, or els so mote I gone
Ye shall it lerne whether ye woll or none
. . . .
After the time, must be temperaunce
To euery wight that can of gouernaunce
(The Frankeleins tale. fol. l[r])

Remarkably, as indicated earlier, a close paraphrase of the fourth through sixth lines above occupies the first directly quoted speech (III.i.25) in the entire fictional existence of Britomart (the God of love, Cupid, being undesirable in the context of III and IV, is metamorphosed into "sweet loue"):

Ne may loue be compeld by maisterie;
For soone as maisterie comes, sweet loue anone
Taketh his wings, and soone away is gone. (III.i.25)

These words are the answer to one female's—Malecasta's—exercise of force (an allegorization of deceitful blandishments—also masterful) to compel men to love her and to give up any former lover. (The latter stipulation is what Britomart chiefly objects to, and what Amoret refuses to cede to Busirane.) More extraordinarily, these words and others in the Chaucerian passage above are paraphrased twice more—something that happens to no other borrowing from another poet in Spenser's entire canon. First, in Book IV, the message is directed at the lover most needing it, Scudamour, but the rightness is unintentional:

For Love is free, and led with selfe delight,
Ne will enforced be with maisterdome or might. (i.46)

Duessa here is trying to stir up trouble (jealousy is Scudamour's trouble—rightly of Busirane, wrongly of Britomart—as Marinell's is denial of life) by correctly reporting that Britomart (a male as far as Scudamour knows here) kisses Amoret and sleeps in the same bed with her during overnight stops on their journey. Spenser counts on his readers to perceive the absence of libido in a routine case of two females sleeping together. (One notes the relation of this to recent speculations about Spenser and Gabriel Harvey's sleeping one night in the same bed in London.)[16] Then, three-quarters of the way through IV, in ix.37, Arthur reproaches the unstable knights who are still fighting over Amoret, to whom Britomart has already granted freedom to choose. To ladies, he says:

The world this franchise ever yeelded,
That of their loves choise they might freedom clame.

The Franklin's words on freedom of amatory choice and the accommodations of friendship are in fact the key to the interpretation of III–IV that I've just provided. Whatever some modern Chaucerians make of the Franklin's Tale, the text of Chaucer that Spenser read would have helped so doctrinal a poet to think that Chaucer was equally doctrinal (as most court poets were expected to be, in addition to being amusing), and that the Franklin's speech was to be taken very seriously. For example, the inclusion in the Thynne *Canterbury Tales* of "The Plowman's Tale" would lead any reader to believe that Chaucer had publicly voiced a fighting opposition to the Roman Church and a preference for what seemed like protestantism. More to the point, what some have considered the crass social climbing and the Host's scoff at it in our own texts of the Franklin's Prologue are not there in Thynne, but in the Merchant's Prologue: the Franklin's attitude is nowhere even possibly derogated. Most importantly, what can be called Thynne's Marriage Group—the tales concerned to present love and marriage in various lights—is printed in a much more pointed sequence than in the texts we read. The group starts with the incomplete Squire's Tale (which Spenser completes as the titular narrative of IV, combining love and friendship in ii–iii) and then goes on: Merchant (having contacts with Spenser's tale of Malbecco, Hellenore, and Paridell), Wife of Bath, Friar, Summoner, Clerk, Franklin. That is, possibly excepting the two fabliaux, all of these are concerned with marriage, and Spenser finishes the first one and paraphrases repeatedly from the last one (encouraged, probably, to believe that its terminal position made it Chaucer's last word on marriage).

It is of course in completing the Squire's Tale that Spenser pays his most conspicuous tribute to Chaucer, saying (deludedly) that Chaucer's spirit is infused in him.[17] More importantly for us, Spenser's Squire's tale, reaffirming the point of the Franklin's speech, turns Chaucer's original into a more obvious member of a more structured Marriage Group, of which the end, the Franklin's Tale, is in its beginning, the Squire's Tale. In his completion of this tale Spenser develops a mechanism for emphasizing the relationship between the moral compulsions of companionship and the biological ones of sexuality. This is the four-group or tetrad, which becomes positively formulaic in ingenious repetitions in at least three further cases throughout IV.[18] In the plainest four-group, the four survivors of the completed Squire's tale are first met, riding, in a rectangular formation of two ranks and two files: friendship rules in each rank, between the two knights in front and between their two ladies in the rear; love rules within members of the two couples in file on left and right. In the tale, Cambel provides a brisk resolution for his sister Canacee out of devotion to her and a wish to end strife among contending aspirants for her: he fights three brothers who are in love with her and dispatches two of them, who magically transfer their souls to their third beloved brother. In battle this brother's and Cambel's mutual hate is pacified magically by the brothers' loving sister, Cambina. The surviving brother marries Canacee; Cambel marries Cambina. All, of course, are united in love and friendship: it is another ratification of the Franklin's words that transforms the Squire's tale into the indubitable first member of the Marriage Group, looking forward to the moral of the last one.

The narratively consolatory kind of four-group found here is a commonplace intertextual phenomenon in Early Modern literature. One need only think of Pyrocles-Philoclea-Musidorus-Pamela in *The Old Arcadia* or Rosalind-Orlando-Celia-Oliver in *As You Like It*. Am I deceived, then, in supposing that Chaucer's Knight's Tale, told by the Squire's father and culminating in a four-group, bears a particularly close relationship to Spenser's completion of the Squire's Tale? Possibly so, but features of the long romance told by the Knight must have been particularly attractive to Spenser: the heavy load of doctrine, with life at first seeming to be one damned thing after another, under the sway of cruel deities (cf. the Cupid we met), but at last amounting, consolatorily, to the best that the highest power of all can do for us in the world of time (cf. Mutability), with the benign help of an earthly authority figure's fellow feeling.

The Knight's Tale is closer to Spenser's Squire's tale than any other narrative that Spenser might have followed, including of course Chaucer's own Squire's Tale. Two brothers by oath, born of two sisters (in place of the new Squire's tale's three brothers), fall in love with one woman, sister-in-law of the authority figure (in place of one woman, sister of the authority figure); this figure wants to help his sister-in-law (in place of his sister) to a choice among them and also to terminate the mischief-breeding strife among aspirants for her (as in the new Squire's tale) and promotes battle to reach resolution (as in the new Squire's tale); the battle in a stately enclosure (in both tales) culminates in an evil preternatural solution (in place of a benign preternatural solution); in the end the surviving lover marries the authority figure's sister-in-law (in place of his sister), and we conclude with a four-group of that figure in amity with the oath-brother-survivor, both married to two sisters (in place of that figure in amity with the brother-survivor, married to each other's sisters).

In Spenser's text of Chaucer, the preceding Father-Knight's Tale is separated from the following Son-Squire's Tale by only three fabliaux (one incomplete) and the Man of Law's Tale. The Knight's and the Squire's are the only mainstream romances in *The Canterbury Tales*. Chaucer, as Spenser would have noted, wrote a similar narrator's trick into the first lines of both of them, and nowhere else: sketching in the general background of the tale, then returning briefly to the frame story of pilgrims needing to tell all their tales on the journey, and finally getting on with the tale proper. Remarkably, Spenser himself starts his Squire's Tale with the words used by the Knight to begin his own tale. Chaucer's Knight: "Whylom, as olde stories tellen vs"; Spenser, substituting a disyllable to make up, probably, for the loss in his own utterance of the final "e" in "olde": "Whylome as antique stories tellen vs" (IV.ii.32).[19] I continue to credit the notion that, whatever got infused into successor-Spenser from predecessor-Chaucer, the consolatory pattern of the Knight's Tale helped him to complete the Knight's son's tale.

Canonical works—the earliest and the most recent—are for me ones in which you can find yourself or reinvent yourself. There are as many ways to do this as there are readers, gazers, and listeners, but not all possible ways work, because some of them are not supported by the artifact properly understood. Then it is not simply that the chain of vatic continuity between Chaucer and Spenser is particularly worth considering because we want to understand the relation between two periods usually considered in isolation. It is also quite possibly the case that we cannot properly find ourselves in the meditation on love and marriage in the middle of *The Faerie Queene* unless we understand its intertextuality with the work of its greatest English predecessor.

Notes

1. I made a similar attempt to clarify such confusions over twenty years ago, but now with new insights. See *Chaucer, Spenser, Milton*, chaps. 2–10, appendices A–B. The relevant parts of this were in part an answer to corresponding parts of

Roche, *Kindly Flame.* Our amicable argument had already begun in an earlier article of his and my response to it. He attempted to find a position upstream from his original one and mine and summarizes this position in his "*The Faerie Queene*, Book III," in *Spenser Encyclopedia*, 273, head of first column ("Some critics"—principally Hieatt; "others"—principally Roche). This article in *Spenser Encyclopedia* (of which I was first an associate editor, then editorial consultant) does not mention Chaucer or give a sense of narrative relation among episodes, although it summarizes Spenser's borrowings from Ariosto and Tasso excellently. Professor Roche's "Amoret" in the same encyclopedia, 29–30, returns to our controversy and to the position that he and I have both psychologized her in too modern a fashion. The editors kindly agree to publish my rejoinder to this in the "Forum" section of *Spenser Studies* XII. Professor Thomas Roche and I are equally amused to find ourselves parting company on a subsidiary question; see note 3. Brill's "Scudamour" (635 in the same work) reflects the puzzlement about the role of this character. The best general discussion of Chaucer's influence on Spenser is Burrow, "Chaucer, Geoffrey," in the same encyclopedia, 144–48. Very numerous interpretations of *Faerie Queene* III–IV, often cognizant of Roche's and my diametrically opposed positions, are adequately noted and summarized in the pages of *Spenser Newsletter.* (In order to focus on the all-important fundamental problem of what actually happens in Spenser's two central books, I avoid taking full account of these interpretations here.) The latest such interpretation known to me is Esolen's "Spenserian Chaos."

2. See Rovang, *Refashioning.*

3. See discussion of this (and references to earlier work) in the "Forum" section of *Spenser Studies*: Hieatt, "Projected Continuation of *The Faerie Queene*"; Roche, "Response"; Hieatt, "Arthur's Deliverance." The contents of the "Forum" section are not listed in the table of contents of *Spenser Studies.*

4. And see my description later in this chapter of recent work by Judith Anderson, below, as well as her earlier work on Spenserian connections with Middle English material, conveniently cited in *Spenser Encyclopedia*, 791.

5. Cf. "assembly" in *Faerie Queene* VII.vii.59.8. All *Faerie Queene* quotations in this chapter follow Edmund Spenser, *The Faerie Queene*, ed. Hamilton. For the now generally accepted conclusion that Spenser habitually read one of the Thynne family of editions—1542, ca. 1550, or 1561 (the most likely)—see Hieatt, *Chaucer, Spenser, Milton*, 19–24. My thanks to Ms. Elizabeth Swaim, who facilitated my use of a 1561 copy (STC 5075) in the Wesleyan University Library Special Collections. All quotations of Chaucer here are from this copy.

Incidentally Dr. Craig Berry, in his chapter in this volume (n. 14) is right in saying that Spenser's "sundry doubts" in *The Faerie Queene* IV.i.4 (a line surely reminiscent of Chaucer's *Canterbury Tales* V.220, Squire's Tale) reproduces the phrase found in other texts of Chaucer, not the "sondry thoughtes" of the Thynne editions. But to suppose that Spenser actually consulted one of these other texts and drew the word *doubts* from it is surely unnecessary (although of course possible). The most enthusiastically alliterative of major English poets would have been driven to "doubts," and would have excluded "thoughts" in the cited hexameter, which contains four other syllabically initial *d* sounds and reads: "So diuersely each one did sundrie doubts deuise." Berry and I might offer a prize for how Spenser could have constructed similar alliterations on the Thynne "thoughtes" or could have reconstructed the whole stanza, but we should have to face up to the likely influence on this line of Chaucer's line 202, similarly alliterating on *d,* with which the passage opens in the 1561 Thynne edition: "Diuers folke diuersely thei demed." Spenser using Chaucer often modifies Chaucer's phrasing. It's not surprising that in doing so Spenser should have lighted on a word that happens to occur in his progenitor's other texts, although readers must consider Berry's alternative carefully.

Ms. Beth Ammerman, Professor Theresa Krier's assistant, kindly provided me with photocopies of this passage in all four Thynne editions. The three earlier ones all reproduce this alliterating "Diuers folke diuersely thei demed," although they spell it quite differently. In studying Spenser's use of Chaucer's words in the Thynne editions, should we use the convenient facsimile of Geoffrey Chaucer, *The Works, 1532*? It may be dangerous to base conclusions on this edition (which actually lists no variants to the Thynne 1532 print), because Spenser is most likely to have used that of 1561, published when he was around nine years old and no doubt available from the printer for long after that. Regularly a printer did not publish a new edition of a text until the entire run of a former edition was sold, so that to have owned one of the earlier editions, Spenser would have had to buy secondhand, or be given, a copy (1545?) published shortly before his birth, one from ten years before he was born (1542), or one twenty of years before (1532). Why take a chance on 1532, the least likely of the four possible Thynne editions, when Elizabethan resetting of texts in successive editions is known to have been so prone to cumulative error?

The photocopies provided by Ms. Ammerman from the Squire's Tale in all four of these Thynne editions happen to include a common passage (corresponding to ll. 242–66 in *The Riverside Chaucer,* with numerous differences in wording and sense). In this particular passage, it's evident that there are almost no changes in wording among 1532, 1542, 1545(?), and 1561. But the virgules (slashes) and the spellings in 1532 have much in common with fifteenth-century manuscripts of Chaucer, particularly in the use of *y* where we should expect *i.* On the other hand, 1561 programmatically uses commas, and *i* in place of *y,* and shows other spelling differences. It is significant that the spellings in 1561 correspond overwhelmingly to those listed, for almost all editions of Spenser's verse works in his lifetime, in Osgood, *A Concordance to the Poems of Edmund Spenser.* Only in the 1561 typesetter's decision for *i* in place of *y* in "they" does Spenser differ. The 1532 passage contains fifteen other words that are spelled differently from the corresponding 1561 ones, and those 1561 spellings agree completely or overwhelmingly in the decisive points with the spellings listed by Osgood. These fifteen 1532 spellings are: medycyns; shulde; rynge (n., worn on finger); thyng; Moyses; kyng [twice]; sayen ("sayne" used twice in *FQ* II and, interestingly, seven times in *Shep-*

heardes Calender, twice in *FQ* III; otherwise no *y* in all other, very numerous cases); lyke (adj.: "like" in *FQ* and almost always elsewhere); al (adj.: always "all" in Osgood); deuyse (never in *FQ* IV; almost never elsewhere); til (conj.: twice in *Shepheardes Calender* and in *FQ* I, otherwise overwhelmingly "till"; aryse (once in *Shepheardes Calender* and in *FQ* II; otherwise overwhelmingly without *y*); royal (once in *FQ* I; otherwise invariably "royall" as, very interestingly, in 1562); tartre (the tribal name; "Tarter" in 1561 and in *FQ* II, the only instance in Osgood).

The 1542 and 1545(?) editions fall midway between 1532 and 1561 in this matter of spellings. The spellings of 1561 are the closest to those Spenserian spellings found in Osgood.

This additional evidence does not decisively demonstrate that Spenser habitually used the 1561 edition. More collations need to be done, particularly since more typesetters than one were probably employed in setting this two-volume work of Chaucer's; but the evidence makes the case much stronger, partly because Spenser, so strongly in love with Chaucer, would have been influenced by him in mobilizing a partly archaic spelling. With such plentiful, widespread examples in the case of Spenser, it seems best to use the 1561 edition of Chaucer both because the spelling seems similar and because the possibility of a misreading exists in the other three editions, particularly 1532. Microfilms of copies of all the Thynne editions in the University of Michigan microfilm collection of STC early English books are available in most large university libraries or can be ordered separately (also in photocopied, but sometimes illegible, form).

6. Anderson, "The 'couert vele'"; see also Cave, *Cornucopian Text*; Greene, *The Light in Troy*.

7. Anderson, "The 'couert vele,'" 648.

8. Quilligan, *Milton's Spenser*, 199. Incidentally, Professor Quilligan and I are agreed in our view of Scudamour's actions against Amoret as described further, later in this chapter. See my review of *Milton's Spenser*, 95. As she says, she derived the notion of this pun from Goldberg, *Endlesse Worke*, 78–79.

9. I suspect "hole" is never used to mean "vagina" or "vulva" in any known Early Modern English text, although this is difficult to determine even from modern reference books. I have never seen an instance. Chaucer once uses the word to mean "anus" of a female (Miller's Tale, 3732, in modern editions). In a song in *Mankind* (in Wickham, ed., *English Moral Interludes*, 16), it is used repeatedly for the male anus. Under Hole, *sb.* 8, *OED* quotes from 1607 an instance referring to an animal's anus.

10. See Hieatt, "Hans Baldung Grien's Ottawa *Eve*," and citations there of earlier studies.

11. The exiguous English painterly tradition makes us wait until William Etty's *Britomart Redeems Fair Amorett* of 1833, in the Tate Gallery, to see a similar visual rendering of Amoret at this narrative point, and it is again heroically decorous. It of course bears no witness to Early Modern symbolizing habits but is worth noting. A grimly professional Britomart in plate armor, with a plumed half-

helmet, braces one foot on the open page of Busirane's overthrown book of magic formulae and threatens his cowering form with an overhead blow of her sword; a respiringly luscious Amoret, draped only from below the hip, receives her heart into her breast magically as the chains fall from her wrists. See Farmer's "Illustrations" in *Spenser Encyclopedia*, ed. Hamilton, 390–91, for citations of other visualizations of this theme.

12. See note 1.

13. For further bearings on Busirane, see Hieatt, *Chaucer, Spenser, Milton*, 130–31, 135–40, 274. On subversion by love sonnets: so industrious a sonneteer as Spenser would scarcely propose this. Anyway, the notion that the exclusively male voice in sonnet sequences is a device for imprisoning women is radically unstable. See the abstract of Ilona Bell's paper, "Spenser's *Amoretti*," 34. Yet of course Spenser sees love lyrics as a device in seduction, as in *FQ* III.x.8.

14. This idea differs in part from the one in Hieatt, *Chaucer, Spenser, Milton*, 123–30.

15. Actually four encounters but three battles against unreconstructed ego: against Malecasta's knights' sexual enforcement, against the consequences of Scudamour's enforcement (Busirane), against Marinell's walling of the self against interpersonal risk, and now against Artegall's enforcement.

16. The contrast is notable between Britomart and Amorett's being in bed together and Malecasta's climbing into bed with a Britomart whom Malecasta assumes to be male. What really happens when Britomart and Amorett find overnight shelter on their journey and share a bed is that as women they share their problems concerning their respective lovers and try to console each other (IV.i.16). When Arthur later takes over the role of Britomart in protecting Amorett in their wanderings (IV.ii.18–19), the most important difference is that, being male and female, he and Amorett cannot sympathetically discuss their problems as lovers. The point is underlined (19.7–9).

17. Burrow, "Chaucer," 148.

18. See Hieatt, "Tetrads," *Spenser Encyclopedia*, 684–85. The three cases are (1) 1. Amyas, 2. Placidas, 3. Aemylia, 4. Poeana; (2) 1. Amoret, 2. Britomart as male, 3. young knight seeking lodging, 4. Britomart as female; and (3) the false four-group, 1. Paridell, 2. Ate, 3. Blandamour, 4. False Florimell.

19. Burrow, "Chaucer," 145.

CHAPTER 9

The Aim Was Song

From Narrative to Lyric in the *Parlement of Foules* and *Love's Labour's Lost*

THERESA M. KRIER

Lyric has ever been the elusive feminine for literary scholarship, and a theoretical challenge to nearly all versions of European literary history. It's likely that even the modest degree of abstraction required to talk about the lyric in general terms does violence to our tacit and corporeal knowledge of it.[1] We struggle with lyric as heirs to the Romantics, a fact both blessing and curse in scholarly discussion. But there is (at least) one historicized way of addressing the topic of lyric without straining to fix its fluidity. Scholars of medieval literatures have made remarkable studies of "the song in the story"—the relationship of lyric to narrative in long, complex works.[2] From these studies emerge some useful principles. One is that lyric can be defined relationally; that is, in the context of any narrative within which it works. Another is that readers need to attend to sequence of literary events and choices within such works, with a heightened sense of strangeness in how exactly one thing leads to another: what poetic, narrative, and psychic conditions could account for just this order of literary events? A third principle is that lyric is less one fixed thing, even within one work or author, than a spectrum of possibilities and shifting relationships to earlier works—family affiliations ready to be activated in the implicit literary genealogy of a work. As John Hollander says, "for poets, words are often like some agents in a larger fiction, not so much an epic or drama, but more a complex romance, of language."[3] This is true not only of words but of tropes, stanza forms, plot motifs, character types, and many other elements.

In this chapter I set together two narratives—one in verse, one in dramatic verse and prose—in which lyric figures prominently, Chaucer's *Parlement of Foules* and Shakespeare's *Love's Labour's Lost,* which

Shakespeare may have written while dwelling in the poetic neighborhood of the *Parlement.* The two works develop similar accounts of mode, specifically of the relation between lyric verse and narrative or dramatic verse, and the relation between mode and amorous experience. Both works are, in an overt sense, intensely lyrical throughout: Shakespeare's play is well known for the many lyric poems created by the characters, for instance, and the three tercels of the *Parlement,* the first long poem in which Chaucer deploys the rime royal stanza, plead their cases in set pieces evolved from French lyric forms, as James Wimsatt notes.[4] But I argue that Shakespeare learned from Chaucer's *Parlement* a certain plotting of poetic language and history: in each work there is an implicit drive from narrative to the release of what each work gradually defines as lyric—a particular historical family of lyric. Within the evident plots about courtly eros, both works discover, as an alternative to the frustrations of courtly or Petrarchan amorous forms, the liberation of a cosmic, creative eros, derived from hexameral and encyclopedic traditions. This liberation takes the form of lyric praise of creatures and seasons, at or near the end of each work. One of my aims here is to offer internal evidence (conclusive proof being unavailable) for the *Parlement* as a crucial precursor to Shakespeare's play; to this end I put greatest emphasis on the dynamic of genre or mode within the two works, a dynamic so specific and unusual that it ought to be weighed not just as an interesting parallel but, in conjunction with other data, as evidence for the relationship of the two works. Such genre patterns are instruments through which writers think their topics and their relations to other poets, and I take the handling of genre or mode as significant in the traditional work of establishing sources.

In order to do justice to this genre narrative, I invoke certain concepts of maternity and infancy from object-relations theory. In each work, for instance, the last and greatest narrative pressure for lyric hymn arises from some form of aggression—boisterous and comic in the *Parlement*'s discussion among the birds, punitive and edgy in the outbursts of ridicule and humiliation near the end of *Love's Labour's Lost.* Literary forms lie behind such aggression—for example, the *débat,* the chivalric romance, courtly/Petrarchan love poetry. But Melanie Klein's ideas about infantile envy and gratitude also help me to account for the feeling-tones of the concluding lyrics, so strikingly different from the narratives that surround them. And proposals by D. W. Winnicott and Christopher Bollas on the mother-child dyad inform my sketch of each writer's argument for the wealth and possible elevation of the English vernacular, his mother tongue. So another aim in this chapter is to articulate the contributions of each work to the thinking within English poetry about the vernacular, about orality and performance as opposed to writing, and about all these things' relations to forms of emotional and ethical life.

But what justifies using any psychoanalytic category in this kind of literary history? The mutual fascination of Renaissance culture and psychoanalysis is of long standing, beginning with Freud's own work, and yields remarkable benefits; it's been much harder to establish pathways between medieval cultures and psychoanalysis.[5] But psychoanalysis is not intrinsically ahistorical or intransitive, and requires no subscription to a single developmental model of subject or family formation, so large and various has its discourse grown. Instead psychoanalysis provides a wide array, the best we have as an instrument of thought for histories of emotions, of (among other things) subjectivities, psychic structures, affects, and capacities for representation. In conjunction with social history, with histories of the family and of women, and with feminist theory, psychoanalysis is, potentially, endlessly historicizable.

For the purposes of this chapter, my initial psychoanalytic premises are few and simple. One is that the impulses and patterns of infantine coming-to-language comprise part of the ground of high poetry, with its access to and integration of archaic forms of language with the complex artifice of forms and traditions.[6] Another premise is that the possible affects and psychic structures available to any person, in part genetically bestowed, are also shaped by preverbal experiences of being handled and cared for (or not) as an infant, chiefly by a mother or other women, in Chaucer's and Shakespeare's cultures. The relatively long time span of this handling is important, a fact relevant not only to psychanalysis but also to biology and cognitive psychology; Christopher Bollas begins his chapter on "the infant-mother culture" with the reminder that "[w]e know that because of the considerable prematurity of human birth the infant depends on the mother for survival."[7] These psychic structures are diachronic—they fit one or another hypothesis of early development—and also synchronic: once formed, they persist in adult life and may inform any adult behavior, including aesthetic creation. A third premise is that, insofar as psychoanalysis offers many divergent explanatory accounts of representation, we can use its concepts to get at the capacities and effects not only of persons or characters but also of tropes and other aesthetic forms. The etiology of representation that I use here derives from Klein, Winnicott, Bion, and Bollas, who elaborate upon rudimentary psychic gestures of projection and introjection, of projective identification, and of fantasized destruction and creation. My third aim, therefore, is to argue that Chaucer's and Shakespeare's poetic narratives show how desire can be for an art, a form, or the conditions that elicit poetic utterance; how a poem or a play can itself be said to desire its perfecting in a specific aesthetic form; that *imitatio* is one of the paths of reading that opens access to the unconscious; that there are nonillusory psychic experiences of achieved plenitude and repletion as well as of lack or absence.[8]

A growing tradition of scholarship attends to Chaucer's *Parlement of Foules* as a poetic manifesto and charts the minutiae of its concern with reading and writing. With these critics, I take as thematic the poem's overt indebtedness to its predecessors, its probing of the relations between philosophy and poetry, its passages simultaneously about love and writing.[9] But one issue of reading and writing in Chaucer's poem needs to be challenged: the claim, made in many arguments, that the relationship between narrative and lyric is represented in the poem—particularly at its end—as being unsatisfactory, frustrating, and alienated. I oppose this apprehension of the feeling-tones and movements of the *Parlement* by addressing the subject of lyric within narrative, an aspect of the poem's exuberance and charm as well as an aspect of its enigmatic reserve. I even hope to answer the perplexing question of what Chaucer's narrator wishes for and hasn't found from his reading, when, frustrated, he moves from his books into sleep and dream.

Broadly speaking, my argument is this: The narrator's dream of Affricanus, Venus, Nature, and the birds unfolds the story of the dreamer's search for release into lyric utterance—a quest that succeeds, and indeed clarifies the poem as such a quest, in the birds' roundel at the dream's end. There are three steps in the itinerary of this dream, steps that to the protagonist of the dream seem random but are actually crucial developmental stages in his advance toward becoming the poet who later writes the poem. For with each step, the dreamer moves into a different literary landscape. First is the Latinate, philosophical realm where he meets Affricanus and receives austere ethical direction. With some blunt help from Affricanus, the dreamer leaves this realm behind for the garden and the second literary stage, that of late medieval, vernacular, courtly love poetry, where Cupid and Venus reign. In the third literary stage, the dreamer leaves what will retrospectively emerge as the static region of the Temple of Venus and finds himself within an expanded, vociferous realm of natural eros, presided over by Dame Nature and her divine creativity. The celebration of creatures here occurs in part through a fusion of vernacular love poetry with Graeco-Roman philosophical and scientific poetry—the two traditions that the narrator has already encountered. The roundel is the poet-dreamer's next step, into the elevation of praise lyric, an utterance that retrospectively releases meanings and narrative momentum in the earlier parts of the narrative.

As the fable unfurls into its immediate narrative future, it also gathers up and makes manifest its past—the just past events laid out on the page but also that literary past which is the path by which the dream and the dreamer came to be. The plot of the dream is haunting because, while represented as seen and thought as if for the first time, full of unexpected turns, it's also familiar. Much of it is familiar, of course, in the sense that Chaucer weaves into his poem venerable literary *topoi*, such as Dame Nature, Venus and her devoted pairs of lovers, catalogues of trees. But the dream is uncannily familiar because its perambulatory processes through poetic history can awaken, in the protagonist as in its readers, partial recognitions of beginnings; that is, traces of infancy's transformative fusions with or absorptions into experience, here a specifically literary experience. The infant's capacity for these absorptions into experience is anterior to a subject's self-awareness; they are processes that constitute "the unthought known," in Bollas's helpful phrase.[10] For all the story's peripatetic relaxation, therefore, it is driven by the pressure of the narrator's desire, or the desire of his dream, for praise song.

The vagrancy of the plot is undergirded by a desire implicit in the plot from the beginning. The aim of lyric bestows meanings imperceptible on initial reading and releases dynamics represented as gradually discovered by the protagonist.[11] At the start of the poem there is a good deal of distance between this figure and the poet who so brilliantly plots a dream logic to his poem. By the end, the seeking dreamer overtakes and fuses with the maker. The poet of the *Parlement,* through a poetic craft that includes his own psychic fusions with poetic antecedents, grants his dreamer a transformative process of fusion with objects in the world he dreams, and the dreamer becomes less conspicuous as an agent in the plot, more important as recipient, witness, and then utterer of the dream. More voice than agent, he moves toward transformation by song.

This desire for fusion with and transformation by song requires complex craft and adult mastery on the part of the poet, but by fusion and transformation I mean something rooted in human infant experience. Here I turn to concepts from the object-relations work of Christopher Bollas and D. W. Winnicott. Bollas inflects Winnicott's concept of a transitional object, linking it to the infant's experience of the mother in the earliest, neonate stages of life. The infant experiences mother "as a process linked to the infant's being and the alteration of his being," rather than as a discrete entity. So the early mother is "a transformational object." The transforming processes of provisioning, protecting, handling, and interacting with the infant, repeated over time, constitute what Winnicott terms a state of "holding"; within this harbor occurs that mysterious dialectic of nature and nurture that structures our psychic, creative, and linguistic resources. Adults may then do more than repetitively seek substitutes for the absent mother, or for a fantasy of preverbal, blissful merger; we can also seek external objects with their own integrity, "when the object is sought for its function as a signifier of transformation. Thus, in adult life, the quest is not [invariably] to possess the object; rather the object [may be] pursued in order to surrender to it as a medium that alters the self."[12]

Hence the hunger to surrender to transformation by reading, and the enigmatic articulation of the protagonist's desire, early in Chaucer's poem: "For bothe I hadde thyng which that I nolde, / And ek I ne hadde that thyng that I wolde" (90–91).[13] The uncertain restlessness of this hunger is made poignant by its expression, adapted from Dante, at the end of a stanza contrasting his fruitless busyness with the beasts' rest as evening falls. The wakeful Chaucerian reader doesn't yet know what object he truly desires, and the first part of his dream, its *insomnium* stage, in which he rehearses characters, texts, and social contexts of his reading, surprisingly works to move him beyond his first, likely objects of desire.

What this amounts to is a display of the unexpected fruitlessness, for this poet-dreamer, of much of the literal *locus classicus* of masculine, Latin, literate culture to which he has provisionally attached himself, when taken by itself. Macrobius's *Commentary on the Dream of Scipio* at first ties him securely in a chain of philosophical writers extending back from Chaucer's own time and place: the narrator on Macrobius, Macrobius on Cicero, Cicero on Plato. The Roman, masculine economy of this cluster of friends and relatives is laden with affective weight. Massinissa takes Scipio "in armes for joie"; there is talk and "blysse"; in the dream, says the protagonist, Scipio meets "Affrycan so deere" (ll. 36–42). The insomnium part of his dream, far from being mere repetition of waking events as the poem had earlier suggested, seems to manifest the protagonist's apparent wish to join a learned Graeco-Roman high culture of writers linked through the centuries. Affricanus's appearance to him and the offer of requiting the narrator's reading labors constitute a promising start, drawing the Chaucerian narrator-poet into that charismatic company of Latinate lovers of philosophy. The recompense that Affrican proffers for his labor would apparently be material for elevated philosophical poetry in the same vein as that of Macrobius: "thus seyde he: 'Thow hast the so wel born / In lokynge of myn olde bok totorn, / Of which Macrobye roughte nat a lyte, / That sumdel of thy labour wolde I quyte'" (109–12).

But retrospectively, the eight stanzas laying out the book and its "sentence" (29–84) turn out to be one of those detours or delays of the dream work's temporality. The inspiration of Macrobius generates little more than a recapitulation, repetition without transformation, of Macrobius's own writing. This is the wrong kind of imitatio; the poet-dreamer must discover how to make the book of the other into his very self, while also honoring the alterity and generativity of old books. It is for this reason that Affricanus, as if a stand-in for Chaucer the maker, propels the dreamer into unpredictably non-Macrobian territory: from a masculine culture of philosophical, narrative poetry, the dream's desire carries the dreamer into a feminine realm of Venus, Nature, and vernacular love poetry within a heterosexual erotic culture. This realm is itself divided into two structures of eros, and two kinds of poetry, represented by Venus and Dame Nature respectively.

One of the implications for this view of the *Parlement* is that a creativity sponsored by Dame Nature, or the mother-as-transformational-object, is not consigned to endless re-creations of essentialist figures for the feminine; it is not chiefly the mother as reified female (the Venerean, Oedipal representation of the mute feminine as mysterious object of sacrificed desire) but the mother as structurer of the infant's aboriginal experience of metamorphosis, through interaction with environment, that underlies the realm of Nature in Chaucer's poem. Affricanus's gesture of getting the dreamer through the gates is more than a movement from a realm of strong fathers and texts to a realm of nurturant mothers and mother tongues. It's also a figure of the dreamer's movement from his stable genre expectation of philosophic discourse in narrative into a realm of transformative process, leading to the precise genre of praise lyric.

Once he is through the gates, the dreamer's itinerary charts the poet's journey through several genres and several vernaculars, all closer to Chaucer's own time than the ancient writers and thinkers he has met. Chaucer the maker seems to shift the balance of his writing allegiances from a narrative aligned with a Latin, philosophical, expository tradition to a narrative aligned with vernacular lyric, from Latin prose to medieval courtly poetry in its many languages and genres. It is this very diversity that signals the dreamer's movement from his initial dream-plot of firm identification within a social group, a genre, and a gender, to his eventual and creative surrender within a matrix of transformation. Literary history provides Chaucer with his adult transformational objects as well as a theory of transformation in poetry: they are the poetic and philosophic works of his predecessors, carried across the centuries and across western Europe into fourteenth-century England. Hence the Macrobian portion of the dream, gathering up several texts from Greek and Latin antiquity, is followed by a section notably indebted to Dante and Boccaccio, who not only wrote in their vernacular but, as Italians, formed a bridge between ancient Latinity and medieval Romance tongues; then by a section indebted to works from (the more northerly) France, the *Roman de la Rose* and Alan of Lille's *De planctu naturae.* Dante, Alan, and the others together form a bridge of *translatio* over which the poet-dreamer passes in his peripatetic movement toward his fusions of genres.

The mediating literary term, the passage by which these literary realms generate new relationships, is cosmological poetry and its traces in Chaucer's brilliant catalogues. The translatio that is the poetic-historical manifestation of transformation sought by Chaucer is most salient in the *Parlement*'s famous catalogues—the catalogue of trees, the sights and sounds that Affrican had shown to Scipio (56–63), the list of those whose *insomnia* are of their own waking concerns. The boldest of these catalogues, the list of birds (330–64) and its narrative adaptations in the birds' debate, arise from an encyclopedic impulse to name the creatures of the world, an impulse toward nouns that also characterizes our earliest ventures into language. Encyclopedic and cosmological catalogues, often structured on the six biblical days of creation, and descended as well from ancient scientific poetry, are frequent enough in medieval writing; their representations of natural generation and plenitude pervade the works of the French Chartrians, the *Roman de la Rose,* and the philosophic Chaucer.[14]

As exultant perpetuators of equally powerful bird catalogues in the courtly-cum-philosophical *Roman de la Rose* and *De planctu naturae,* Chaucer's bird catalogues celebrate a fusion of courtly and philosophical genres, shift the trope of birdsong from courtly to hexameral lyric, and bring to English poetry a further fusion of a line of ancient scientific poetry (for example, Hesiod, Lucretius, Virgil) with a line of biblical namings of creatures. The bird catalogues manifest the adult poet's joyous mastery in the experience of fusion, now transformed from the infant's relatively passive, nonverbal knowledge of fusion to the adult's active, poetic making, which is yet a surrender to particular materials of his world. Insofar as the utterance of celebratory naming in lists, whether in short poems or long, is a root impulse of lyric, and insofar as it takes a further step away from the poem's early, relatively less ardent catalogues, we may take Chaucer's bird catalogue in the *Parlement* as another important movement toward the lyric of praise near the end, as well as a further clarification of his true desire for the achieved lexical simplicity and elevation of lyric, with all its complex fusions of genres.[15]

These birds dwell in the precincts of the garden presided over by the goddess Nature, her maternal realm a region of transformation. In the poem's plot, transformation is bound up with the noisiness of utterances—Nature's own commands, declamatory speeches, flyting, debates, animal sounds emphasizing the corporeality of language, jokes, and finally song. Although the realm of Venus is highly literary-historical and intertextual, it's also eerily silent, its lack of capacity for the vagaries of sound and speech somehow consistent with its tableaulike, reified images of the feminine and courtly desire. These images are another detour, toward a mistaken object, of the dream's desire. Nor is it simply that there are sounds here; Dame Nature actively sponsors and evokes a wide range of verbal activities and exchanges in her part of the poem.

Psychoanalytic and feminist theorists now theorize "the sonorous envelope" of the mother's voice, at first surrounding and lapping the neonate, then eliciting, echoing, and shaping the infant's sounds into speech, later mediating the child's formative encounters with objects in the world, teaching the young child language in part through nursery rhyme, poetry, story.[16] The mother (and her female surrogates in caretaking) structures a "potential space" in relationship with the child, a harbor for the growing exchanges of language, and also teaches more directly, as namer, as charter of pathways into the world, as the active transmitter of "the mother tongue." Indeed, psychoanalytic theory here extends and participates in the venerable trope that links acquisition of the vernacular with maternal figures and feeding.[17] (In *Love's Labour's Lost,* Moth will mock lovers' urge to sing in a particular style "as if you swallowed love with singing love" [3.1.12–13].) Here I want to expand "the sonorous envelope" to encompass the *child's* acts of giving voice in the presence and presiding of the mother, and not limit the sonorous envelope to the infant-encompassing song of the mother. I do this for several reasons. First, the envelope surrounding the dependent neonate swiftly gives way to those equally important wordings with which the mother sustains and helps to give deep structure to the child's increasing experience of the world. Second, long-lived and related tropes in all the arts—for example, the mother tongue or the singing woman who orders the world—seem to suggest that the sonorous envelope experienced by the infant may come to be internalized, a potential affective spring of the emergent subject's literal voice, creative action, and authority.[18] Thus Winnicott includes the young child's earliest lallations among "transitional phenomena," those crucial objects and events that, for the child, are created within but are also discovered without.[19] Third, an expansion of the idea of the sonorous envelope into an environment within the child that encourages *giving voice*—say, in debate or in song—helps to account for the noisy self-assertiveness of Chaucer's fowls and the eventual empowerment that their vigorous talk imparts to the formel. Acquisition of language, as Nancy Chodorow observes, comes from others but is not intrinsically alienating, a view that acknowledges the child's discovery of literal voice within her own body.[20] For Chaucer in the late fourteenth century, as for Shakespeare in the late sixteenth century, embodiment of the voice in lyric song, and an implicit claiming of that voice's authority, are of the first importance.

In Chaucer's poem, it is aggression, in the form of the vigorous clash of the fowls' views on love and marriage, that somehow frees the formel to speak in her own voice, for the first and only time in the poem, and to make the decision to defer marital choice. At first she has been tongue-tied and blushing with embarrassment—"She neyther answerde wel, ne seyde amys, / So sore abasht was she" (446–47)—but after the debate she articulates in thirteen eloquent lines a choice that hadn't been among those initially offered, and she does it "with dredful vois" (638). I think this independence and determination arise less from any argument that's been put forward about marriage than from the heating up of the emotional atmosphere in the vociferous debate and the concomitant changes in poetic devices. In these stanzas, so far from the serene celestial harmonies contemplated in the Macrobian part of the dream, conflict gains poetic energy from an intensification of colloquialisms, from the hurling of insults, from the onomatopoeic words evoking the bodily sounds of the most raucous birds ("Kek kek! kokkow! quek quek!," 499). This is an aggression that changes and refreshes the verse texture, opening it up to what Chaucer would have understood as the vernacular's lower levels of diction and sound. The narrator changes as well, as he moves closer to becoming the poet who writes the entire *Parlement:* he becomes the poet who can fashion the lyric that is vernacular but not coarse, uttered by the birds with a sound system that moves away from the raucous gutterals and stops of the debate to the liquids, sibilants, and labials of the roundel.

This poetic movement toward song, presided over and made possible by the inclusive Dame Nature, supersedes yet embraces the world described by Macrobius's Roman fathers. Macrobius's big subjects—the knowledge of the heavens, the soul's immortality, the ethical choices following upon awareness of the cosmos, the "commune profit," the notably inaudible music of the spheres—are deferred in favor of a poetry and poetic subjects founded at earlier levels of discovery of the world, subjects sought and understood via the mother tongue and embodied sound. The scientific features of this kind of ancient work, generally focused on the celestial canopy, are preserved but brought down to earth, wedded to the realm of mutable Nature. The movement from Affrican to Dame Nature is a recovery of what Bollas would call the "unthought known": the infant's earliest relations, formative of subjectivity, cognition, and language, to the maternal. The poem's passage is from narrative to lyric; from a presumed desire to be among fathers and sons and their literary genres to an anterior desire for those transformations and fusions—fusions of genre by the poet, fusions of poet and genre together—that lead to praise lyric, in a full-throated ease that echoes the poet's and reader's discovery of access to the plenitude of the natural world. Paradoxically, this is not a regression but an enlargement of adult apprehension and mastery.

As simple as the song itself is in its lexical and affective dimensions, it is a purposive consequence to all the movements of genre and affect throughout the poem. Allied variously to ancient philosophic contemplation of the way things are, to the medieval encyclopedic and hexameral traditions, to the mythopoeic works of the Chartrians, and to the courtly genres of late medieval continental Europe, Chaucer's lyric lodges eros under the aegis of Nature's resplendent creativity and brings to the natural ways of the mating birds the Christian endowment of "Saynt Valentyn" (683). A rondeau in form, its gratitude and ritual elevations ("As yer by yer was alwey hir usaunce," 674) make it a hymn in impulse.[21] As a speech act, it is also a welcome or salute to the wealth of the birds' natural world. The dreamer himself has shifted from the position of a son welcomed by father figures into a world that they provide for him to an identification with the creatures who, assured and at home, welcome the summer's warmth and vitality—a position of greater poise and fluency, if less status and cultural authority, than he had occupied in the Macrobian portion of the poem. Though the melody, if there was one, may have existed before the words and was "imaked in Fraunce" (677), as was the rondeau form itself, these words for music perhaps are those of the English vernacular poet: "The wordes were swiche as ye may heer fynde, / The nexte vers, as I now have in mynde" (678–79). The chief marker of his newly voiced desire and inventive authority is the unanticipatable shift into lyric: "Now welcome, somer, with thy sonne softe. . . . Wel han they cause for to gladen ofte" (680, 687).

"Our wooing doth not end like an old play," laments a rueful Berowne near the end of Shakespeare's *Love's Labour's Lost.* But more than one reader has suggested that it does end like Chaucer's old poem, *The Parlement of Foules.*[22] Taking seriously the possibility that Shakespeare formed the interplay of genres in his comedy via Chaucer's poem, I link the play's beautifully elaborated meditation on genre and poetic mode with the movement I've traced in the *Parlement:* a plotting of narrative (here in dramatic verse and prose) seeking elevation, closure, and composure in one family of lyric, the cataloguing of creaturely life. It is easy enough to discern the need for composure of some sort among the anxious, nervy characters of the play, caught up as they are in exchanging ridicule, contempt, gestures of superiority, all through a virtuoso range of verbal attacks and games. But composure is also the goal of the genre plot, as it seeks a poetic stance that offers release from the restless Petrarchism and exaggeratedly pretentious, learned humanist modes. Of course, as I said at the start, the play is in one way intensely lyric from its opening lines, filled with ambitious poems composed by the characters. But there is also a plot momentum toward the famous concluding songs of Winter and Spring—so incongruously homely and yet so right, as readers have always attested—providing just the precise kind of lyric release that the overwrought poets within the play require. To arrive at these songs, I first sketch the sequence of events and linguistic issues that make them necessary.

Navarre's tendentiously masculine "little academe," devoted to bookish philosophy, fasting, and sequestration from the company of women, holds a place in the plot analogous to the opening, Macrobian episode of Chaucer's dream. An idealized, noble, male company of learners—Berowne refers to "these earthly godfathers of heaven's lights" (1.1.88)—Navarre's academy is immediately waylaid by the vigorous intrusions of Costard, Armado, Moth, and their companions and by the charisma of the ladies who plant themselves in the wideness of the fields, like Dame Nature, apart from the cloistered court. When the young men do venture forth from the site of their vows, they try vainly to create with the ladies a court of Cupid, filled with "revels, dances, masks, and merry hours" (4.3.375), in the process creating idealizing love lyrics and acting out many other forms of medieval and Renaissance courtship. The various attempts of the men at flirtation in these exchanges with the ladies actually stall the action they think should follow from such witty disguise and banter, since the women's caustic refusals block the men's plot expectations. These encounters among the aristocrats constitute the equivalent of Chaucer's regions of Cupid and Venus: "Saint Cupid, then! and, soldiers, to the field!" (4.3.362). Eros in this courtly vein is not so much wrong as it is jejune; Cupid "hath been five thousand year a boy" (5.2.11).

The finer resolution in the aristocratic plot lies in the turn that has most reminded readers of Chaucer's *Parlement:* the crucial choice of the ladies to defer marital commitment for a year. It's in part this striking breach of dramaturgic decorum (at least as the men characters think) that leads to the unexpected ending of the Winter-Spring lyrics, just as in the *Parlement* it's the contentious social energies of the birds prior to the formel's similar choice that leads the poem into the rondeau to summer. Lyrics pointedly not in the Petrarchan mode but in a vein cataloguing the vicissitudes of the seasons offer Shakespeare's stalled lovers a new framework of attitudes toward mature eros. Like the dream that unfolds as if to transform the wakeful reader within Chaucer's poem, the Shakespearean seasonal songs of the locals proffer a transformative matrix to the witty courtiers, whose penitential acts should draw them into the temporal processes and embodied sufferings of their fellows.

The exacerbations of the plot have created so much hostility that some resolution other than a set of four marriages is called for.[23] In this play laden with high-spirited combativeness from the start, social aggression has reached a pitch with the extended exposures and humiliations of the lords, the subsequent punitive turn of the lords against the locals during the Pageant of the Nine Worthies, and Costard's exposure and humiliation of Armado. These conflicts threaten to escalate into a brawl, and though the disconcerting entry of Marcade, with his news of the death of the old King, diverts any physical violence, social dissonance remains. Shakespeare the dramaturge has understood the boisterous social combat of the birds' debate in Chaucer's *Parlement* anew, as a dramatic motivation, a psychically compelling movement into the release and fresh composure of seasonal lyric. The vigorous winds of attraction, aggression, envy, sharp wit, and malice fly about in linguistic forms that parallel, in plot functions, the movements of Chaucer's *Parlement* through vernacular poetic and amatory traditions.

Shakespeare's articulation of his precise role in the genre-historical issues raised by Chaucer marks not only the temporal distance of two centuries between himself and Chaucer but also the genre difference between a written, narrative poem and a performed comedy; Shakespeare contemplates his place as dramatist in *poetic* genre history. He carries a step further the Chaucerian declaration for the vernacular over Latinity, for lyric over discursive mode, for (the fiction of) sung over written utterance, for cosmological over courtly eros—though both writers cherish, preserve, and disseminate to later writers even the losing terms of these binarisms. Shakespeare's play carries the cosmological/encyclopedic tradition from twelfth-century, learned, Latin and French works further into the vernacular (hence, for example, the flowers of the Spring song taken from John Gerard's popular *Herball*), and to insist on the performative aspect of the songs.[24] They are not only literate but also oral songs; for the working playwright, they exist in the breaths and bodies of his singers.

Orality and literacy, Latinity and the vernacular become topics in this play; Costard's exultation in his presumed discovery—"Remuneration! O that's the Latin word for three farthings: three farthings, remuneration" (3.1.132–34)—is only the most famous instance. These topics are not simply displayed as variously comic or charming set pieces; they are also deployed as terms in an unfolding argument about their respective worths and tasks in the history of English. Thus one of the many linguistic contests that Shakespeare stages is that between the humanist, Latinate, written style, championed by the pedant Holofernes, and the native, vernacular, unlettered speech that is the only mode available to a character like Dull. Hence Holofernes versifies *extempore* in what the Arden editor calls "mathematical typography" (4.2.53–60); he thinks in letters as much as in words.[25] In the conversations of Holofernes, as Terence Hawkes argues, "the resonant world of speech is comically opposed to the silent world of writing."[26] True enough, but this binarism is complicated by the fact that in Holofernes' speech, and for that matter in that of Armado, Moth, Costard, and Nathaniel, Latinity evinces a positive pressure to become part of the spoken vernacular. Holofernes is an extreme and parodic case, but the stylistic habit of interleaving Latin phrases with English was at this time being transformed into a racy, colloquial prose style, by Thomas Nashe, among others. It is perhaps Nashe's greatest contribution to his mother tongue; Shakespeare, Nashe's greatest pupil, evidently ponders Nashe's lexical and colloquial gifts (as well as his person, in the character of Moth), throughout this play.[27] Latin enters spoken English, transforming not simply the lexicon but phrasings, sentence rhythms, range of allusive resonance:

> *Hol.* The deer was, as you know, *sanguis,* in blood; ripe as the
> pomewater, who now hangeth like a jewel in the ear of *coelo,*

the sky, the welkin, the heaven; and anon falleth like a crab on the face of *terra,* the soil, the land, the earth.

Nath. Truly, Master Holofernes, the epithets are sweetly varied, like a scholar at the least: but, sir, I assure ye, it was a buck of the first head.

Hol. Sir Nathaniel, *haud credo.*

Dull. 'Twas not a *haud credo.* 'twas a pricket. . . . I said the deer was not a *haud credo;* 'twas a pricket. (4.2.3–21)

As A. L. Rowse first suggested to the scholarly world, Dull hears this *haud credo* as "awd [old] grey doe," and the Latin/English pun is more than a lamentable Shakespearean quibble.[28] Dolores Warwick Frese argues for a Chaucerian *topos* that puns on the name of Grisel or Griselda—"old gray"—as an involucral pun for the ancient, lowly vernacular, the mother tongue.[29] It has become a critical commonplace that the notion of a maternal tongue informs figures of and claims for the European vernaculars throughout the Middle Ages and the Renaissance; Moth invokes one in his homespun invocation to the Muses: "My father's wit and my mother's tongue assist me" (1.2.90). It is lore so familiar by Shakespeare's time that I propose Dull's "old grey doe" as one of these figures for the mother tongue, brilliantly naturalized in a comic dialogue embodying the very contest of Latinity with native English.

This suggestion carries more force when the old grey doe is aligned with other references to maternity and its clustered associations in the play, for example Moth's appeal to the generativity of his father's wit with his "mother's tongue." Holofernes taps the same figurative fund when he characterizes the source of his linguistic gifts in a trope of pregnancy:

Hol. This is a gift that I have, simple, simple; a foolish extravagant spirit, full of forms, figures, shapes, objects, ideas, apprehensions, motions, revolutions: these are begot in the ventricle of memory, nourished in the womb of *pia mater,* and delivered upon the mellowing of occasion. But the gift is good in those in whom it is acute, and I am thankful for it. (4.2.64–70)

This is striking for its sustained conceit of maternity and childbirth, its affect of maternal tenderness, and the action of feeding. Holofernes speaks from a sense of the inward plenitude of the brain-space, of its protection and encompassing by a containing physiological structure, and of its taking nourishment into itself. Winnicott would call this an instance of holding: Holofernes experiences his own spirit as held and has the capacity to hold his own spirit in a generative internal environment. It is significant that Holofernes ends with an expression of gratitude, in a scene dense with elaborations of feeding, literally in the evening's anticipated dining, figuratively in the "dainties that are bred in a book" (4.2.23).

Katherine Maus has recently pondered Renaissance men writers' various appropriations of birthing figures for their own achievements in writing.[30] What psychic conditions would make Holofernes' use of this trope in speaking about his creativity true, interpretable, dramatically fit? Melanie Klein's polarity of envy and gratitude is useful here (see chapter 1 of this volume); in Holofernes' gratitude we can find a clue to his vocabulary as well as to his comic complacency. Although a minor character, Holofernes represents a capacity for gratitude that has developed as if through complex exchanges between infant and a good, feeding maternal figure. It is not accidental that it is Holofernes, at home with his own creative resources, upon whom the lords later unleash their most strident envy and hostility, during the pageant that he has written out of the wealth of his *pia mater.* However sentimental the character may be at this moment, he is Shakespeare's clear expression of an achieved gratitude, balanced in the play by the lords' aggressive, anxious envy in response to the imaginative gifts of others.[31]

I will return to the envy of the lords; here I continue with Shakespeare's linkages of female lineage with the vernacular. Taken alone, each of these can seem slight, but each is an instance of that brilliant Shakespearean way of offhandedly naturalizing literary traditions and tropes, something he studied closely in Chaucer. Taken together, and in light of the instances cited above, these examples form a delicate but unmistakable thread joining maternity with the play's apprehension of being *grounded* in the mother tongue. Many of these occur in the low linguistic register of bawdy joke; one job of bawdy in this play is to resist the lords' vaunting poetic pretensions. Maria is, in a bawdy exchange, "her mother's daughter" (2.1.200–1); the Princess is on an embassy as her father's daughter; Katherine had a sister who "might ha' been a grandam ere she died" were it not for Cupid's cruelty to her (5.2.17). Boyet interrupts Moth's stammering attempt to deliver a memorized paean to the ladies, "Once to behold with your sun-beamed eyes,—with your sun-beamed eyes—" with "They will not answer to that epithet; / You were best call it 'daughter-beamed eyes'" (5.2.169–72). Berowne, straining for a grotesque riposte to Dumain's lyrical praise of Katherine that she is "upright as the cedar," comments acerbically, "Stoop, I say; / Her shoulder is with child" (4.3.86–88). The ladies have entered on a deceptively frivolous compliment from Boyet: "Be now as prodigal of all dear grace / As Nature was in making graces dear / When she did starve the general world beside, / And prodigally gave them all to you" (2.1.9–12). This dame Nature also provides lodging for these ladies: since Navarre will not allow them within his court, they effectually establish an alternative court in "the wide fields" (2.1.91).

This ground outside the lords' court is base, as the Princess notes. But the negative sense of baseness—as of personal honor, of language, of love—is confounded throughout the play, with the result that what Holofernes calls "the face of *terra,* the soil, the land, the earth" (4.2.6–7) is drawn into the orbit of mother-tongue imagery and makes possible the mutual enrichments of Latinity with native English. Thus Armado's letter, read aloud by Navarre, incidentally reveals Armado's devotion to earth and includes a Shakespearean bow to medieval English roots with its archaism "ycleped": "I . . . betook myself to walk. The time when? About the sixth hour; when beasts most graze, birds best peck, and men sit down to that nourishment which is called supper. . . . Now for the ground which? which, I mean, I walked upon: it is ycleped thy park" (1.1.228–36). Armado's ideas about language cause him to condemn the "base and obscure vulgar" (4.1.69–70), but in the practice of his speech, as in love, he tends to adore the base with a touching gallantry. Thus he loves Jaquenetta in her very "lowliness" (4.1.80), and gestures grandly that he will "profane my lips on [her] foot" (4.1.84–85). It's not inappropriate that this particular lover commits himself to three years at the plough, for her love. And in the pageant of the Nine Worthies, Armado's grandiloquent self-abasement ("I do adore thy sweet grace's slipper," he says in an access of gratitude to the Princess who is kind to him when the lords have reviled him) becomes a moving devotion to the human acts of heroism and imagination grounded, both literally and figuratively, in corporeal mortality: "The sweet war-man is dead and rotten; sweet chucks, beat not the bones of the buried; when he breathed, he was a man" (5.2.653–55).

In the delirium of synonymy afflicting so many speakers in this play, Armado has named Jaquenetta "a child of our grandmother Eve, a female . . . a woman" (1.1.257–58). Female lineage casts the imagination back to the mother of mothers and to the play's park. The park is a figure for the essential finitude of all the characters and for the ubiquitousness of the mother tongue. The park is also the link between these themes and that of the just season, most eloquently voiced by Berowne:

King. Berowne is like an envious sneaping frost
That bites the first-born infants of the spring.

Ber. Well, say I am; why should proud summer boast
Before the birds have any cause to sing?
Why should I joy in any abortive birth?
At Christmas I no more desire a rose
Than wish a snow in May's new-fangled shows;
But like of each thing that in season grows. (1.1.100–107)

The fulfillment of these lines, with their topoi of winter's grudging envy of spring and of birdsong acknowledging the warm season with joy, occurs in the play's final movement, the movement into seasonal lyric and lyric catalogue; the final steps leading to that turn into song make it clear that the lords need to come down off the high horses, as it were, of humanist aspiration, to stand firmly on "the soil, the land, the earth" of their vernacular, "sans 'sans'" (5.2.416). But this is a painful process; at the ladies' hands the lords suffer public ridicule, exposure, insult, and shame. The courtesy of the play requires that their response to these sufferings be similarly public, witty, and high-spirited but that the aggression they find awakened in themselves not be directed at the ladies. In the lines about the proper generative cycle of the seasons, Berowne has been unjustly accused of envy, which Renaissance ethics, anticipating Klein, cast as the defining counterpart to gratitude and as an impulse to spoil and degrade (rather than acknowledge and celebrate) the object. Klein says that envy is aimed especially at spoiling of the envied one's creativity, precisely because creativity is felt not to be within oneself.[32] Now, near the play's end, envy is truly awakened in Berowne and the other lords. Refused a kind of nourishment by the ladies, they turn against the offspring of the locals' *pia mater,* those "forms, figures, shapes, objects" that constitute the Pageant of the Nine Worthies. Berowne is lucid about this displacement of envious aggression in himself and his friends: "Their form [the pageant] confounded makes most form in mirth, / When great things labouring perish in their birth" (5.2.515–16). This is not only wittily nasty; it is also a ferocious turning against the seasonable linguistic generativity that he had articulated near the play's beginning. And his articulation of motive comes as a response to the King's embarrassment at the hands of the ladies: "We are shame-proof, my lord; and 'tis some policy / To have one show worse than the king's and his company" (5.2.507–9).

Hanna Segal says that for Klein, envy is "purely destructive and aimed at the object of love and admiration."[33] But Shakespeare shows us, in the spoiling attacks of the lords, an adult derivative, in which envy of the ladies and the bounty they are felt to possess is displaced onto persons whose spoiling would be less of a threat to the lords than a spoiling attack on the ladies would be. Holofernes, Nathaniel, and their associates are a safer target because they are not idealized by the lords, as are the ladies; but they are also a worthwhile target in that they are strikingly creative—throughout the play but most evidently and grandly in the pageant. It is appropriate, in this work so full of play on proper names and nomenclature, a play in which "every godfather can give a name" (1.1.93), that one of the cruelest manifestations of the lords' envy against the Worthies escalates from a purposeful mistaking of the names of Judas Iscariot and Judas Maccabaeus (in Elizabethan English, to misname or mistake in this way is to "nickname"), and ends with a pun on "Jude-ass" (5.2.590–621). The massed verbal attack on Holofernes' face ("a cittern-head," "the head of a bodkin," "a death's face in a ring," and so on) is finally and justly rebuked by the victim himself: "This is not generous, not gentle, not humble" (5.2.623). In the ethical and linguistic terms that the play links, we might hear in "not generous" an indictment of the lords' failure in gratitude, so common a theme throughout Shakespeare's works; in "not humble" we are reminded that the lords still need to learn something like Armado's commitment to earth, to a style and deportment low or *humilis*. The play has yet to find or invent its fullest satisfaction of desire, which will be release into performed song in English.

The aggressions of this penultimate moment, paralleling the comic aggressions of the *Parlement*'s fowls at a similar stage of the narrative, are variously and swiftly developed. Armado appears as Hector (a formalization of aggression in role-playing).[34] Costard reveals Jaquenetta's pregnancy and Armado's responsibility for it (an "infamonizing" or defaming of Armado); they prepare to fight (hostility made physical); Armado is further humiliated by the discovery of his wool shirt, bespeaking his poverty; Marcade enters with news of death. These are all discords and, with the exception of Marcade's news, articulations of envy. But they also open up a space in their tense episode for the creatural vulnerabilities to which all the mortal characters are subject: Hector dead and buried, Jaquenetta pregnant, Armado impoverished, the Princess bereaved, her father dead. The apparently dark triumph of finitude is the crucial plot link between the dead end of the lords' amatory plot and the disarray of the Worthies, on the one hand, and the closure of the final songs, on the other.

The songs also conclude Shakespeare's imitatio of the genre plot of Chaucer's *Parlement*. Chaucer had emphasized his lyric's fusion of French melody and English words; Shakespeare's songs take us from a putatively French setting to an emphatically English one, a metamorphosis that occurs partly by means of the rustic English proper names: "Dick the shepherd blows his nail, / And Tom bears logs into the hall . . . / While greasy Joan doth keel the pot . . . / And Marian's nose looks red and raw" (5.2.905–16). The move to an English landscape occurs also by means of the floral nomenclature of the catalogue: "daisies pied and violets blue / And lady-smocks all silver-white / And cuckoo-buds of yellow hue" (5.2.886–88). This native nomenclature of flowers Shakespeare culled from John Gerard's *Herball* (1597), a book itself devoted to the project of drawing Latinity through continental vernaculars into English and even into English regionalisms. This linguistic desire to name obtains in the very composition of the book, the history of which is an intricate web of translation from one vernacular into another, along with a longtime scholarly movement away from the taxonomies of (Mediterranean) antiquity and toward the documentation of local (northern European) flora.[35]

Latinity thus becomes part of the vernacular, and this way of confounding opposed categories emerges in other aspects of the songs. As befits a composition by the lovers of Latin Holofernes and Nathaniel, the two seasons are introduced as "*Hiems,* Winter" and "*Ver,* the Spring" (5.2.883). The pieces are sung, but prior to singing was their "compiling" by "the two learned men" (5.2.878): a triumphant vindication of their idiosyncratic devotion to humanist ideals of learning. The songs were, furthermore, compiled also by Shakespeare himself, in writing. So although the lyric is intended to be voiced, any simple opposition between oral and written is confounded. What critics universally celebrate as Shakespeare's "great feast of language" is not only synchronic but also diachronic: it gathers up and forms a commentary upon poetic history, the life of the vernacular, and the transformation of the most prosaic language into the elevations of song.

For the singers of both Chaucer's and Shakespeare's songs, the stance of the singers toward the givenness of the natural world is one of gratitude—an earned gratitude, made possible in the unfolding of dynamics and stresses in each work. Their aim is to be "Thankynge alwey the noble goddesse of kynde" (*Parlement,* 672). The trope of birdsong, coupled with the figure of bird catalogues, seems to have become available as a trope for gratitude itself, taken as a creative generosity antithetical to envy. Among the many appearances of birdsong and bird catalogues in the sixteenth century, the thematic cluster of gratitude, envy, performed orality in the vernacular, and markers of temporality like the seasons is a particularly Chaucerian bequest.[36] Strikingly, while we can see well enough the way that these lyrics slow the temporal momentum of the story or draw it toward closure, as lyric commonly does within narrative, the three lyrics treated here honor what Milton would call "grateful vicissitude"—the very processes of temporality. In Chaucer and Shakespeare these are the seasons, always changing yet always the same: extended figures for a matrix of transformation, which is the mortal condition of those, like Chaucer and Shakespeare, who reflect on the internal generative resources of their own creativity.

Shakespeare fashions and holds a place in literary history in which the mythopoeic, philosophic, infolded density of Dame Nature—the goddess of Chaucer and his medieval continental predecessors—is naturalized into the Princess and ladies of *Love's Labour's Lost.* These ladies possess the poise and wit of the lively Franco-English goddesses, social endowments to comic heroines for centuries; but they also remain rooted in the emblematic, authoritative richness of Chaucer's Dame Nature. She is the transformative cause not only of the fowls' roundel but also of Chaucer's dreamer's waking emotions:

I wok, and othere bokes tok me to,
To reede upon, and yet I rede alwey.
I hope, ywis, to rede so som day
That I shal mete some thyng for to fare
The bet, and thus to rede I nyl nat spare. (695–99)

It is commonplace to read this stanza in the gloomiest possible sense, as an expression of frustration, dissatisfaction, or lack.[37] But there is no evidence compelling us to take the lines in this way.[38] Chaucer's final lines are rather an expression of happily surprised gratitude for the discovery of the fruits of reading and writing, unpredictable and wayward as they are.

Notes

1. Mark Jeffreys has two helpful essays on this subject; see "Songs and Inscriptions" and "Ideologies of Lyric." See also Menocal's *Shards of Love*, offering one interesting alternative to traditional kinds of close reading, a procedure of limited use with many kinds of lyric.

2. *The Song in the Story* is the title of Maureen Boulton's book; see also, among many others, Huot, *From Song to Book*; Kinney, *Strategies of Poetic Narrative.*

3. Hollander, *Melodious Guile*, 180.

4. Wimsatt, *Chaucer and His French Contemporaries*, 139, 183, passim.

5. For helpful surveys of work on, and analysis of, the relationship of Renaissance culture to psychoanalysis, see, e.g., the introduction to *Desire in the Re-*

naissance, ed. Finucci and Schwartz, 3–15; Schiesari, *The Gendering of Melancholia*, 21–32, passim; Bellamy, *Translations of Power*, 1–31.

6. On poetry's relations to early language formations, see Welsh, *Roots of Lyric*; I am also indebted to Ellen Martin's unpublished paper "The Shady Trope of Spenser's Trees."

7. Bollas, *Shadow of the Object*, 18. At first Bollas regularly refers to the mother; later, especially in clinical examples, he shifts to sporadic use of "mother and father," "the mother-father," "the parental care system." In this chapter I stay with the mother, partly because this articulates better what happens in the language of the works studied here and partly because I argue specifically about consequences arising from the infant's very earliest weeks of life, when traditionally (i.e., in both Chaucer's and Shakespeare's cultures) the mother (or her surrogate) handles the infant most, for reasons arising from both the infant's physical need and, potentially, the mother's own desire.

8. On the claim that poetry in any period offers access to the unconscious, it is helpful to have Bollas's distinction, one that would make possible the historicizing of the unconscious: "the unconscious ego differs from the repressed unconscious in that the former refers to an unconscious form and the latter to unconscious contents" (*Shadow of the Object*, 8). The form or "idiom of the ego" is constituted through a dialectic between "inherited disposition" and environment; the ego in this sense "develops and establishes a highly complex system of organization all of which precedes the 'birth' of the subject or the presence of the self" (8). It is unthought but intimately known as the very ground of one's experience, the fashioner of one's idiom.

9. See, e.g., Polzella, "'Craft So Long to Lerne,'" Neuss, "Images of Writing," Kiser, *Truth and Textuality*, and especially Lawton, *Chaucer's Narrators*.

10. Bollas, *Shadow of the Object*, 60, passim. See also note 9.

11. This is a plot movement described throughout Freud's *Interpretation of Dreams*. See also Brooks, *Reading for the Plot*, and Kinney, *Strategies*, 21.

12. Bollas, *Shadow of the Object*, 14. On holding, see Winnicott, "Theory of the Parent-Infant Relationship."

13. Chaucer is cited from the *Riverside Chaucer.*

14. See Barney, "Chaucer's Lists." On the encyclopedists, see Hurst, "Encyclopaedic Tradition." On hexameral arts generally, see McColley, *A Gust for Paradise*, 135–51, passim; Williams, *Common Expositor.*

15. I concur with McDonald and Farrell, in contrasting the bird catalogue—which Farrell calls "vital, fresh, and functionally important" at page 70—with earlier catalogues in the poem. See McDonald, "Interpretation of Chaucer's *Parlement*"; Farrell, "Chaucer's Use of the Catalogue." Martin's "Shady Trope of Spenser's Trees" traces the much different narrative functions and affects of anxiety and ambivalence in Chaucer's and Spenser's tree catalogues. On naming in lyric, see Welsh, *Roots of Lyric*, 243–51, passim.

16. See, e.g., Silverman, *Acoustic Mirror*, particularly the chapter "The Fantasy of the Maternal Voice"; Spitz, "A Cycle of Songs."

17. Essential essays on this trope and its link with childrearing in the Renaissance include Ong, "Latin Language Study," and Kerrigan, "Articulation of the Ego."

18. Twentieth-century instances would include Stevens's "The Idea of Order at Key West" and, apropos to the avian elevations of Chaucer's poem, Frost's "Never Again Would Birds' Song Be the Same," about how Eve gave song to the birds of Eden.

19. Winnicott, "Transitional Objects," 2.

20. Chodorow, *Feminism and Psychoanalytic Theory*, 189–90.

21. On the concluding song, it is worth noting that the sixteenth-century printed versions, which acknowledge Chaucer's term *roundel*, print it as an eight-line stanza; the roundel form with which we are familiar in recent scholarly editions was devised by Skeat. Thanks to Helen Cooper for reminding me of this.

22. See, e.g., Coghill, "Shakespeare's Reading"; Presson, "Conclusion of *Love's Labour's Lost*"; Thompson, *Shakespeare's Chaucer*, 78–80, 85.

23. For a theory of Shakespearean comedy based on curative exacerbation, see Nevo, *Comic Transformations in Shakespeare.*

24. The discovery regarding the flowers, and its implication for a dating of the play's composition or revision in or after 1597, we owe to Lever, "Three Notes on Shakespeare's Plants."

25. Richard David, in his edition of *Love's Labour's Lost*, 78. Citations are taken from the *Riverside Shakespeare.*

26. Hawkes, *Shakespeare's Talking Animals*, 54; see also Montrose, "*Curious-Knotted Garden*," 58–59.

27. Among many studies of the Nashe-Harvey topicality of the play, see Nicholl, *A Cup of News*, 208–20. Holmer, "Nashe as 'Monarch of Witt,'" argues for the relevance of Nashe's character and work to *Romeo and Juliet*; she details Shakespeare's minute lexical dismemberments and rememberings of Nashe's work, a large, peculiar, and underestimated aspect of Shakespeare's imitative practice.

28. A. L. Rowse, letter to *Times Literary Supplement*, 18 July 1952; cited in David's edition of the play, 73.

29. Frese, "Names of Women," 165; also her unpublished lecture "Three Men and a Baby." The relevance of lexical patterns (including puns) in Shakespeare has always been acknowledged; for recent studies of the work that they do, including the carrying of implicit accounts of literary relationships, see Holmer, "Nashe as 'Monarch of Witt'"; Mahood, *Shakespeare's Wordplay*; Parker, *Shakespeare from the Margins*; Booth, "Exit, Pursued by a Gentleman Born."

30. Maus, *Inwardness and the Theater*, 182–209. On the *pia mater*, see Sacks, *Shakespeare's Images of Pregnancy*, 182–209. On the association of matter and *mater* in Shakespeare, see Ferguson, "*Hamlet*: Letters and Spirits."

31. Holofernes' gratitude would be an instance of the first of Klein's kinds of gratitude, that which exists innate in the newborn and is elaborated directly in exchange with the reliable feeding mother. It is this formulation that leads to

Winnicott, I think; Holofernes does not have anything to show us about Kleinian gratitude as a defensive formation, that is for the lords and the role of the seasonal songs in relation to the lords' envy.

32. Klein, *Envy and Gratitude*, 40. This is a crucial book—one that Elizabeth Bishop called "superb in its horrid way," rightly enough. (Letter of 30 March 1959 to Robert Lowell; in *One Art*, 371.) See also Klein, "On Observing the Behaviour of Young Infants," in Klein et al., *Developments in Psycho-Analysis*, 237–70, on the formative consequences of the infant's repeated experiences, of loss and regaining, greed and gratification; "A Contribution to the Psychogenesis of Manic-Depressive States."

33. Segal, *Melanie Klein*, 146.

34. The interruption of the pageant is also the falling apart of the learned locals' last attempt at a performative identification with classical antiquity; their love for this tradition makes all the more striking their composition of the vernacular songs.

35. For this history, see Anderson, *Illustrated History*, and Woodward, *Gerard's Herball.*

36. If Shakespeare used the 1532 edition of William Thynne or one of its successors, he would have found another treatment of birdsong and birds' marital choices on St. Valentine's Day in the poem that immediately follows *The assemble of foules—The floure of Curtesy*, a poem that ends with a "Balade symple." But this embedded lyric remains in the courtly complaint mode, rather than offering an alternative to it. See *Works, 1532*, fol. cclxxxiiii^{v}. Birdsong, bird catalogues, lyric praises of the created world, marital choice, St. Valentine's Day, and the love of old books recur in various combinations in the Thynne editions in *The complaynt of mars and venus*, *The legende of good women*, the *Romaunt of the Rose.*

37. The happy exception is Lawton, *Chaucer's Narrators*, 44–45: "Rather than bathos, Chaucer's return to his library is, in its quiet way, as positive an event as the preceding roundel. Rather than contradicting the dream, the narrator corroborates it."

38. Nor does the frustration reading take into account the startling fact that the stanza provides a conclusion at all, an element so conspicuous by its rarity in Chaucer's work. R. A. Shoaf, in a response to a presentation from this chapter in Kalamazoo in 1995, has suggested that it is the particular, positive relation of the poet to the maternal-transformational in this poem that makes this satisfying closure possible at all.

CHAPTER 10

Jacobean Chaucer

The Two Noble Kinsmen and Other Chaucerian Plays

HELEN COOPER

> It has a noble breeder and a pure,
> A learned, and a poet never went
> More famous yet 'twixt Po and silver Trent.
> Chaucer, of all admired, the story gives:
> There constant to eternity it lives.
> *Two Noble Kinsmen*

The encomium of Chaucer in the Prologue to *The Two Noble Kinsmen* is not belied by the play that follows. For both Shakespeare and John Fletcher, the work marked a continuing interest in Chaucerian themes and plots, but here they treat such material with unique respect. In the other plays in which the dramatists draw on Chaucer, plots and characters are changed at will, and scarcely a line of Chaucer comes through in recognizable form. Their dramatization of the Knight's Tale is different. Chaucer here is given authoritative status comparable to Plutarch in Shakespeare's Roman plays (though Plutarch is never accorded an encomium). The playwrights add a subplot, of the Jailer's Daughter who engineers Palamon's escape from prison, and of a country morris-dance that fills out Chaucer's May observances; but otherwise the plot, the structure, the characterization, and the ideas of the play are all closely derived from the Knight's Tale.[1] Derivation in this instance, however, does not mean copying. It is rather that the play enters into a continuing and detailed dialogue with its original. The Knight's Tale is a poem about the intellectual, human and theological problems that until this century were held to be the paramount questions of human existence: issues of free will; providential justice; rationality, affection, and passion in both men and women. *The Two Noble Kinsmen* not only carries over these problems but makes them sharper; the untied thematic ends of Chaucer's original are not just left loose but rendered jagged.

The play was not the first dramatic version of the Knight's Tale to be staged, two versions (both now lost) having been produced in the reign of Elizabeth.[2] One of these, Richard Edwardes' *Palamon and Arcite,* was performed before the Queen at Oxford in 1566 and was never intended for the public stage. The second was presented by the Admiral's Men in September 1594, just a few weeks after they had split off from the company that was to become the Chamberlain's Men—Shakespeare's company. The two companies had been running a combined operation in association with Philip Henslowe, who commissioned the 1594 *Palamon,* until the middle of that year, and it may have been the current dramatic interest in the Knight's Tale that drew Shakespeare's attention to it for his writing of *A Midsummer Night's Dream,* probably dating from 1594–95.[3] By the time he returned to the Knight's Tale some twenty years later, he had looked to Chaucer on a number of other occasions, for *Troilus and Cressida* and many of the later plays; but never with the kind of detailed attention that he pays to Chaucer's text in *The Two Noble Kinsmen.*

At about the same time that Shakespeare and Fletcher were adapting the Knight's Tale, Fletcher himself was collaborating on the *Four Plays, or Moral Representations, in One,* which includes as its "Triumph of Honor" a free reworking of the Franklin's Tale.[4] His collaborator in this instance was probably Nathan Field, who was about to become a member of Shakespeare's company and is listed as one of the leading actors of his plays in the First Folio. Field is the likely author of this particular "moral representation," but Fletcher presumably had full access to his scheme of composition. Some six years later, Fletcher was to write a similarly free adaptation of the Wife of Bath's Tale entitled *Women Pleased.*[5] *The Two Noble Kinsmen* stands out from all these other Chaucerian plays, however, as an anomaly in both the Shakespeare and the Fletcher corpus, and not just by virtue of its faithfulness to its original. The other dramatizations, *Troilus and Cressida* famously excepted, press toward a full resolution of the problematic elements that are central to their Chaucerian source poems; it seems to have been the unresolvable problems in the Knight's Tale that caught the attention of the playwrights.[6]

All these plays share a common plot, in the love of two men for one woman—the classic love triangle. This is obvious in most instances: Palamon and Arcite's love for Emily; Troilus's love for Criseyde/Cressida and Diomede's sexual interest in her; the faithful marriage of Dorigen and Arveragus in the Franklin's Tale (or of Dorigen and Sophocles in *The Triumph of Honor*) threatened by the desire of Aurelius, the *Triumph's* Martius. *A Midsummer Night's Dream* starts off similarly, with both

Lysander and Demetrius as suitors for Hermia's hand, and continues with them both in pursuit of Helena. The Wife of Bath's Tale might seem to contain a very different plot, but not by the time Fletcher had finished with it. His hero Silvio is not a rapist, but is condemned rather for attempting to elope with the Duke of Siena's promised bride, the princess Belvidere; and the *dénouement* threatens the complementary problem, of Silvio's being promised in marriage to two women, his beloved and the old hag who has helped him to solve the traditional riddle of what women most desire.

Women Pleased shows with particular clarity how Fletcher can produce a full resolution, in terms of both plot and theme, to a more problematic original. This is achieved partly by cutting the story free of its context: many of the tantalizing questions raised by Chaucer's original have to do with the tale's relationship to its teller, the Wife of Bath, defender of matrimony and of the rights of wives both in practice and in theory. The main plot of the play is thus rendered free to develop the romance elements of its action, wifely dominance being associated with lower-style genres such as fabliau. Fletcher does not ignore the issue of wives' rights, but he moves it into a subplot: a subplot which, interestingly, is itself based on a pseudo-Chaucerian old wife's tale, from the prose *novelle* told by the passengers traveling down the Thames in the anonymous *Cobbler of Canterbury.*[7] Fletcher alters the old woman's story of female wiles (itself based on the *Decameron*) to provide its wife with a sympathetic motivation for her matrimonial discontent: the wife of his subplot is tempted to infidelity by her miserly and jealous husband's refusal to allow her adequate food or clothing, and the aim of the episode is to teach him (and other husbands with him) to treat his wife with proper respect. The issue, in fact, is more one of human decency than a battle of ideologies between male dominance and female self-assertion such as is charted by the Wife of Bath's Prologue. Fletcher also omits the hag's pillow-talk on the independence of true nobility, *gentillesse,* from noble birth, which takes up a full quarter of the Wife's tale. Something of the same idea is present in the gap in social rank between the gentleman Silvio and the princess Belvidere, and in the lesson in good matrimonial manners administered to everyone in the subplot; but the absorption of the moral discourse into the action softens the revolutionary potential of the original speech into a more sentimental appeal to audience sympathy for thwarted young lovers and ill-treated wives.

The riddle that Silvio is set after being arrested for his attempted elopement is the same as in the Wife of Bath's Tale—to find what women most desire; and the answer is the same too, to have their will. But this potential promotion of female sovereignty is again rendered safe by Fletcher, both by the phrasing of the riddle and by the twists of the plot. The question is not revealed until the last act of the play, when the answer is given too:

Question
Tell me what is that onely thing,
  For which all women long;
Yet having what they most desire,
  To have it do's them wrong.
Answer
Tis not to be chaste, nor faire,
  Such gifts malice may impaire;
Richly trim'd, to walke or ride,
  Or to wanton unespi'd;
To preserve an honest name,
  And so to give it up to fame;
These are toyes. In good or ill
  They desire, to have their will;
Yet when they have it, they abuse it,
  For they know not how to use it. (V.i.126–41)

There is a remarkable moralistic tone to this, in contrast to the nonjudgmental nature of Chaucer's riddle and its answer: the question takes as its premise that women's desire for their own way "do's them wrong" when it is achieved, and the reply further insists that they necessarily abuse their freedom. Yet this apparent sellout to conventional misogynist views, while it may be designed to remove any overt threat from the issue of women's sovereignty, is not supported by the action of the play itself. Belvidere knows exactly what she wants—Silvio—and she runs away from her mother's control to win him, adopting the disguise of a loathly lady to do so (she herself, in fact, is the hag); the choice she offers him at the end, the Chaucerian options of being fair and wanton or ugly and virtuous, has minimal force behind it when she is indeed his faithful Belvidere and has no intention of being otherwise. Although Silvio has been the central character of the play in the sense that he is the one whose actions are followed, it is the women who engineer the whole plot. Belvidere disguises herself, with the aid of a female friend, to follow her beloved; and at the very end the Duke of Siena, who has been wreaking revenge on the country for the disappearance of his promised bride, is bought off by his acceptance of the "mastry" of her widowed mother, the Duchess of Florence, who offers him her own hand and with it "a husbands freedome" (V.iii.82–102). The husbands in the subplot are prepared by the end to joke about giving "our wives the breeches too" so long as they "rule with vertue" (V.ii.104–5). Young love and women's moral clear-sightedness keep the plot on course and are duly rewarded at the end.

It is likewise a strong woman who engineers the happy conclusion of *The Triumph of Honor* in *Four Plays in One*. "Honor" here means less chivalric reputation (as it does in the Franklin's Tale) or a masculine code of military uprightness (though that seems at first to be crucial for the play) than it does female chastity. The corporal in its subplot similarly equates dishonor with his wife's unfaithfulness (i.266). The setting for the story is shifted both in time and place to the conquest of Greece by Rome; the play opens with the more-than-human refusal of Sophocles, Duke of Athens (the same title held by Theseus in the Knight's Tale and its derivative plays), to beg for mercy from his conqueror Martius. Sophocles' wife Dorigen has more in common with the tough-minded Volumnia of *Coriolanus* than with Chaucer's gentle heroine, as the following early exchange shows when she pleads for her husband's life:

> *Martius*: He would not live.
> *Dorigen*: He would not beg to live.
> When he shall so forget, then I begin
> To command, Martius; and when he kneels,
> Dorigen stands; when he lets fall a tear,
> I dry my eyes, and scorn him. (i.132–36)

When Martius propositions her, her rejection of him is fierce and proud—"Hath Dorigen never been written, read, / Without the epithet of chaste, chaste Dorigen?" (ii.65–66)—but she is also prescient in her assessment of male bonding above that of husband and wife:

> Is this Martius?
> I will not tell my Lord; he'll swear I lye,
> Doubt my fidelitie, before thy honour. (ii.54–56)

This bonding of fellow soldiers that Dorigen posits between Martius and Sophocles is the same as that which leads Claudio to believe Hero unfaithful when Don John calumniates her in *Much Ado about Nothing*, or Othello to trust Iago above Desdemona, or Posthumus in *Cymbeline* to believe Iachimo rather than Imogen. Like those plays, however, *The Tri-*

umph of Honor vindicates the woman's faithfulness above such blind male trust. Misogyny is presented critically, and the play implies blame for Sophocles' equally blind mistrust of women beyond anything the upright Dorigen ever makes explicit.

As in the Franklin's Tale, Dorigen promises to love her suitor if he removes "these rocks we see so fix'd" (ii.85), and the promise functions as an unequivocal part of her rejection of him; the rocks have received no earlier mention in the play, and serve no purpose except to guarantee her oath. Yet Martius goes ahead to create an illusion of their disappearance since "the Athenians are religious in their vows, / Above all nations" (ii.152–53), and he believes he has her trapped by her own culturally instilled piety. Her immediate response (with none of the original Dorigen's lamenting) is to tell her husband, but, as she has already suspected, his response is an aside—overheard by her—in which he gives way to jealousy. His command to her to keep her promise shows, not the victory over human weakness of his initial refusal to ask for life, but cold brutality: "For chaste, and whore, are words of equal length" (iii.16). Dorigen snatches back the initiative by pretending that his jealousy is well-founded, and she immediately obeys her husband by going off to Martius. She disobeys him just as decisively, however, in breaking his prohibition on saying that he has sent her:

> Hail, General of Rome; from Sophocles
> That honours Martius, Dorigen presents
> Her self to be dishonour'd: do thy will;
> For Sophocles commands me to obey.
> Come, violate all rules of holinesse,
> And rend the consecrated knot of love. (iv.1–6)

She intends by this to shake Martius back into his senses, but he signally fails to respond to her challenge; not until she is on the point of stabbing herself, Lucretia-like, so that her "chaste name lives to posterity" (iv.18), is he converted back to the path of virtue. The jealous Sophocles then bursts in to take revenge, but he is now soothed by Martius's assurances that his wife is innocent as he had failed to be by her own protestations. As in *Women Pleased,* however, even at this point, when the woman appears to hold all the moral high ground, a piece of misogynist flippancy is allowed in, in Martius's backhanded compliment to Sophocles on his wife:

> Heaven has not stuff enough
> To make another such; for if it could,
> Martius would marry too. (iv.50–52)

This discord in the final harmony is immediately drowned out by the following "Shew of Honours Triumph" under Diana's aegis, in which Sophocles is celebrated for Valour, Martius for Clemency, and Dorigen, crowned, for both Chastity and Constancy. Chaucer's concluding question as to which of his male characters was the "mooste fre"[8] could have no place in the Field-Fletcher version; the men here have all disgraced themselves to some degree, and only Dorigen has set an unambiguous moral standard.

An equivalent emphasis on the women as carrying the values endorsed by the close of the play is found in many of Shakespeare's comedies, most persistently in the late plays closest in time to these of the Fletcher canon and to *The Two Noble Kinsmen.* While none of Shakespeare's romances uses a Chaucerian model directly, they do share with the Man of Law's tale of Constance and the Clerk's of Griselda both the motif of the calumniated woman and the stress on patience. These are key elements in *The Winter's Tale, Cymbeline, Pericles,* and that other Shakespeare-Fletcher collaboration, *Henry VIII.*[9] The association comes partly through the common base of both Chaucer's and the dramatists' stories in the "Eustace-Constance-Florence-Griselda" group of romances, but partly too from direct knowledge of Chaucer's texts.[10] Both tales had indeed been popular enough in 1599–1600 for Dekker and others to dramatize them, in *Patient Grissil* (the second play to be given the title) and the lost *Fair Constance of Rome.*[11] In contrast to the Chaucerian heroines of the Fletcher canon, however, the women at the center of these late plays of Shakespeare's are important less for what they do—as the stress on patience indicates, they are much more sufferers than agents—than for what they are and what they represent. The key thematic changes between the Franklin's Tale and the Field-Fletcher *Triumph of Honor* stem from Dorigen's insistence on dominating the action; the scope for female initiative is enlarged from the Wife of Bath's Tale into *Women Pleased.* Hermione, Imogen, Pericles' wife and child and himself too, Katherine of Aragon, are all to an extent victims who can have little positive response other than patient endurance. Even the least victimlike of Shakespeare's late heroines, Perdita, matters far less for her actions than for the symbolic weight she carries, as the embodiment of the returning cycle of spring and fertility, as Flora or Proserpina, the child of "great creating Nature."[12]

The contemporary use by Shakespeare of the Knight's Tale would seem to fit with such a presentation of his women protagonists more than it does with Fletcher's. Chaucer's Emily, too, carries an emblematic power beyond anything she does. What she does, indeed, matters singularly little for the story: she has to be seen, she has to accept the suitor who wins the combat—her role is to be acted on, not to act. She is never presented as a martial Amazon in either text, though the Hippolyta of *The Two Noble Kinsmen* is war-hardened in the grimmest sense (her inability to weep at starving mothers' cannibalism of their own children, for instance, I.iii.18–22). Yet Emily's introduction into the Knight's Tale is much more powerful than that passivity would suggest.

> It fil ones, in a morwe of May,
> That Emilye, that fairer was to sene
> Than is the lylie upon his stalke grene,
> And fressher than the May with floures newe—
> For with the rose colour stroof hire hewe,
> I noot which was the fyner of hem two—
> Er it were day, as was hir wone to do,
> She was arisen and al redy dight,
> For May wile have no slogardie anyght . . .
> . . . .
> This maked Emelye have remembraunce
> To doon honour to May . . . (*CT* I.1034–42, 1046–47)

The alternating references to Emily and to May associate her indissolubly with the month of love; the lilies and roses to which she is compared (and which the "white and rede" flowers she is gathering for her garland also suggest) associate her further with purity and love. Set beside Perdita's associations with flowers and the spring, however, Emily is strikingly static. She is less a fully fledged character than an idea in the minds of the cousins who see her from their prison with the force of a revelation, or in the minds, of the readers who share the narrator's gaze. The initial symbolic presentation of her is designed to make her infinitely desirable, but in a way that stays within the bounds of the tale. The wider context of the *Canterbury Tales* as a whole puts firmer limits on her still: in the Second Nun's Tale, earthly garlands of roses and lilies are transcended by heavenly ones that will not wither or die, as the mortal is rejected for the immortal. Emily is redefined retrospectively, as an object of pleasure that will not last. Perdita, by contrast, does not gather flowers but distributes them. For her, the language describing her actions invites mythic associations of the return of "the spring to the earth" (*WT* V.i.150), and her frank engagement with the regenerative processes of this world turns even the traditional strewing of the corpse with flowers into an act of procreation,

like a bank for love to lie and play on,
Not like a corpse—or if, not to be buried,
But quick and in mine arms. (*WT* IV.iv.130–32)

The vibrant sexuality that those lines suggest, or the vigor of the new life contained in the return of spring, is missing from the Knight's Tale.

It is missing too from *The Two Noble Kinsmen.* There are moments when such a promise of mythic regeneration appears to be made, but they are always ironic, canceled out by the tragic movement of events unforeseen by the characters. The speech that Shakespeare offers as the equivalent of Chaucer's description of Emily in the garden is more markedly subjective than the narratorial account in the Knight's Tale: it is spoken by Arcite in soliloquy, after his return to Thebes in disguise, as he recalls the absent Emily to his imagination.[13]

O, Queen Emilia,
Fresher than May, sweeter
Than her gold buttons on the boughs, or all
Th'enamelled knacks o'th' mead or garden—yea,
We challenge too the bank of any nymph
That makes the stream seem flowers; thou, O jewel
O'th' wood, o'th' world . . . (III.i.4–10)

Within the play this recalls the initial strewing of flowers by the masque figure of Hymen at the nuptial procession of Theseus and Hippolyta:

Oxlips, in their cradles growing,
Marigolds, on deathbeds blowing,
Lark's-heels trim;
All dear nature's children sweet,
Lie fore bride and bridegroom's feet. (I.i.10–14)

That Perdita-like image of "nature's children," however, had been interrupted by the appearance of the "three Queens in black," who immediately override Hymen's dismissal of the crow and raven to describe the birds of carrion that feed on the corpses of their husbands. The larger dramatic context for Arcite's apostrophe to his beloved is similarly chilling. He goes on to congratulate himself on the favor shown him by Lady Fortune and to describe the steed that Emilia has bestowed on him, but it is this horse that will cause his death at the end of the play. The image of the nymph of the stream is likewise tainted, when the Jailer's Daughter is found "like the fair nymph / That feeds the lake with waters" (IV.i.86–87) and surrounded by flowers, but in a state of Ophelia-like madness in which she comes close to drowning herself. Where the flowers that surround Chaucer's Emily define her as mortal and those that Perdita strews suggest the cyclical triumph of nature over death, Arcite's speech foreshadows the madness and death that are to dominate the last two acts of the play, and its life-giving imagery is undercut by the tragic irony of a blindness that forms one of the central themes of the Knight's Tale: "We seken faste after felicitee, / But we goon wrong ful often, trewely"(*CT* I.1266–67). Arcite's lyric evocation of felicity as he dreams in the forest of Emilia is just so precisely misplaced.

The Jailer's Daughter is not a character who will be familiar to readers of Chaucer. She is created to fill out the bare hint in the Knight's Tale as to how Palamon escapes from prison, "by helpyng of a freend" (*CT* I.1468), but her effect on the play is much larger than any plot mechanism, and her feeling for Palamon is not just friendship but passionate love. In marked contrast to Emilia, she knows exactly which one of the cousins she loves; Arcite never gets so much as a mention from her after she first corrects her father as to which of them is which. Already promised to a man identified only as the "Wooer," she knows perfectly well that her obsession with Palamon will get her nowhere—"To marry him is hopeless, / To be his whore is witless" (II.iv.4–5)—but she still embarks on the desperate course of releasing him, although she knows her father may be executed as a result. She attempts to follow him to the forest, but fails to find him, and loses her mind from the combined effects of passion, fear, and desperation—"wood within this wood" in a more literal fashion than the lovers of *A Midsummer Night's Dream* ever experience (*MND* II.i.192). She is eventually cured by the Wooer's pretending to be Palamon and courting her under that name, to the point of making love to her. The scenes of her madness tread a narrow line of pathos between the incipient tragedy suggested by the parallels with Ophelia and the incipient comedy of the bawdy cure; but the line is held, and the recent stagings of the play after its long neglect have proved the theatrical power of the scenes. Her madness makes literal the irrationality of the passion felt by all the lovers of the play, and shows the force of that passion when she has no outlet for it such as the men can find in fighting. Unusually both for a woman and for a character from a subplot, she is given most of the play's soliloquies, being completely alone in her love (Palamon never so much as acknowledges her existence until he is about to be executed after losing the battle). She also provides a lower-class commentary on the aristocratic posturings of the cousins, both through the intensity of her passions and through her final cure.

What she does not do is provide any resolution to the main plot. It might seem that the ideal way to resolve a love triangle is to provide a fourth term, to turn it into a square: this indeed is what Fletcher does when he has Belvidere's mother offer herself to the Duke of Siena, what Shakespeare does when Demetrius and Hermia, Lysander and Helena finally get themselves sorted out into pairs. The same happens in a Restoration version of *The Two Noble Kinsmen,* William Davenant's *The Rivals,* in which the Jailer's Daughter is upgraded to a Provost's Daughter so that the knights can have a wife apiece at the happy ending, Philander-Palamon being prepared to marry for honor the woman who freed him from prison since he cannot persuade Heraclia-Emilia to reciprocate his love.[14] The impossibility of such an outcome in *The Two Noble Kinsmen*—an impossibility made explicit by the gap in rank and by Palamon's general blindness to the Daughter's existence—is the corollary of what actually does happen: the love triangle is resolved, not by the addition of a second woman to provide a comedic ending in marriage all round, but by the reduction of the triangle to a single couple. *The Triumph of Honor* takes this way out, with Martius removing himself as a sexual contender; and in *Women Pleased,* Silvio finds that his two promised brides, Belvidere and the loathly lady, are one and the same. Theseus aims to achieve a similar result by executing the loser in the battle for Emilia; "the gods" intervene to remove Arcite instead. That the subplot furnishes a further couple in the persons of the Wooer and the recovered Daughter only heightens the injustice of the play: there is no moral or chivalric reason for Palamon to be rewarded while Arcite dies. Arcite wins the battle; Palamon takes the prize. The Daughter loses her heart to Palamon; the man who loves her has to adopt Palamon's name to lie with her and win her back. There is a sense in which Palamon gets both the women, Arcite neither.

Once there is more than one couple in a play, then the possibilities of various geometrical arrangements are opened up, not just across the sexes but between them. As its title implies, *The Two Noble Kinsmen* is a play about male friendship: as in the Knight's Tale, the relationship between the cousins is established before ever they set eyes on Emilia. The play, however, debates much more fully the issue of same-sex friendship as against the love of "sex dividual" (I.iii.82).[15] Chaucer's knights argue about the rights of love over friendship, with self-interest winning out over any theory—"ech man for hymself, ther is noon oother" (*CT* I.1182). Shakespeare and Fletcher supplement their quarrel with a broad range of debates between other characters and of examples that offer different attitudes to the question. Pirithous, Theseus' friend, is an active character in the play, not the shadowy background figure of the poem; and Hippolyta and Emilia are given a substantial discussion as to whether same-sex or heterosexual love is stronger. Hippolyta is prepared to believe that Theseus' love for his friend is equal to that for herself. Emily coolly suggests otherwise—"Doubtless / There is a best, and reason has no manners / To say it is not you" (I.iii.47–49)—but she goes on to insist that she will never love any man as she loved her childhood friend Flavina, now dead. Hippolyta is much less ready to accept same-sex friendship as equivalent to heterosexual love when it takes the form of such woman-to-woman affection; she responds by elevating the love of man and woman both in Theseus' own relationship with her and in any future bond Emilia may have. That the play requires Emilia's eventual marriage might seem to endorse Hippolyta's views, but it is not in practice so straightforward:[16] indeed, Shakespeare and Fletcher show signs of disagreeing over the nature of Emilia more than anything else in the whole collaboration, with Shakespeare steering her toward preserving the "virgin's faith" of her mind whatever the plot may impose on her, and Fletcher promoting a change of heart to a more conventional image of nuptial womanhood. So in Fletcher's Act IV, she is prepared to be in love with both the cousins rather than with neither (IV.ii.1–54); in Shakespeare's Act V, when she believes Palamon must die, she regards the only advantage in remaining alive herself as being that she can comfort Arcite for the loss of his friend (V.v.141–44). In the work of both dramatists, however, her linguistic habits constantly show her identifying herself by gender, as she frequently appeals to a sisterhood of women or a standard of female judgment in a way that one would think of as more twentieth-century feminist than seventeenth-century Amazon.[17]

In evaluating the rival claims of love and friendship, Fletcher would seem to have past Shakespearean practice on his side: the comedies regularly show young men having to grow from callow male comradeship into mature relationships with women—*Love's Labour's Lost* is perhaps the clearest instance. So far as women are concerned, however, matters are not so straightforward. In *The Two Gentlemen of Verona*, the other play that debates the rivalry of love and friendship most fully (and that itself has some element of the Knight's Tale in its ancestry), the strongest contrast is between any relationship that involves the male protagonists and any that involves the female ones: the men come out of both friendship and love distinctly badly, Proteus because he is treacherous in both, Valentine because his casual handing over of the woman who loves him to his friend calls all his emotions, and their moral basis, into question. Julia and Silvia, by contrast, are unhesitatingly faithful to their first loves, and Silvia's sympathy for the betrayed Julia suggests the same kind of woman-to-woman bonding that Emilia invokes. Shakespeare does not give it such good press in *A Midsummer Night's Dream,* when Helena makes a sentimental appeal to her childhood friendship with Hermia in a speech that offers the closest parallel in his works to Emilia's on Flavina (*MND* III.ii.203–19). In this play, however, the clash of love and friendship has no broader repercussions for the human characters, and its Hippolyta is given no male rival in Theseus' love. Matters are somewhat more problematic in the fairy world, where Oberon's obsession with the "little changeling boy" has wrecked his matrimonial relationship with Titania, she being determined to care for the child for the sake of his dead mother (II.i.122–37). It would be a brave critic who attempted to draw any conclusions from, or even define, the amatory relationships of the fairies;[18] but the lines in which Titania speaks of her "votaress" do carry a rhetorical conviction lacking in Helena's too much protesting, and this friendship, like Flavina's, has been rendered immutable by death. *The Two Noble Kinsmen* represents a rare moment in the Shakespeare canon in showing the "maturely seasoned" love between male friends, Theseus and Pirithous (I.iii.56), and there is no suggestion that Emilia's evaluation of her childhood love is itself childish; but the play endorses neither those values nor any others. It is too full of counterexamples to turn such moments into fixed principles, in the bitter rivalry of Palamon and Arcite and Emilia's enforced yielding to marriage—how enforced, will depend on the production: she has reluctantly agreed to marry the victor in the combat, but like Isabella in *Measure for Measure,* she remains silent at the end of the play when she is led off to marriage by a bridegroom she has not expected. Heterosexual passion may be presented in the play as stronger than friendship both for the cousins and for the course of the plot, but there is no confirmation that it is better.

The Knight's Tale already provides the raw material for such a questioning of the nature of friendship and love, in the instant collapse of the cousins' sworn faith to each other and in the emblematic presentation of the nastiness of sexual love in the decoration of Venus's temple, with its folly, rape, pimping, lies and jealousy (*CT* I.1918–54). *The Two Noble Kinsmen* transfers such a cynical view of the topic to where one might least expect it, the lovers themselves. The casual masculine flippancy about women that puts in appearances in both *Women Pleased* and *The Triumph of Honor* is given a much higher profile in this play, and placed where it can do more damage. When Arcite succors Palamon in the forest, they drink to "the wenches / We have known in our days" (III.iii.28–29), and compare notes on former loved and abandoned mistresses—women of the same social rank as the Jailer's Daughter; while she is losing her mind, they are laughing at her counterparts in their past lives. Palamon's address to Venus before the tournament, describing her power over gods and men, is notorious for its unpleasantness, an unpleasantness much more specific than that of Chaucer's temple since Fletcher gives human examples rather than personifications. While it may at first be possible to accept his protestation at the birth of a child to an eighty-year-old man and his fourteen-year-old bride—"I / Believed it was his, for she swore it was, / And who would not believe her?" (V.ii.48–50)—the decorous interpretation is rapidly undermined by his further reference to the couple as "those that would and cannot" (53), whether "those" refers to impotent husbands or unfulfilled wives.

In such moments of the cousins' badinage or Palamon's analysis of Venerean love, the compatibility of misogyny with the idealization of women becomes explicit. The play itself does not endorse such views; it treats its women with consistent respect, even the Jailer's Daughter, whose class might seem to push her toward low-life sexual comedy such as provided a staple ingredient of Jacobean drama (even *The Triumph of Honor* finds space for such a subplot). It does, however, ask uncomfortable questions about men's attitudes, questions that prevent the audience from taking the kinsmen's love for Emilia as ideal or even admirable, and that make the play appear an aberration in the context of much of Fletcher's work and, in particular, of Shakespeare's other late plays. Not only is Emilia inactive, and her symbolic power undercut by tragic irony; she does not even affect her lovers sufficiently to make them respect women. *The Winter's Tale, Cymbeline, Pericles,* as well as *Women Pleased* and *The Triumph of Honor,* achieve their happy endings largely through a demonstration of women's strength. The aristocratic heroines of *The Two Noble Kinsmen* may be Amazons, but they have been defeated by Theseus, "born to uphold creation" in reasserting male superiority (I.i.82–83), and it is not their values that triumph.

With that failure goes a radical shift away from comedy, and from any satisfying closure. Like *Pericles,* the play carries no kind of generic designation. It is commonly associated with Jacobean tragicomedy, but it differs from both Fletcher's and Shakespeare's tragicomic practice elsewhere. Fletcher's definition of the genre requires that it should lack deaths, a condition contradicted by Arcite's fatal accident.[19] Shakespeare's other late plays offer a tragicomic structure, in the sense that a happy ending is attached to serious or potentially tragic subject matter (a structure that did not prevent the editors of the First Folio from classifying *Cymbeline* as straight tragedy). Such an upbeat ending is found even in *Henry VIII,* the plot of which ends with Henry triumphant and Katherine of Aragon dead; but before or alongside that, Katherine has a vision of her blissful entry into heaven, and Cranmer utters a prophecy of the blessings that England will receive from the infant Elizabeth. It is a given of the story of Palamon and Arcite that a happy ending for one can only be achieved at the expense of the other; but it is Shakespeare and Fletcher's innovation in the story that both *cannot* survive, that the loser in the combat must die—that the archetypal comic marriage has to be counterbalanced by the archetypal tragic death. The snatching of Palamon from the block after his defeat by Arcite might appear to offer a way out of Theseus' decree of execution for the loser, just as the harsh conditions set at the start of other comedies are superseded or forgotten by the end (Theseus' citation of the Athenian law in *A Midsummer Night's Dream,* for instance, that Hermia must marry in accordance with her father's wishes or else be executed or immured in a nunnery); and the rescue of Palamon looks at first glance as if it parallels the resurrections of the other late plays, Hermione's or Imogen's or Thaisa's. His life, however, has been paid for by the death of his friend, and his survival appears not as any kind of working out of a providential ordering of the world, of a reward for patience or penitence, or of a mythic cycle of rebirth, but as arbitrary: an act of capriciousness on the part of whatever forces, if any, govern the world.

Chaucer had made the apparent arbitrariness in the ordering of the world a major theme of the Knight's Tale, in his organization of the plot, in narrative comment, and above all in the characters' own consciousness of the lack of any predictable moral order. His provision of a set of gods who parallel the human characters intensifies the problems; there is nothing providential or benign about his Mars or Venus, certainly not Saturn—they represent power without responsibility or care. At the end, Chaucer has Theseus assert instead a Boethian principle of love, which he identifies with Jove, and which binds the universe despite all appearances to the contrary. It is still a problematic enough ending, not least in that it does not answer the questions the rest of the work has raised, but it does at least recognize its own problems: the Tale indeed puts them at its center. That Shakespeare was intrigued by the dramatic possibilities of such a structure is shown by *A Midsummer Night's Dream,* where the human characters believe they are acting with free will while in fact the fairies and the magic Love-in-idleness control much of the action, sometimes for better (Oberon's intention to sort the lovers out into pairs), sometimes for worse (Puck's general delight in mischief, the "translation" of Bottom), sometimes by accident (when the love-juice goes to the wrong person). In the structure of the play, Oberon and Titania match Theseus and Hippolyta, and are often doubled in the acting; their direct ancestors also include the Pluto and Proserpina of the Merchant's Tale, who themselves bear a close parallel relationship to the wintry January and his consort "fresshe May." There is however minimal unease created in the *Dream* by the fact that the humans are little more than puppets, love a matter of getting the right sets of eyes properly enchanted: the play is simply too delightful, and the audience (even an Elizabethan audience) know that they are only suspending their disbelief in fairies. The gods, by contrast, have at least a potential real existence, as astrological influences, as personifications of the most powerful human attributes or actions, or as metaphors for whatever forces (blind chance, malign misfortune, a fully Christian Providence) do govern the world. In Shakespeare's late romances, the gods play an active but benign role, Apollo's oracle confirming Hermione's chastity, Diana appearing in person to direct Pericles to Ephesus, Jupiter descending "in thunder and lightning, sitting upon an eagle" to leave a prophetic tablet on Posthumus's breast (*Cymbeline* V.v). The harder metaphysical questions that Chaucer was asking eliminate any possibility of such a providentially guided ending for *The Two Noble Kinsmen.* Chaucer makes his gods active but grim participants in the Knight's Tale; Shakespeare and Fletcher cut them out as physical presences, allowing them only an emblematic response to each supplicant in the scene of the prayers in the temple (V.ii), but leave their motivation, and with that the purpose (if any) behind human events, inscrutable and potentially meaningless. The problems are pushed forward with some urgency by the action, but the characters, in marked contrast to Chaucer's, never comment on the tragic ironies that entrap them, and Theseus' final complacent summing up does not so much attempt to find a way through the metaphysical maze as deny that it exists.

The contrast shows particularly clearly since many of the lines in the play about the ordering of the world draw directly on the Knight's Tale, but they are placed in different contexts and resonate in different ways. Chaucer's Palamon, for instance, accuses the gods of treating men like beasts for slaughter, as little valued as sheep:

> What is mankynde moore unto you holde
> Than is the sheep that rouketh in the folde?
> (*CT* I.1307–8)

Shakespeare transfers the image from Palamon in prison to Theseus after his victory over Creon, turns the herdsmen-gods into agents of justice, and reinterprets the accusation of absence of involvement as the presence of impartiality:

> Th'impartial gods, who from the mounted heavens
> View us their mortal herd, behold who err
> And in their time chastise. (I.iv.4–6)

Given Creon's tyranny, an attribute confirmed even by the Theban cousins, such an alteration might seem to signal a genuine shift from arbitrariness to just order. It emerges over the course of the play, however, that *justice* to Theseus is a term of convenience, a Hobbesian definition of order as being the will of the ruler. The justice he offers to the defeated party in the tournament is instant execution (V.v.132). This serves the purely pragmatic purpose of preventing one suitor from causing further trouble, but it would appear to be wholly purposeless, and indeed downright tyrannous, so far as the supporting champions are concerned (V.v.132, III.vi.218–22, 287–96). The lovers in Chaucer are effectively indistinguishable, so that no outcome can be deserved; the factor that decides which shall have Emily is one of intellectual, not moral, error, Arcite praying for the means to the end (winning the combat) while Palamon prays for the end itself (winning the lady). Shakespeare and Fletcher generally make Arcite sweeter-natured, more conciliatory, while Palamon is more bitter and irascible,[20] and although the difference is small enough to be obliterated by a production that so chooses, the change highlights the problem of rightful reward—especially as here the deciding factor in the outcome is said to be one of "right," of moral due. Theseus thus sees no problem at all:

> The gods have been most equal. Palamon,
> Your kinsman hath confessed the right o'th' lady
> Did lie in you, for you first saw her. (V.vi.115–17)

The question of justice becomes a purely formalist one, of who first saw Emilia; but no principle or law ever laid down that priority of sight confers the right to marriage, or that the infringement of such a law incurs death. Theseus has here shifted from the discourse of love to that of colonialism, in which first sight confers the right of appropriation, rival claimants can justifiably be killed, and the unexplored country is frequently figured—not least by Shakespeare's contemporaries—as a virgin awaiting sexual discovery.[21]

Theseus' final words recall, not the attempt of his counterpart in the Knight's Tale to find a way through or beyond such apparent arbitrariness, but an earlier point in the poem, Arcite's complaint that mankind cannot know the best path to happiness (*CT* I.1251–72). Chaucer's lover notes that Fortune, or the "crueel goddes," may give men "wel bettre than they kan hemself devyse," though the examples he gives are all of men receiving *worse* than they devise—riches causing murder, for instance; and he likens the inability of the human race to identify what is truly desirable to a drunk man's being unable to find his home. The Theseus of the play notes the phenomenon, but without any of the urgency of the tale, and he is happy to dismiss the issues it raises:

> O you heavenly charmers,
> What things you make of us! For what we lack
> We laugh, for what we have, are sorry; still
> Are children in some kind. Let us be thankful
> For that which is, and with you leave dispute
> That are above our question. (V.vi.131–36)

The change of tone between tale and play can be measured by the shift of image for mankind from drunkard to child, and for the gods from cruelty to charm (presumably in the sense—not specifically attested in the *OED*—of astrological influence, but still a much weaker term than Chaucer's Arcite uses). Yet it is not a tone that is comfortable, or that provides a resolution. Theseus' very insistence on justice calls attention to its absence; and his final refusal to continue the debate ("with you leave dispute") is a reminder that the problems are not easily resolved. The Knight's Tale is about the difficulty, even the impossibility, of perceiving any order in the world; *The Two Noble Kinsmen* allows enough of a glimpse of the issue to remind the audience forcefully that it exists, but refuses to focus on it. The closing words, outside the action, indicate that the playwrights recognize that they have sold their audience short somewhere along the way. Chaucer ends by redefining his Knight's tale as a "noble storie," worth further thought (*CT* I.3109–12), and the prologue to the play insists on the need to uphold that nobleness (15). Its epilogue, by contrast, declares that the play is no more than a tale, important only for its market value (8–13), and promises a better to follow.

The shift from nobility to mercantilism is a significant one. It suggests that the play itself charts the decline from the age of chivalry to the age of capitalism, the urban world of self-interest and sharp dealing that the Jacobean stage specialized in representing. Nothing comparable is found in the other Chaucerian plays. *The Triumph of Honor* might seem to participate in such a world, since its subplot corporal regards himself as being doubly defrauded of his property by a debtor he suspects of enjoying his wife's sexual favors: "I say, thou hast dishonour'd mee, and since honour now adaies is only repaired by money, pay mee, and I am satisfied" (i.266–67). The point here, though, is the contrast of such a pecuniary ideology with the rigid codes of martial honor of the characters of the main plot, codes that also saturate their language and imagery. In *The Two Noble Kinsmen,* the market takeover is more insidious.[22] The Knight's Tale offers pilgrimage as a metaphor for the life of its human characters, as an alternative to the plot images of passion and strife or the cousins' sense of themselves as helpless victims:

> This world nys but a thurghfare ful of wo,
> And we been pilgrymes, passynge to and fro.
> Deeth is an ende of every worldly soore. (*CT* I.2847–49)

The words are intended as comfort by their speaker, the aged Egeus, after the death of Arcite; and if they promise no more than death as an end, they do at least, in the larger context of the *Canterbury Tales,* have the power to resonate with Christian ideas of the pilgrimage to Heaven. The equivalent lines offered by Shakespeare occur early in the play, at the end of Act I, when the three queens who have petitioned Theseus for help against Creon take the bodies of their husbands to burial:

> This world's a city full of straying streets,
> And death's the market-place where each one meets. (I.v.15–16)

A pilgrimage route has a clear aim; these "straying streets" carry more of the resonances of Arcite's speech on the drunk man unable to find his way home, only now there is no home for him to find in this nightmare city where the streets themselves thwart direction. In this darker Jacobean world, ancient Athens and contemporary London become the model for a city of death. Egeus's words are offered as reconciliation: Arcite is dead, and even grief for him must end. The queen's words are predictive: whatever path the characters of the play, or indeed the members of the audience, may seek to take, all ways lead alike to extinction. From the very first act of the play, it does not ultimately matter which of the cousins will win Emilia, for both are condemned to death by the simple fact of being alive. Palamon's unexpected salvation from execution is not the metaphorical resurrection of Shakespeare's other late plays, but just one more turning that will delay for a little his arrival in the marketplace of death.

Notes

The epigraph is from the prologue to *Two Noble Kinsmen*, quoted from Shakespeare, *Complete Works*, ed. Wells and Taylor. I have also consulted the editions by Bowers in *Beaumont and Fletcher*, 7:145–298; by Waith, *Two Noble Kinsmen*; and by Leech, *Two Noble Kinsmen.*

1. Thompson, *Shakespeare's Chaucer*, 171–208, gives a scene-by-scene analysis of the relationship; and see also Edwards, "On the Design of *The Two Noble Kinsmen.*" Hillman, in *Intertextuality and Romance*, 136–54, argues for a "radical discontinuity" from Chaucer rather than a shift of emphasis (141).

2. See Thompson, *Shakespeare's Chaucer*, 29–30.

3. Chambers, *Elizabethan Stage,* 2:138–46. The combined company up until 1594 had consisted of Lord Strange's and the Admiral's Men; Shakespeare is first mentioned in connection with the acting companies as a leading actor of the Chamberlain's Men at Christmas 1594. See also Gurr, *Shakespearian Playing Companies*, 68–71. On the parallels with the Knight's Tale, see Brooks's edition of *A Midsummer Night's Dream*, lxxvii–ix, 129–34, and Donaldson, *Swan at the Well*, 30–49.

4. *Four Plays*, ed. Hoy, in *Beaumont and Fletcher*, 8:223–344 (the Chaucerian *Triumph of Honour* is on 247–67). On the date, probably 1613, see McMullan, *Politics of Unease*, 215.

5. *Women Pleased*, ed. Gabler, in *Beaumont and Fletcher*, 5:441–538. The likely date of 1619–23 is rendered uncertain by some evidence that suggests its existence by 1604; see 443–45.

6. Clark notes this quality of the play in relation to its treatment of desire in *Plays of Beaumont and Fletcher*, 132–35.

7. *Cobler of Caunterburie,* 69–74. It was first published in 1590 and reprinted eight years later; Robert Greene was accused of the authorship but denied it. See also Cooper, "Shape-shiftings of the Wife of Bath," esp. 172–75.

8. *Canterbury Tales* V.1622 (*Riverside Chaucer*).

9. See Cooper, *Canterbury Tales*, 422–24, and Baldwin, "From the *Clerk's Tale* to *The Winter's Tale.*"

10. On the "Eustace-Constance-Florence-Griselda" group of romances, see Severs, ed., *Manual of the Writings in Middle English*, 1:120–22.

11. See Thompson, *Shakespeare's Chaucer,* 20–27.

12. *The Winter's Tale*, IV.iv.88; see also II.ii.63, IV.iv.2–3, 116–19, 140–43, 489–92.

13. I accept the customary division of authorship, i.e., Shakespeare: I; II.i; III.i–ii; V.i.34–173, iii–iv; Fletcher: prologue; II.ii–vi; III.iii–vi; IV.i–ii; V.i.1–33, ii; epilogue. IV.iii is accepted as Shakespearean by Waith but not by Bowers or Wells and Taylor; Wells and Taylor also assign V.iv to Fletcher. See Waith, *Two Noble Kinsmen*, 8–23; Bowers, *Two Noble Kinsmen*, 156–58; Wells and Taylor, *William Shakespeare*, 625.

14. William Davenant, *The Rivals* (1668).

15. I use "same-sex" rather than "homosexual" to foreground the absence of any overt sexual element in these friendships, whether the mature love of Theseus and Pirithous or the childhood affection of Emilia and Flavina; the Elizabethans and Jacobeans perceived a wide gap between close same-sex friendship, which was accepted as an ideal and admirable relationship, and sodomy, which was condemned as an abomination. See also Waith's discussion in his introduction to *Two Noble Kinsmen*, 49–54, and his "Shakespeare and Fletcher on Love and Friendship"; and, for a fuller account of Elizabethan friendship literature and its relationship to the play, Weller, "*The Two Noble Kinsmen.*"

16. See Donaldson, *Swan at the Well*, 61–65.

17. See, e.g., I.i.125; III.vi.191–94, 245–50; IV.ii.4–6, 35–36.

18. Donaldson is the bravest and best; see *Swan at the Well*, 33–36, 44–47.

19. The definition appears in the epistle "To the Reader" that prefaces *The Faithful Shepherdess* (*Beaumont and Fletcher*, 2:497). McMullan and Hope note that Fletcher's definition should not be taken as normative even for his own practice: see their introduction to their collection *Politics of Tragicomedy*, 1–7. Interestingly, John Lane's nondramatic continuation of Chaucer's Squire's Tale, which is almost exactly contemporary with *The Two Noble Kinsmen*, is also described as a tragicomedy, both in one of its original commendatory poems and by Lane himself when he came to rewrite its dedication in 1630 (*John Lane's Continuation*, 5, 7); the use of the term here would seem to draw on the fact that so many Jacobean tragicomedies took the form of nonnaturalistic romances.

20. Though cf. Donaldson, *Swan at the Well*, 56–58.

21. See, for a colonialist example, Sir Walter Ralegh's comment that Guiana "is a country that hath yet her maidenhead" (*The Discovery of . . . Guiana*, in *Sir Walter Ralegh*, ed. Hammond, 120); and for a sexual example of the same comparison, Donne's famous extended conceit on "his Mistress going to bed" as "my America, my new found land" (Elegy 19, 1.27, in *Complete English Poems*, 125). My thanks to David Wallace for pointing out the colonialist tendency in Theseus' phrasing. Potter notes the interchangeability of women and cities in "Topicality or Politics?"

22. See Abrams, "*The Two Noble Kinsmen* as Bourgeois Drama."

Contributors

Judith H. Anderson, who received her doctorate from Yale University, is professor of English at Indiana University. She is author of many studies in medieval and Renaissance poetry, including *The Growth of a Personal Voice: "Piers Plowman" and "The Faerie Queene"* (1976), *Biographical Truth: The Representation of Historical Persons in Tudor-Stuart Writing* (1984), *Words That Matter: Linguistic Perception in Renaissance English* (1996), and a series of essays on Chaucer and Spenser. She is coeditor (with Elizabeth Kirk) of E. Talbot Donaldson's translation *Will's Vision of Piers Plowman,* and coeditor (with Donald Cheney and David A. Richardson) of *Spenser's Life and the Subject of Biography* (1996). She is currently working on historicized metaphor in early modern England.

Craig A. Berry is an independent scholar with a doctorate from Northwestern University. He has published essays on medieval and Renaissance poetry.

Helen Cooper, with a D.Phil. from Cambridge University, is a fellow of University College, Oxford. She is the author of numerous studies of medieval and Renaissance writing, including *Pastoral: Mediaeval into Renaissance* (1977), *The Structure of "The Canterbury Tales"* (1983), and the *Canterbury Tales* volume in the Oxford Guides to Chaucer series (1989; 2d ed., 1996). She is currently working on Shakespeare and romance in the sixteenth century.

A. Kent Hieatt, whose Ph.D. is from Columbia University, is professor emeritus of English at the University of Western Ontario and fellow of the Royal Society of Canada. He has published widely on medieval and Renaissance poetry and art history, including *Short Time's Endless Monument: The Symbolism of the Numbers in Edmund Spenser's "Epithalamion"* (1960) and *Chaucer, Spenser, Milton: Mythopoeic Continuities and Transformations* (1975). He also coedited, with Constance B. Hieatt, an edition of *The Canterbury Tales* (1981) and (with Maristella P. Lorch) translated Lorenzo Valla's *De voluptate* (1977). He was editorial consultant for *The Spenser Encyclopedia*, and in 1985 his essay "The Genesis of

Shakespeare's *Sonnets:* Spenser's *Ruines of Rome: by Bellay*" won PMLA's William Riley Parker Prize.

Clare R. Kinney, with a doctorate from Yale University, is associate professor of English at the University of Virginia, where she teaches medieval and Renaissance literature. Her publications include *Strategies of Poetic Narrative: Chaucer, Spenser, Milton, Eliot* (1992) and articles on *Beowulf, Sir Gawain and the Green Knight,* Chaucer, Shakespeare, and Sidney.

Theresa M. Krier (Ph.D. from University of Michigan) is associate professor of English at the University of Notre Dame. She is the author of *Gazing on Secret Sights: Spenser, Classical Imitation, and the Decorums of Vision* (1990) and essays on Renaissance poetry. She is currently working on maternity in pre-modern narrative poetry.

Carol A. N. Martin, with a Ph.D. from the University of Notre Dame, is assistant professor of English at Bowdoin College. She studies the hermeneutics of late medieval to early Renaissance authors and discourses.

Glenn Steinberg, who earned his doctorate at Indiana University, teaches medieval and Renaissance literature at St. Thomas University. He is at work on a study of authority and canonicity in medieval literature.

John Watkins, whose Ph.D. comes from Yale University, is assistant professor of English at the University of Minnesota. He is the author of *The Specter of Dido: Spenser and the Virgilian Epic* (1995) and essays on medieval and Renaissance English poetry. He is at work on a book about seventeenth-century representations of Queen Elizabeth.

Bibliography

I. Texts

Anon. *The Cobler of Caunterburie and Tarltons Newes out of Purgatory*, ed. Geoffrey Creigh and Jane Belfield. Medieval and Renaissance Texts 3, 69–74. Leiden: E. J. Brill, 1987.

Ariosto, Ludovico. *Orlando Furioso*, trans. Sir John Harington, ed. Robert McNulty. Oxford: Clarendon Press, 1972.

Ascham, Roger. *The Scholemaster.* In his *English Works*, ed. William Aldis Wright. Cambridge: Cambridge University Press, 1904.

Bale, John. *Illustrium Maioris Britanniae Scriptorum . . . Summarium.* London, 1548.

Boccaccio, Giovanni. *Boccaccio on Poetry: Being the Preface and the Fourteenth and Fifteenth Books of Boccaccio's "Genealogia deorum gentilium libri,"* trans., introd., and commentary by Charles G. Osgood. New York: Liberal Arts Press, 1930.

———. *Genealogie deorum gentilium libri.* Bari: Guis. Laterzi, 1951.

Bowers, Fredson, ed. *The Dramatic Works in the Beaumont and Fletcher Canon.* 9 vols. Cambridge: Cambridge University Press, 1966–.

Brewer, D. S. *Chaucer: The Critical Heritage.* 2 vols. London: Routledge and Kegan Paul, 1978.

Brown, Rawdon, ed. *Calendar of State Papers and Manuscripts Existing in the Archives and Collections of Venice, 1509–1519.* London, 1867.

Calvin, John. *Commentary upon the Epistle of Saint Paul to the Romans*, trans. Christopher Rosdell (1583), ed. Henry Beveridge. Edinburgh: Calvin Translation Society, 1844.

Chaucer, Geoffrey. *Chaucer's Poetry: An Anthology for the Modern Reader*, ed. E. Talbot Donaldson. New York: Ronald Press, 1958.

———. *The Riverside Chaucer.* 3d ed., general ed. Larry D. Benson. Boston: Houghton Mifflin, 1987.

———. *Troilus and Criseyde*, ed. R. A. Shoaf. East Lansing: Colleagues Press, 1989.

———. *The Workes of Our Ancient and learned English Poet, Geffrey Chaucer*, ed. Thomas Speght. London, 1602.

———. *The Workes of our Antient and Lerned English Poet, Geffrey Chavcer, Newly Printed*, ed. Thomas Speght. London, 1598.

———. *The Works, 1532 (ed. William Thynne), with supplementary material from the editions of 1542, 1561, 1598, and 1602*, ed. D. S. Brewer. London: Scolar Press, 1969; rpt. 1976.

——. *The Works of Geoffrey Chaucer*, ed. Thomas Speght. London: John Harefinch, 1687. From *English Books 1641–1700*, C3736 Wing Reel No. 59. Ann Arbor: University Microfilms.

Dante Alighieri. *The Divine Comedy*, trans. and commentary Charles Singleton. Vol. II, *Purgatorio*. Vol. III, *Paradiso*. Princeton: Princeton University Press, 1970–75.

Davenant, William. *The Rivals* (1668). Intro. Kenneth Muir. Facsimile. London: Cornmarket Press, 1970.

Donne, John. *The Complete English Poems,* ed. A. J. Smith. Harmondsworth, Middlesex: Penguin, 1971.

The Geneva Bible: A Facsimile of the 1560 Edition, intro. Lloyd E. Berry. Madison: University of Wisconsin Press, 1969.

Howard, Henry, Lord Surrey. *Poems*, ed. Emrys Jones. Oxford: Clarendon Press, 1964.

Lane, John. *John Lane's Continuation of Chaucer's Squire's Tale*, ed. F. J. Furnivall. Chaucer Society, 2d ser. 23. London: Kegan Paul, Rench, Trübner, 1888.

Leland, John. *Commentarii de Scriptoribus Britannicis.* 1545. Rpt. Oxford, 1709.

McCarl, Mary Rhinelander, ed. *The Plowman's Tale: The c. 1532 and 1606 Editions of a Spurious Canterbury Tale*. New York and London: Garland Publishing, 1997.

Peacham, Henry. *The Garden of Eloquence* (1593), ed. W. G. Crane. Gainesville, Fla.: Scholars' Facsimiles and Reprints, 1954.

Puttenham, George. *The Arte of English Poesie.* In *Elizabethan Critical Essays*, ed. Smith, vol. 2.

Ralegh, Sir Walter. *Sir Walter Ralegh: Selected Writings*, ed. Gerald Hammond. Harmondsworth, Middlesex: Penguin, 1986.

Shakespeare, William. *The Complete Works*, ed. Stanley Wells and Gary Taylor. Oxford: Clarendon Press, 1986.

——. *Love's Labour's Lost*, ed. Richard W. David. The Arden Shakespeare. London: Methuen, 1951; rpt. 1987.

——. *A Midsummer Night's Dream*, ed. Harold F. Brooks. The Arden Shakespeare. London: Methuen, 1979.

——. *The Riverside Shakespeare*, ed. G. Blakemore Evans et al. Boston: Houghton Mifflin, 1974.

——. *The Winter's Tale*, ed. J. H. P. Pafford. The Arden Shakespeare. London: Methuen, 1963; rpt. 1978.

Shakespeare, William, and John Fletcher. *The Two Noble Kinsmen*, ed. Clifford Leech. New York: New American Library, 1972.

——. *The Two Noble Kinsmen*, ed. Eugene M. Waith. Oxford: Clarendon Press, 1989.

Sidney, Sir Philip. *Apologie for Poetrie.* In *Elizabethan Critical Essays,* ed. Smith, q.v., vol. 1.

Skeat, Walter W., ed. *Chaucerian and Other Pieces, Being a Supplement to the Works of Geoffrey Chaucer.* 7 vols. Oxford, 1894–97.

Smith, G. Gregory, ed. *Elizabethan Critical Essays.* 2 vols. Oxford: Oxford University Press, 1904.

Spenser, Edmund. *The Faerie Queene*, ed. A. C. Hamilton. London and New York: Longman, 1977.

———. *Poetical Works*, ed. J. C. Smith and E. de Selincourt. 1912; rpt. Oxford: Oxford University Press, 1970.

———. *The Works of Edmund Spenser: A Variorum Edition*, ed. Edwin Greenlaw, F. M. Padelford, C. G. Osgood, et al. 11 vols. 1932–49. Rpt. Baltimore: Johns Hopkins University Press, 1966.

Spurgeon, Caroline. *Five Hundred Years of Chaucer Criticism and Allusion, 1357–1900.* New York: Russel and Russel, 1960.

Thynne, Francis. *Animadversions upon the Annotations and Corrections to Some Imperfections of Chaucer's Works* (1598), ed. F. J. Furnivall, with a preface by G. H. Kingsley. Early English Text Society. London: Humphrey Milford, 1875.

Wickham, Glynne, ed. *English Moral Interludes.* London: Dent; Totowa, N.J.: Rowman and Littlefield, 1976.

Wyatt, Sir Thomas. *Collected Poems*, ed. Kenneth Muir and Patricia Thomson. Liverpool: Liverpool University Press, 1969.

———. *The Complete Poems*, ed. A. Rebholz. New Haven: Yale University Press, 1981.

II. Studies

Abrams, Richard. "*The Two Noble Kinsmen* as Bourgeois Drama." In *Shakespeare, Fletcher*, ed. Frey, q.v., 145–62.

Aers, David. "A Whisper in the Ear of Early Modernists; Or Reflection on Literary Critics Writing the 'History of the Subject.'" In *Culture and History, 1350–1600: Essays on English Communities, Identities, and Writing*, ed. Aers, 177–202. Detroit: Wayne State University Press, 1992.

Allen, David G., and Robert A. White, eds. *The Work of Dissimilitude: Essays from the Sixth Citadel Conference on Medieval and Renaissance Literature.* Newark: University of Delaware Press, 1992.

Allen, Robert J. "A Recurring Motif in Chaucer's *House of Fame.*" *Journal of English and Germanic Philology* 55 (1956): 393–405.

Anderson, Frank J. *An Illustrated History of the Herbals.* New York: Columbia University Press, 1977.

Anderson, Judith H. "The 'couert vele': Chaucer, Spenser, and Venus." *English Literary Renaissance* 24 (1994): 638–59.

———. "'A Gentle Knight was pricking on the plaine': The Chaucerian Connection." *English Literary Renaissance* 15 (1985): 166–74.

———. *The Growth of a Personal Voice: "Piers Plowman" and "The Faerie Queene."* New Haven: Yale University Press, 1976.

———. "'Myn auctour': Spenser's Enabling Fiction and Eumnestes' 'Immortall Scrine.'" In *Unfolded Tales*, ed. Logan and Teskey, q.v., 16–31.

———. "'Nat worth a boterflye': *Muiopotmos* and *The Nun's Priest's Tale.*" *Journal of Medieval and Renaissance Studies* 1 (1971): 89–106.

———. "Prudence and Her Silence: Spenser's Use of Chaucer's Melibee." *English Literary History* 62 (1995): 29–46.

———. "What Comes After Chaucer's *But:* Adversative Constructions in Spenser." In *Acts of Interpretation: The Text in Its Contexts 700–1600: Essays on Medieval and Renaissance Literature in Honor of E. Talbot Donaldson,* ed. Mary J. Carruthers and Elizabeth Kirk, 105–18. Norman, Okla.: Pilgrim Books, 1982.

———. *Words That Matter: Linguistic Perception in Renaissance English.* Stanford: Stanford University Press, 1996.

Anderson, Judith H., Donald Cheney, and David Richardson, eds. *Spenser's Life and the Subject of Biography.* Amherst: University of Massachusetts Press, 1996.

Anderson, Luke, O. Cist. "Enthymeme and Dialectic: Cloister and Classroom." In *From Cloister to Classroom,* ed. Elder, q.v., 239–74.

Ascoli, Albert Russell. *Ariosto's Bitter Harmony: Crisis and Evasion in the Italian Renaissance.* Princeton: Princeton University Press, 1987.

Bakhtin, M. M. *The Dialogic Imagination*, trans. Caryl Emerson and Michael Holquist, ed. Michael Holquist. Austin: University of Texas Press, 1981.

———. *Rabelais and His World,* trans. Helene Iswolsky. Cambridge: M.I.T. Press, 1993.

Baldwin, Anna. "From the *Clerk's Tale* to *The Winter's Tale.*" In *Chaucer Traditions,* ed. Morse and Windeatt, q.v., 199–212.

Barney, Stephen A. *Allegories of History, Allegories of Love.* Hamden, Conn.: Archon Books, 1979.

———. "Chaucer's Lists." In *The Wisdom of Poetry: Essays in Early English Literature in Honor of Morton W. Bloomfield,* ed. Larry D. Benson and Siegfried Wenzel, 189–224, 297–307. Kalamazoo: Medieval Institute Publications, 1982.

———, ed. *Chaucer's "Troilus": Essays in Criticism.* Hamden, Conn.: Archon Books, 1980.

Barthes, Roland. *Roland Barthes by Roland Barthes*, trans. Richard Howard. New York: Hill and Wang, 1977.

Bell, Ilona. "Spenser's *Amoretti:* 'By Her Undone.'" Abstract, *Spenser Newsletter* 26, 1 (1995): 34.

Bellamy, Elizabeth J. *Translations of Power: Narcissism and the Unconscious in Epic History.* Ithaca: Cornell University Press, 1992.

Bennett, J. W. *The Evolution of "The Faerie Queene."* Chicago: University of Chicago Press, 1942.

Bennington, Geoffrey. *Sententiousness in the Novel: Laying Down the Law in Eighteenth-Century French Fiction.* Cambridge: Cambridge University Press, 1985.

Benskin, Michael, and M. L. Samuels, eds. *So meny people longages and tonges: Philological Essays in Scots and Mediaeval English Presented to Angus McIntosh*. Edinburgh: By the eds., 1981.

Benson, C. David, and Barry A. Windeatt. "The Manuscript Glosses to Chaucer's *Troilus and Criseyde*." *Chaucer Review* 25 (1990): 31–53.

Berger, Harry, Jr. "'Kidnapped Romance': Discourse in *The Faerie Queene*." In *Unfolded Tales*, ed. Logan and Teskey, q.v., 208–56.

———. "Narrative as Rhetoric in *The Faerie Queene*." *English Literary Renaissance* 21 (1991): 3–48.

———. *Revisionary Play: Studies in the Spenserian Dynamics*. Berkeley: University of California Press, 1988.

Berlin, Normand. "Chaucer's *The Book of the Duchess* and Spenser's *Daphnaïda*." *Studia Neophilologica* 38 (1966): 282–89.

Berry, Craig. "Borrowed Armor/Free Grace: The Quest for Authority in *The Faerie Queene* I and Chaucer's Tale of Sir Thopas." *Studies in Philology* 91 (1994): 136–66.

Bieman, Elizabeth. *Plato Baptized: Towards an Interpretation of Spenser's Mimetic Fictions*. Toronto: University of Toronto Press, 1988.

Bion, Wilfred. *Learning from Experience*. London: Heinemann, 1962.

Bishop, Elizabeth. *One Art: Letters*, ed. Robert Giroux. New York: Farrar Strauss Giroux, 1994.

Blodgett, James E. "William Thynne (d. 1546)." In *Editing Chaucer*, ed. Ruggiers, q.v., 32–52.

Bloomfield, Morton W. "Chaucer's *Squire's Tale* and the Renaissance." *Poetica* 12 (1981): 28–35.

Bollas, Christopher. *Cracking Up: The Work of Unconscious Experience*. New York: Hill and Wang, 1995.

———. *The Shadow of the Object: Psychoanalysis of the Unthought Known*. New York: Columbia University Press, 1987.

Bono, Barbara J. "The Birth of Tragedy: Tragic Action in *Julius Caesar*." *English Literary Renaissance* 24 (1994): 449–70.

Booth, Stephen. "Exit, Pursued by a Gentleman Born." In *Shakespeare's Art from a Comparative Perspective*. Proceedings of the Comparative Literature Symposium, vol. 12, ed. Wendell M. Aycock, 51–66. Lubbock: Texas Tech Press, 1981.

Boughner, D. C. "The Background of Lyly's Tophas." *PMLA* 54 (1939): 967–73.

Boulton, Maureen. *The Song in the Story: Lyric Insertions in French Narrative Fiction, 1200–1400*. Philadelphia: University of Pennsylvania Press, 1993.

Brewer, Derek. "Images of Chaucer 1386–1900." In his *Chaucer and Chaucerians: Critical Studies in Middle English Literature*, 240–70. London: Thomas Nelson, 1966.

Brill, Lesley. "Scudamour." In *Spenser Encyclopedia*, ed. Hamilton, q.v., 635.

Bronson, Bertrand. "*The Book of the Duchess* Re-Opened." *PMLA* 67 (1952): 863–81.

Brooks, Peter. *Reading for the Plot: Design and Intention in Narrative.* Cambridge: Harvard University Press, 1984.

Bruns, Gerald L. *Heidegger's Estrangements: Language, Truth and Poetry in the Later Writings.* New Haven: Yale University Press, 1989.

———. *Hermeneutics Ancient and Modern.* New Haven: Yale University Press, 1992.

Burke, Séan. *Death and the Return of the Author: Criticism and Subjectivity in Barthes, Foucault and Derrida.* Edinburgh: Edinburgh University Press, 1992.

Burrow, John A. "Chaucer, Geoffrey." In *Spenser Encyclopedia,* ed. Hamilton, q.v., 144–48.

———. "*Sir Thopas* in the Sixteenth Century." In *Middle English Studies Presented to Norman Davis in Honour of His Seventieth Birthday,* ed. Douglas Grey and E. G. Stanley, 69–91. Oxford: Clarendon Press, 1983.

Butler, Judith. *Bodies That Matter: On the Discursive Limits of "Sex."* New York: Routledge, 1993.

———. *Gender Trouble: Feminism and the Subversion of Identity.* New York: Routledge, 1990.

Cain, Thomas H. *Praise in "The Faerie Queene."* Lincoln: University of Nebraska Press, 1978.

Carruthers, Mary J. *The Book of Memory: A Study of Memory in Medieval Culture.* Cambridge: Cambridge University Press, 1990.

Cave, Terence. *The Cornucopian Text: Problems of Writing in the French Renaissance.* Oxford: Clarendon Press; New York: Oxford University Press, 1979.

Chambers, E. K. *The Elizabethan Stage.* Oxford: Clarendon Press, 1923.

Cheney, Donald. Afterword to *Spenser's Life*, ed. Anderson, Cheney, and Richardson, q.v., 172–77.

Cheney, Patrick. "Spenser's Completion of *The Squire's Tale:* Love, Magic, and Heroic Action in the Legend of Cambell and Triamond." *Journal of Medieval and Renaissance Studies* 15 (1985): 135–55.

———. *Spenser's Famous Flight: A Renaissance Idea of a Literary Career.* Toronto: University of Toronto Press, 1993.

Chodorow, Nancy. *Feminism and Psychoanalytic Theory.* New Haven: Yale University Press, 1989.

Clanchy, M. T. *From Memory to Written Record: England, 1066–1307.* Oxford: Basil Blackwell, 1993.

Clark, John W. "Does the Franklin Interrupt the Squire?" *Chaucer Review* 7 (1972): 160–61.

Clark, Sandra. *The Plays of Beaumont and Fletcher: Sexual Themes and Dramatic Representation.* London: Harvester Wheatsheaf, 1994.

Coghill, Nevill. "Shakespeare's Reading in Chaucer." In *Elizabethan and Jacobean Studies Presented to Frank Percy Wilson in Honour of His Seventieth Birthday,* ed. Herbert Davis and Helen Gardner, 86–99. Oxford: Clarendon Press, 1959.

Colish, Marcia. *The Mirror of Language: A Study in the Medieval Theory of Knowledge.* Lincoln: University of Nebraska Press, 1983.

Constable, Giles. *Three Studies in Medieval Religious and Social Thought.* Cambridge: Cambridge University Press, 1995.

Cooper, Helen. *The Oxford Guides to Chaucer: The Canterbury Tales.* Oxford: Clarendon Press, 1989; corrected edition, 1991; 2d ed., 1996.

———. "The Shape-Shiftings of the Wife of Bath, 1395–1670." In *Chaucer Traditions,* ed. Morse and Windeatt, q.v., 168–84.

———. "Wyatt and Chaucer: A Reappraisal." *Leeds Studies in English* 13 (1982): 104–23.

Coulter, Cornelia C. "The Genealogy of the Gods." In *Vassar Mediaeval Studies,* ed. Christabel Forsythe Fisk, 317–41. New Haven: Yale University Press, 1923.

Crampton, Georgia Ronan. *The Condition of Creatures: Suffering and Action in Chaucer and Spenser.* New Haven: Yale University Press, 1974.

Crane, Mary Thomas. *Framing Authority: Sayings, Self and Society in Sixteenth-Century England.* Princeton: Princeton University Press, 1993.

David, Alfred. *The Strumpet Muse: Art and Morals in Chaucer's Poetry.* Bloomington: Indiana University Press, 1976.

Delany, Sheila. *Chaucer's "House of Fame": The Poetics of Skeptical Fideism.* Chicago: University of Chicago Press, 1972; rpt., Gainesville: University Press of Florida, 1994.

———. *The Naked Text: Chaucer's "Legend of Good Women."* Berkeley: University of California Press, 1994.

de Man, Paul. "Pascal's Allegory of Persuasion." In *Allegory and Representation,* ed. Greenblatt, q.v., 1–25.

———. "The Rhetoric of Temporality." In *Interpretation,* ed. Singleton, q.v., 173–209.

DeNeef, A. Leigh. *Spenser and the Motives of Metaphor.* Durham, N.C.: Duke University Press, 1982.

Donaldson, E. Talbot. "Adventures with the Adversative Conjunction in the General Prologue to the *Canterbury Tales;* or, What's Before the *But?*" In *So meny people,* ed. Benskin and Samuels, q.v., 355–66.

———. "Chaucer the Pilgrim." *PMLA* 69 (1954): 928–36.

———. *The Swan at the Well: Shakespeare Reading Chaucer.* New Haven: Yale University Press, 1985.

Donaldson, E. Talbot, and Judith J. Kollmann, eds. *Chaucerian Shakespeare: Adaptation and Transformation.* Medieval and Renaissance Monograph Ser. 2. Detroit: Michigan Consortium for Medieval and Early Modern Studies, 1983.

Duncan, Charles F., Jr. "'Straw for Your Gentilesse': The Gentle Franklin's Interruption of the Squire." *Chaucer Review* 5 (1970): 161–64.

Duncan-Jones, Katherine. *Sir Philip Sidney: Courtier Poet.* New Haven: Yale University Press, 1991.

Edwards, Phillip. "On the Design of *The Two Noble Kinsmen.*" *Review of English Literature* 5 (1964): 89–105.

Elder, E. Rozanne, ed. *From Cloister to Classroom: Monastic Approaches to Truth.* Kalamazoo: Cistercian Publications, 1986.

Esolen, Anthony. "The Disingenuous Poet Laureate: Spenser's Adoption of Chaucer." *Speculum* 87 (1990): 285–311.

———. "Spenserian Chaos: Lucretius in *The Faerie Queene*." *Spenser Studies* 11 (1994): 31–51.

Evans, Robert C. "Ben Jonson's Chaucer." *English Literary Renaissance* 19 (1989): 324–45.

Farmer, Norman K. "Illustrations." In *Spenser Encyclopedia,* ed. Hamilton, q.v., 390–91.

Farrell, William J. "Chaucer's Use of the Catalogue." *Texas Studies in Literature and Language* 5 (1963): 64–78.

Ferguson, Margaret. "*Hamlet:* Letters and Spirits." In *Shakespeare and the Question of Theory*, ed. Parker and Hartman, q.v., 292–309.

———. *Trials of Desire: Renaissance Defenses of Poetry.* New Haven: Yale University Press, 1983.

Fineman, Joel. "The Structure of Allegorical Desire." In *Allegory and Representation,* ed. Greenblatt, q.v., 26–60.

Finucci, Valeria, and Regina Schwartz, eds. *Desire in the Renaissance: Psychoanalysis and Literature.* Princeton: Princeton University Press, 1994.

Flesch, William. *Generosity and the Limits of Authority: Shakespeare, Herbert, Milton.* Ithaca: Cornell University Press, 1992.

Fox, Alastair. *Politics and Literature in the Reigns of Henry VII and Henry VIII.* Oxford: Basil Blackwell, 1989.

———. "Thomas More's *Dialogue* and the *Book of the Tales of Caunterbury:* 'Good Mother Wit' and Creative Imitation." In *Familiar Colloquy: Essays Presented to Arthur Edward Barker,* ed. Patricia Bruckmann, 15–24. Ottawa: Oberon Press, 1978.

Fradenburg, Louise. "'Voice Memorial': Loss and Reparation in Chaucer's Poetry." *Exemplaria* 2 (1990): 169–202.

Frank, Manfred. *What Is Neostructuralism?* trans. Sabine Wilke and Richard Gray, foreword by Martin Schwab. Minneapolis: University of Minnesota Press, 1989.

French, W. H. "The Man in Black's Lyric." *Journal of English and Germanic Philology* 56 (1957): 231–41.

Frese, Dolores Warwick. *An "Ars Legendi" for Chaucer's "Canterbury Tales": Reconstructive Readings.* Gainesville: University Press of Florida, 1991.

———. "The Names of Women in the *Canterbury Tales*: Chaucer's Hidden Art of Involucral Nomenclature." In *"A Wyf Ther Was": Essays in Honour of Paule Mertens-Fonck*, ed. Juliette Dor, 155–66. Liège: Université de Liège, 1992.

———. "Three Men and a Baby: Boccaccio, Petrarch, Chaucer and the Making of Patient Griselda." Presented as the Grellet-Simpson Lecture in Medieval Literature, Mary Washington College, Virginia, 1995.

Freud, Sigmund. *The Interpretation of Dreams.* In *The Standard Edition of the Complete Psychological Works of Sigmund Freud,* vols. 4–5, ed. James Strachey. London: Hogarth Press, 1900.

Frey, Charles H. *Shakespeare, Fletcher and "The Two Noble Kinsmen."* Columbia: University of Missouri Press, 1989.

Frye, Susan. *Elizabeth I: The Competition for Representation.* Oxford: Oxford University Press, 1993.

Fyler, John M. "Domesticating the Exotic in the *Squire's Tale.*" *English Literary History* 55 (1988): 1–26.

———. Explanatory Notes and Textual Notes to *The House of Fame.* In *Riverside Chaucer,* 977–90, 1139–43.

Gallacher, Patrick J., and Helen Damico. *Hermeneutics and Medieval Culture.* Albany: State University of New York Press, 1989.

Giamatti, A. Bartlett. *Play of Double Senses: Spenser's "Faerie Queene."* New York: Norton, 1975.

Goldberg, Jonathan. *Endlesse Worke: Spenser and the Structures of Discourse.* Baltimore: Johns Hopkins University Press, 1981.

Goodman, Jennifer R. "Chaucer's *Squire's Tale* and the Rise of Chivalry." *Studies in the Age of Chaucer* 5 (1983): 127–36.

Graff, Gerald. *Professing Literature: An Institutional History.* Chicago: University of Chicago Press, 1987.

Graves, Thornton S. "Some Chaucer Allusions (1561–1700)." *Studies in Philology* 20 (1923): 469–78.

Greenblatt, Stephen, ed. *Allegory and Representation.* Baltimore: Johns Hopkins University Press, 1981.

———. "Psychoanalysis and Renaissance Culture." In *Literary Theory/Renaissance Texts,* ed. Parker and Quint, q.v., 210–24.

———. *Renaissance Self-Fashioning: From More to Shakespeare.* Chicago: University of Chicago Press, 1980.

Greene, Thomas. *The Light in Troy: Imitation and Discovery in Renaissance Poetry.* New Haven: Yale University Press, 1982.

———. *The Vulnerable Text: Essays on Renaissance Literature.* New York: Columbia University Press, 1986.

Greenfield, Concetta Carestia. *Humanist and Scholastic Poetics, 1250–1500.* Lewisburg, Pa.: Bucknell University Press, 1981.

Gross, Kenneth. *Spenserian Poetics: Idolatry, Iconoclasm, and Magic.* Ithaca: Cornell University Press, 1985.

Gurr, Andrew. *The Shakespearian Playing Companies.* Oxford: Clarendon Press, 1996.

Hamilton, A. C., Donald Cheney, W. F. Blissett, David A. Richardson, and William Barker, eds. *The Spenser Encyclopedia.* Toronto: University of Toronto Press, 1990.

Hammond, Eleanore Prescott. *Chaucer: A Bibliographical Manual.* New York: Macmillan, 1908.

Hammond, Gerald. *Fleeting Things: English Poets and Poems, 1616–1660.* Cambridge: Cambridge University Press, 1990.

Haraway, Donna J. *Simians, Cyborgs, and Women: The Reinvention of Nature.* New York: Routledge, 1991.

Harrier, R. C. *The Canon of Sir Thomas Wyatt's Poetry.* Cambridge: Harvard University Press, 1975.

Harris, Duncan, and Nancy Steffen. "The Other Side of the Garden: An Interpretive Comparison of Chaucer's *Book of the Duchess* and Spenser's *Daphnaïda.*" *Journal of Medieval and Renaissance Studies* 2 (1981): 17–36.

Harrison, Thomas. *They Tell of Birds: Chaucer, Spenser, Milton, Drayton.* Austin: University of Texas Press, 1956.

Hawkes, Terence. *Shakespeare's Talking Animals: Language and Drama in Society.* Totowa, N.J.: Rowman and Littlefield, 1973.

Heberle, Mark. "The Limitations of Friendship." *Spenser Studies* 8 (1987): 101–18.

Helgerson, Richard. *Forms of Nationhood: The Elizabethan Writing of England.* Chicago: University of Chicago Press, 1992.

———. *Self-Crowned Laureates: Spenser, Jonson, Milton, and the Literary System.* Berkeley: University of California Press, 1983.

Henderson, Katherine Usher, and Barbara F. McManus. *Half Humankind: Contexts and Texts of the Controversy about Women in England.* Urbana: University of Illinois Press, 1985.

Herman, Peter C., ed. *Rethinking the Henrician Era: Essays on Early Tudor Texts and Contexts.* Urbana: University of Illinois Press, 1994.

Hetherington, John Rowland. *Chaucer 1532–1602: Notes and Facsimile Texts.* Birmingham: By the author, 1964.

Hieatt, A. Kent. "Arthur's Deliverance of Rome? (Yet Again)." *Spenser Studies* 9 (1988): 243–48.

———. *Chaucer, Spenser, Milton: Mythopoeic Continuities and Transformations.* Montreal: McGill-Queen's University Press, 1975.

———. "Hans Baldung Grien's Ottawa *Eve* and Its Context." *Art Bulletin* 65 (1983): 290–304.

———. "The Projected Continuation of *The Faerie Queene*: Rome Delivered?" *Spenser Studies* 8 (1987): 335–42.

———. Review of *Milton's Spenser: The Politics of Reading,* by Maureen Quilligan. *Milton Quarterly* 18 (1984): 94–95.

———. "Tetrads." In *Spenser Encyclopedia,* ed. Hamilton, q.v., 684–85.

Higgins, Anne. "Spenser Reading Chaucer: Another Look at the *Faerie Queene* Allusions." *Journal of English and Germanic Philology* 89 (1990): 17–36.

Hillman, Richard. *Intertextuality and Romance in Renaissance Drama.* New York: St. Martin's Press, 1992.

Hollander, John. *Melodious Guile: Fictive Pattern in Poetic Language.* New Haven: Yale University Press, 1988.

Holmer, Joan Ozark. "Nashe as 'Monarch of Witt' and Shakespeare's *Romeo and Juliet.*" *Texas Studies in Literature and Language* 37 (1995): 314–43.

Howard, Donald R. *Chaucer: His Life, His Works, His World.* New York: Dutton, 1987.

Hume, Anthea. *Edmund Spenser: Protestant Poet.* Cambridge: Cambridge University Press, 1984.

Huot, Sylvia. *From Song to Book: The Poetics of Writing in Old French Lyric and Lyrical Narrative Poetry.* Ithaca: Cornell University Press, 1987.

Huppé, Bernard, and D. W. Robertson Jr. *Fruyt and Chaf.* Princeton: Princeton University Press, 1963; rpt. New York: Kennikat, 1972.

Hurst, Peter W. "The Encyclopaedic Tradition, the Cosmological Epic, and the Validation of the Medieval Romance." *Comparative Criticism* 1 (1979): 53–71.

Jauss, Hans Robert. *Question and Answer: Forms of Dialogic Understanding*, trans. Michael Hayes. Minneapolis: University of Minnesota Press, 1989.

Javitch, Daniel. *Proclaiming a Classic: The Canonization of "Orlando Furioso."* Princeton: Princeton University Press, 1991.

Jeffreys, Mark. "Ideologies of Lyric: A Problem of Genre in Contemporary Anglo–phone Poetics." *PMLA* 110, 2 (1995): 196–205.

———. "Songs and Inscriptions: Brevity and the Idea of Lyric." *Texas Studies in Literature and Language* 36 (1994): 117–34.

Johnson, Lynn Staley. *"The Shepheardes Calender": An Introduction.* University Park: Pennsylvania State University Press, 1990.

Jordan, Robert M. "Lost in the Funhouse of Fame: Chaucer and Postmodernism." *Chaucer Review* 18 (1983): 100–115.

Kane, Sean. *Spenser's Moral Allegory.* Toronto: University of Toronto Press, 1989.

Kay, Dennis. *Melodious Tears: The English Funeral Elegy from Spenser to Milton.* Oxford: Clarendon Press, 1990.

———. "Wyatt and Chaucer: *They Flee from Me* Revisited." *Huntington Library Quarterly* 47 (1984): 211–25.

Kenny, Anthony, and Jan Pinborg. "Medieval Philosophical Literature." In *The Cambridge History of Later Medieval Philosophy.* Cambridge: Cambridge University Press, 1982.

Kerrigan, William. "The Articulation of the Ego in the English Renaissance." In *Literary Freud,* ed. Smith, q.v., 261–308.

King, John. *Spenser's Poetry and the Reformation Tradition.* Princeton: Princeton University Press, 1990.

Kinney, Arthur F. *Humanist Poetics: Thought, Rhetoric, and Fiction in Sixteenth-Century England.* Amherst: University of Massachusetts Press, 1986.

Kinney, Clare. "Lost in Translation: The Vicissitudes of the Heroine and the Immasculation of the Reader in a Seventeenth-Century Paraphrase of *Troilus and Criseyde.*" *Exemplaria* 5 (1993): 343–63.

———. *Strategies of Poetic Narrative: Chaucer, Spenser, Milton, Eliot.* Cambridge: Cambridge University Press, 1992.

Kiser, Lisa J. *Truth and Textuality in Chaucer's Poetry.* Hanover, N.H.: University Press of New England, 1991.

Klein, Melanie. "A Contribution to the Psychogenesis of Manic-Depressive States" (1935). In *Love, Guilt and Reparation and Other Works, 1921–1945*, 262–89. London: Hogarth Press, 1975.

———. *Envy and Gratitude: A Study of Unconscious Sources.* New York: Basic Books, 1957.

———. "On Observing the Behaviour of Young Infants." In Klein, Paula Heimann, Susan Isaacs, and Joan Rivière, *Developments in Psycho-Analysis*, ed. Rivière, 237–70. 1952. Rpt. London: Karnac Books and the Institute of Psycho-Analysis, 1989.

Koch, Carl. *Die Zeichungen Hans Baldung Griens* [The drawings of Hans Baldung Grien]. Berlin: Deutscher Verein für Kunstwissenschaft, 1941.

Kretzmann, Norman, and Eleonore Stump. *The Cambridge Translations of Medieval Philosophical Texts.* Vol. I, *Logic and the Philosophy of Language.* Cambridge: Cambridge University Press, 1988.

Krier, Theresa M. "Orality and Chaucerian Textuality in *The Faerie Queene* IV.i–iii: Spenser's Quest for Mothers to Think Back Through." Paper presented at the conference of the Modern Language Association, San Francisco, 1991.

Lasater, Alice E. "The Chaucerian Narrator in Spenser's *Shepheardes Calender.*" *Southern Quarterly* 12 (1974): 189–201.

Lawton, David. *Chaucer's Narrators.* Cambridge: D. S. Brewer, 1985.

Lee, Judith. "The English Ariosto: The Elizabethan Poet and the Marvelous." *Studies in Philology* 80 (1983): 277–99.

Leff, Gordon. *The Dissolution of the Medieval Outlook: An Essay on Intellectual and Spiritual Change in the Fourteenth Century* New York: Harper and Row, 1976.

Leicester, Marshall, Jr. *The Disenchanted Self: Representing the Subject in the "Canterbury Tales."* Berkeley: University of California Press, 1990.

Lerer, Seth. *Chaucer and His Readers: Imagining the Author in Late Medieval England.* Princeton: Princeton University Press, 1993.

Lethaby, W. R. "Chaucer's Tomb." *Times Literary Supplement*, 21 February 1929, 137.

Levao, Ronald. "Sidney's Feigned *Apology.*" In *Sir Philip Sidney: An Anthology of Modern Criticism,* ed. Dennis Kay, 127–46. Oxford: Clarendon Press, 1987.

Lever, J. W. "Three Notes on Shakespeare's Plants." *Review of English Studies* 3 (n.s. 1952): 117–29.

Lewis, C. S. *English Literature in the Sixteenth Century Excluding Drama.* Oxford: Clarendon Press, 1954.

Leyerle, John. "Chaucer's Windy Eagle." *University of Toronto Quarterly* 40 (1971): 247–65.

Loewenstein, Joseph. "Echo's Ring: Orpheus and Spenser's Career." *English Literary Renaissance* 15 (1986): 287–302.

———. "Spenser's Retrography: Two Episodes in Post-Petrarchan Bibliography." In *Spenser's Life,* ed. Anderson, Cheney, and Richardson, q.v., 99–130.

Logan, George M., and Gordon Teskey, eds. *Unfolded Tales: Essays on Renaissance Romance.* Ithaca: Cornell University Press, 1989.

Lynch, Kathryn L. "East Meets West in Chaucer's *Squire's* and *Franklin's Tales.*" *Speculum* 70 (1995): 530–31.

Machan, Tim William. "Kynaston's *Troilus,* Textual Criticism and the Renaissance Reading of Chaucer." *Exemplaria* 5 (1993): 161–83.

Mahood, Molly. *Shakespeare's Wordplay.* London: Methuen, 1957.

Manning, Stephen. "*Troilus,* Book V: Invention and the Poem as Process." *Chaucer Review* 18 (1984): 288–303.

Marcus, Leah. "Renaissance/Early Modern Studies." In *Redrawing the Boundaries: The Transformation of English and American Literary Studies,* ed. Stephen Greenblatt and Giles Gunn, 41–63. New York: Modern Language Association, 1992.

Marrone, Steven P. "Kilwardby, Robert." *Dictionary of the Middle Ages,* ed. Joseph R. Strayer. 13 vols. 7:253. New York: Scribner, 1982–89.

Martin, Ellen. "The Shady Trope of Spenser's Trees: Inside the Catalogue at *Faerie Queene* I.i.viii–ix." Paper presented at Thirtieth International Congress on Medieval Studies, Kalamazoo, Michigan, May 1995.

———. "Spenser, Chaucer, and the Rhetoric of Elegy." *Journal of Medieval and Renaissance Studies* 17 (1987): 83–109.

Martz, Louis L. "The *Amoretti:* 'Most Goodly Temperature.'" In *Form and Convention in the Poetry of Edmund Spenser: Selected Papers from the English Institute,* ed. William Nelson, 146–68, 180. New York: Columbia University Press, 1961.

Mason, H. A. *Humanism in the Early Tudor Period.* London: Routledge and Kegan Paul, 1959.

Maus, Katharine Eisaman. *Inwardness and the Theater in the English Renaissance.* Chicago: University of Chicago Press, 1995.

Mauss, Marcel. *The Gift: Forms and Functions of Exchange in Archaic Societies.* London: Cohen and West, 1954; rpt. New York: Norton, 1990.

Maynard, Theodore. *The Connection between the Ballade, Chaucer's Modification of It, Rime Royal, and the Spenserian Stanza.* Washington, D.C.: Catholic University of America, 1934.

McColley, Diane Kelsey. *A Gust for Paradise: Milton's Eden and the Visual Arts.* Urbana: University of Illinois Press, 1993.

McDonald, Charles. "An Interpretation of Chaucer's *Parlement of Foules.*" *Speculum* 30 (1955): 444–57.

McMullan, Gordon. *The Politics of Unease in the Plays of John Fletcher.* Amherst: University of Massachusetts Press, 1994.

McMullan, Gordon, and Jonathan Hope. *The Politics of Tragicomedy: Shakespeare and After.* London: Routledge, 1992.

Menocal, María Rosa. *Shards of Love: Exile and the Origins of the Lyric.* Durham, N.C.: Duke University Press, 1994.

Miller, David Lee. "The Earl of Cork's Lute." In *Spenser's Life,* ed. Anderson, Cheney, and Richardson, q.v., 146–71.

Miller, Helen. *Henry VIII and the English Nobility.* Oxford: Basil Blackwell, 1986.

Miskimin, Alice. *The Renaissance Chaucer.* New Haven: Yale University Press, 1975.

Montrose, Louis Adrian. *"Curious-Knotted Garden": The Form, Themes, and Contexts of Shakespeare's "Love's Labour's Lost."* Elizabethan and Renaissance Studies 56. Salzburg: Institut für Englissche Sprache und Literatur, 1977.

Morrison, Karl F. *History as a Visual Art in the Twelfth-Century Renaissance.* Princeton: Princeton University Press, 1990.

Morse, Ruth, and Barry Windeatt, eds. *Chaucer Traditions: Studies in Honour of Derek Brewer.* Cambridge: Cambridge University Press, 1990.

Muir, Kenneth. *The Life and Letters of Sir Thomas Wyatt.* Liverpool: Liverpool University Press, 1963.

Muscatine, Charles. *The Book of Geoffrey Chaucer: An Account of the Publication of Geoffrey Chaucer's Works from the Fifteenth Century to Modern Times.* San Francisco: Book Club of California, 1963.

Nadal, Thomas. "Spenser's *Daphnaïda* and Chaucer's *Book of the Duchess.*" *PMLA* 23 (1908): 646–61.

———. "Spenser's 'Muiopotmos' in Relation to Chaucer's *Sir Thopas* and *The Nun's Priest's Tale.*" *PMLA* 25 (1910): 640–56.

Nelson, William. *The Poetry of Edmund Spenser.* New York: Columbia University Press, 1963.

———. "Spenser *ludens.*" In *A Theatre for Spenserians,* ed. Judith M. Kennedy and James A. Reither, 83–100. Toronto: University of Toronto Press, 1973.

Neuss, Paula. "Images of Writing and the Book in Chaucer's Poetry." *Review of English Studies* 32 (n.s. 1981): 385–97.

Nevo, Ruth. *Comic Transformations in Shakespeare.* London: Methuen, 1980.

Nicholl, Charles. *A Cup of News: The Life of Thomas Nashe.* London: Routledge and Kegan Paul, 1984.

Norris, Christopher. *Derrida.* Cambridge: Harvard University Press, 1987.

Ong, Walter. "Latin Language Study as a Renaissance Puberty Rite." *Studies in Philology* 56 (1959): 103–24.

Oram, William. "*Daphnaïda* and Spenser's Later Poetry." *Spenser Studies* 2 (1981): 141–58.

Ord, Hubert. *Chaucer and the Rival Poet in Shakespeare's Sonnets: A New Theory.* London: J. M. Dent, 1921; rpt. New York: AMS Press, 1973.

Osborn, Marijane. "The Squire's 'Steed of Brass' as Astrolabe: Some Implications for *The Canterbury Tales.*" In *Hermeneutics and Medieval Culture,* ed. Gallacher and Damico, q.v., 121–31.

Osgood, Charles Grosvenor. *A Concordance to the Poems of Edmund Spenser.* 1915; rpt. Gloucester, Mass.: Peter Smith, 1963.

Parker, Patricia. "Literary Fat Ladies and the Generation of the Text." In *Literary*

Fat Ladies: Rhetoric, Gender, Property, ed. Parker, 8–35. London: Methuen, 1987.

———. *Shakespeare from the Margins: Language, Culture, Conflict*. Chicago: University of Chicago Press, 1996.

Parker, Patricia, and Geoffrey Hartman, eds. *Shakespeare and the Question of Theory*. London: Routledge, 1985.

Parker, Patricia, and David Quint, eds. *Literary Theory/Renaissance Texts*. Baltimore: Johns Hopkins University Press, 1986.

Paster, Gail Kern. *The Body Embarrassed: Drama and the Disciplines of Shame in Early Modern England*. Ithaca: Cornell University Press, 1993.

Patterson, Lee. *Chaucer and the Subject of History*. Madison: University of Wisconsin Press, 1991.

———. "'What Man Artow?': Authorial Self-Definition in *The Tale of Sir Thopas* and *The Tale of Melibee*." *Studies in the Age of Chaucer* 11 (1989): 177–75.

———, ed. *Literary Practice and Social Change in Britain, 1380–1530*. Berkeley: University of California Press, 1990.

Pearsall, Derek. *The Life of Geoffrey Chaucer: A Critical Biography*. Oxford: Basil Blackwell, 1992.

———. "Thomas Speght (ca. 1550–?)." In *Editing Chaucer*, ed. Ruggiers, q.v., 71–92.

Peterson, Joyce E. "The Finished Fragment: A Reassessment of the *Squire's Tale*." *Chaucer Review* 5 (1970): 62–74.

Phillips, Adam. *On Kissing, Tickling, and Being Bored: Psychoanalytic Essays on the Unexamined Life*. Cambridge: Harvard University Press, 1993.

Pigman, George W. III. *Grief and English Renaissance Elegy*. Cambridge: Cambridge University Press, 1985.

Polzella, Marion. "'The Craft So Long to Lerne': Poet and Lover in Chaucer's 'Envy to Scogan' and *Parliament of Fowls*." *Chaucer Review* 10 (1976): 279–86.

Potter, Lois. "Topicality or Politics? *The Two Noble Kinsmen*." In *Politics of Tragicomedy*, ed. McMullan and Hope, q.v., 77–91.

Presson, R. K. "The Conclusion of *Love's Labour's Lost*." *Notes and Queries* 7 (1960): 17–18.

Prior, Sandra Pierson. "*Routhe* and *Herte-Huntyng* in *The Book of the Duchess*." *Journal of English and Germanic Philology* 85 (1986): 3–19.

Pyles, Thomas. "Dan Chaucer." *Modern Language Notes* 57 (1942): 437–39.

Quilligan, Maureen. *Milton's Spenser: The Politics of Reading*. Ithaca: Cornell University Press, 1983.

Remley, Paul G. "Mary Shelton and Her Tudor Literary Milieu." In *Rethinking the Henrician Era*, ed. Herman, q.v., 40–77.

Renna, Thomas. "The Idea of Jerusalem: Monastic to Scholastic." In *From Cloister to Classroom*, ed. Elder, q.v., 96–109.

Roche, Thomas P., Jr. "Amoret." In *Spenser Encyclopedia*, ed. Hamilton, q.v., 29–30.

———. "*The Faerie Queene*, Book III." In *Spenser Encyclopedia*, ed. Hamilton, 273.

———. *The Kindly Flame: A Study of the Third and Fourth Books of "The Faerie Queene."* Princeton: Princeton University Press, 1964.

———. "A Response to A. Kent Hieatt." *Spenser Studies* 8 (1987): 343–47.

Roney, Lois. *Chaucer's "Knight's Tale" and Theories of Scholastic Psychology.* Tampa: University of South Florida Press, 1990.

Ross, Diane M. "The Play of Genres in the *Book of the Duchess.*" *Chaucer Review* 19 (1984): 1–13.

Rotman, Brian. *Signifying Nothing: The Semiotics of Zero.* New York: St. Martin's Press, 1987; rpt. Stanford: Stanford University Press, 1993.

Rovang, Paul R. *Refashioning "Knights and Ladies Gentle Deeds": The Intertextuality of Spenser's "Faerie Queene" and Malory's "Morte Darthur."* Madison, N.J.: Fairleigh Dickinson University Press; London: Associated University Presses, 1996.

Rowland, Beryl, ed. *Companion to Chaucer Studies*, rev. ed. London: Oxford University Press, 1979.

Rowse, A. L. Letter to *Times Literary Supplement*, 18 July 1952. Cited in Shakespeare, *Love's Labour's Lost*, ed. David, q.v., 73–74.

Ruggiers, Paul, ed. *Editing Chaucer: The Great Tradition.* Norman, Okla.: Pilgrim Books, 1984.

Ruskin, John. *Love's Meinie* and *Proserpina.* London: George Allen, 1906.

Russell, J. Stephen. *English Dream Vision: Anatomy of a Form.* Columbus: Ohio State University Press, 1988.

Ryan, Francis X., S.J. "Sir Thomas More's Use of Chaucer." *Studies in English Literature 1500–1900* 35 (1995): 1–17.

Ryan, Lawrence V. "Chaucer's Criseyde in Neo-Latin Dress." *English Literary Renaissance* 17 (1987): 288–302.

Sacks, Elizabeth. *Shakespeare's Images of Pregnancy.* New York: St. Martin's Press, 1980.

Sanders, Arnold A. "Ruddymane and Canace, Lost and Found: Spenser's Reception of Gower's *Confessio Amantis* 3 and Chaucer's *Squire's Tale.*" In *Work of Dissimilitude*, ed. Allen and White, q.v., 196–215.

Scarisbrick, J. J. "Henry VIII and the Vatican Library." *Bibliothèque d'humanisme et rénaissance* 24 (1962): 211–16.

Scarry, Elaine. *The Body in Pain: The Making and Unmaking of the World.* Oxford: Oxford University Press, 1985.

Schiesari, Juliana. *The Gendering of Melancholia: Feminism, Psychoanalysis, and the Symbolics of Loss in Renaissance Literature.* Ithaca: Cornell University Press, 1992.

Schless, Howard H. *Chaucer and Dante.* Norman, Okla.: Pilgrim Books, 1984.

Seaman, David M. "'The Wordes of the Frankeleyn to the Squier': An Interruption?" *English Language Notes* 24 (1986): 12–18.

Seaton, Ethel. "Medieval Poems in the Devonshire Manuscript." *Review of English Studies* 7 (1956): 55–56.

Segal, Hanna. *Melanie Klein.* Harmondsworth, Middlesex: Penguin, 1979.

Sessions, William A. "Surrey's Wyatt: Autumn 1542 and the New Poet." In *Rethinking the Henrician Era*, ed. Herman, q.v., 168–93.

Severs, J. Burke, ed. *A Manual of the Writings in Middle English 1050–1350.* Vol. I, *Romances.* New Haven: Connecticut Academy of Arts and Sciences, 1967.

Seznec, Jean. *The Survival of the Pagan Gods: The Mythological Tradition and Its Place in Renaissance Humanism and Art*, trans. Barbara F. Sessions. Princeton: Princeton University Press, 1953.

Shoaf, R. A. "'Mutatio Amoris': 'Penitentia' and the Form of *The Book of the Duchess.*" *Genre* 14 (1981): 163–89.

———. Response to panel on Chaucer and Spenser at Thirtieth International Congress on Medieval Studies, Kalamazoo, Michigan, May 1995.

Shook, Laurence K. "*The House of Fame.*" In *Companion to Chaucer Studies,* ed. Rowland, q.v., 341–54.

Silberman, Lauren. *Transforming Desire: Erotic Knowledge in Books III and IV of "The Faerie Queene."* Berkeley: University of California Press, 1995.

Silverman, Kaja. *The Acoustic Mirror: The Female Voice in Psychoanalysis and Cinema.* Bloomington: Indiana University Press, 1988.

Sinfield, Alan. "The Cultural Politics of the *Defense of Poetry.*" In *Sir Philip Sidney and the Interpretation of Renaissance Culture: The Poet in His Time and Ours*, ed. Gary F. Waller and Michael D. Moore, 124–43. Totowa, N.J.: Barnes and Noble, 1984.

Singleton, Charles S. *Interpretation: Theory and Practice.* Baltimore: Johns Hopkins University Press, 1969.

Smalley, Beryl. *English Friars and Antiquity in the Early Fourteenth Century.* Oxford: Basil Blackwell, 1960.

Smith, Joseph H., ed. *The Literary Freud: Mechanisms of Defense and Poetic Will.* New Haven: Yale University Press, 1980.

Smith, Paul. *Discerning the Subject.* Minneapolis: University of Minnesota Press, 1988.

Southall, Raymond. *The Courtly Maker.* Oxford: Oxford University Press, 1963.

———. "The Devonshire Manuscript Collection of Early Tudor Poetry, 1532–41." *Review of English Studies* 15 (1964): 142–50.

Spearing, A. C. *Medieval to Renaissance in English Poetry.* Cambridge: Cambridge University Press, 1985.

———. "The Poetic Subject from Chaucer to Spenser." In *Subjects on the World's Stage: Essays on British Literature of the Middle Ages and the Renaissance*, ed. David G. Allen and Robert A. White, 13–37. Newark: University of Delaware Press; London: Associated University Presses, 1995.

Spitz, Ellen Handler. "A Cycle of Songs." In *Image and Insight: Essays in Psychoanalysis and the Arts*, ed. Spitz, 127–48. New York: Columbia University Press, 1991.

Stone, Lawrence. *The Crisis of the Aristocracy, 1558–1641.* Oxford: Clarendon Press, 1965.

Strohm, Paul. *Hochon's Arrow: The Social Imagination of Fourteenth-Century Texts.* Princeton: Princeton University Press, 1992.

———. "Politics and Poetics: Usk and Chaucer in the 1380s." In *Literary Practice and Social Change,* ed. Patterson, q.v., 83–112.

———. *Social Chaucer.* Cambridge: Harvard University Press, 1989.

Stump, Eleonore, ed. and trans. *Boethius's "De topicis differentiis."* Ithaca: Cornell University Press, 1978.

Taylor, Karla. *Chaucer Reads "The Divine Comedy."* Stanford: Stanford University Press, 1989.

———. "Proverbs and the Authentication of Convention in *Troilus and Criseyde.*" In *Chaucer's "Troilus,"* ed. Barney, q.v., 277–96.

Teskey, Gordon. "Irony, Allegory, and Metaphysical Decay." *PMLA* 109 (1994): 397–408.

Thompson, Ann. *Shakespeare's Chaucer: A Study in Literary Origins.* Liverpool: Liverpool University Press, 1978.

Tobler, Alfred. *Geoffrey Chaucer's Influence on English Literature.* Berne, 1905; rpt. New York: AMS Press, 1973.

Tribble, Evelyn B. *Margins and Marginality: The Printed Page in Early Modern England.* Charlottesville: University Press of Virginia, 1993.

Waith, Eugene M. "Shakespeare and Fletcher on Love and Friendship." *Shakespeare Studies* 18 (1986): 235–49.

Wallace, David. *Chaucerian Polity: Absolutist Lineages and Associational Forms in England and Italy.* Stanford: Stanford University Press, 1997.

Warton, Thomas. *Observations on the Fairy Queen of Spenser.* 2d ed. London: R. and J. Dodsley, 1762; facsimile rpt. New York: Greenwood Press, 1968.

Watkins, John. *The Specter of Dido: Spenser and Virgilian Epic.* New Haven: Yale University Press, 1995.

Wawn, Andrew N. "Chaucer, *The Plowman's Tale,* and Reformation Propaganda: The Testimonies of Thomas Godfray and *I Playne Piers.*" *Bulletin of the John Rylands University Library of Manchester* 56 (1973): 174–93.

———. "The Genesis of *The Plowman's Tale.*" *Review of English Studies* 2 (1972): 21–40.

Weiner, Andrew D. *Sir Philip Sidney and the Poetics of Protestantism.* Minneapolis: University of Minnesota Press, 1978.

Weller, Barry. "*The Two Noble Kinsmen,* the Friendship Tradition, and the Flight from Eros." In *Shakespeare, Fletcher,* ed. Frey, q.v., 93–108.

Wells, Stanley, and Gary Taylor. *William Shakespeare: A Textual Companion.* Oxford: Clarendon Press, 1987.

Welsh, Andrew. *The Roots of Lyric: Primitive Poetry and Modern Poetics.* Princeton: Princeton University Press, 1978.

Whiting, Bartlett J. *Chaucer's Use of Proverbs.* Cambridge: Harvard University Press, 1934.

Williams, Arnold. *The Common Expositor: An Account of the Commentaries on Genesis, 1527–1633*. Chapel Hill: University of North Carolina Press, 1948.

Wimsatt, James. *Chaucer and His French Contemporaries: Natural Music in the Fourteenth Century*. Toronto: University of Toronto Press, 1991.

Windeatt, Barry. "Chaucer Traditions." In *Chaucer Traditions*, ed. Morse and Windeatt, q.v., 1–20.

Winnicott, D. W. "The Beginnings of a Formulation of an Appreciation and Criticism of Klein's Envy Statement." In his *Psycho-Analytic Explorations*, ed. Clare Winnicott, Ray Shepherd, and Madeleine Davis, 447–57. Cambridge: Harvard University Press, 1992.

———. "The Theory of the Parent-Infant Relationship." In his *The Maturational Processes and the Facilitating Environment: Studies in the Theory of Emotional Development*, 37–55. New York: International Universities Press, 1965. 37–55.

———. "Transitional Objects and Transitional Phenomena." In his *Playing and Reality*, 1–25. London: Tavistock, 1971.

———. "The Use of an Object and Relating through Identifications." In his *Playing and Reality*, 86–94.

Woodward, Marcus. *Gerard's Herball: The Essence Thereof Distilled*. From the 1636 ed. London: Spring Books, 1964.

Wright, Herbert G. *Boccaccio in England from Chaucer to Tennyson*. London: University of London Athlone Press, 1957.

———, ed. and intro. *A Seventeenth-Century Modernisation of the First Three Books of Chaucer's "Troilus and Criseyde."* Bern: Francke Verlag, 1960.

Wright, Louis B. *Middle Class Culture in Elizabethan England*. Chapel Hill: University of North Carolina Press, 1935.

Yeager, R. F. "Literary Theory at the Close of the Middle Ages: William Caxton and William Thynne." *Studies in the Age of Chaucer* 6 (1984): 135–64.

Zagorin, Perez. "Sir Thomas Wyatt and the Court of Henry VIII: The Courtier's Ambivalence." *Journal of Medieval and Renaissance Studies* 23 (1993): 113–41.

Žižek, Slavoj. *The Sublime Object of Ideology*. London: Verso, 1989.

Index